Fundamentals of Great Vocal Technique

The Teachings of Michael Trimble

Complied & Edited by Richard di Renzi and Christopher Arneson

Inside View Press
Delaware, Ohio

Fundamentals of Great Vocal Technique
The Teachings of Michael Trimble

www.InsideViewPress.com

ISBN: 978-0-9910876-0-0

Printed in the United States of America
Delaware, Ohio

Cover design by Jordana Grosso

To Pamela

Acknowledgements

It seemed to be that they would not be my readers, but readers of their own selves, my book being merely a magnifying glass.

Marcel Proust
In Search of Lost Time

When I began to write, it was for my own pleasure. Poetry was my first interest, and I managed to get some of it published before I became so discouraged trying to justify my own criticisms. My darling wife, Pamela, had encouraged me during my excursions into the world of rhyme and delicate expression. In fact, it was she who pushed the poetry into publication.

Pamela was still a presence in the small space of my mind I dedicated to fantasy, even though I had decided to stop writing. She was relentlessly there with her passionate and persistent encouragements to keep my secret mind active and in its searching mode. She seemed to really want me to find the world through my own looking glass. I always thought of myself as a medium through which the music of great composers could reach an audience. It was my intention to clarify where there might be doubt or misunderstanding. I succeeded at times as a performer, and it was gratifying in a way that only a fellow performer could understand. Pamela was and is a performer in every sense of the word, and that identity gives her a unique insight into my needs and desires to communicate and express my responses to music and text.

Due to severe health problems, I ended my performance career in as dignified a manner as possible. The termination of that terrible emotional upheaval was painfully accomplished, but I was left with the undiminished need to communicate my feelings about music and character to the world. Teaching became an avenue for me to express my talents and concerns to other performers. I had taught singing since I first began to sing—when I was just nineteen. It seemed natural for me to impart information to students and colleagues, and they all were appreciative of my efforts.

An unavoidable consequence of my fascination with the biomechanical process of singing led me to ask questions of every professional singer I met about vocal technique. Some were unfriendly or simply not interested in discussing their psychological and physical approach to the production of musical sounds with the voice. However, some were very willing, even anxious, to help a young singer discover the secrets of vocal freedom and the fulfillment of professional criteria. The most influential singers in my life were Richard Tucker, Helge Roswänge, George London, and Lauritz Melchior. Not only did these great singers teach me their physical approach to vocalism, but they also introduced me to many of their colleagues. Victor Trucco, one the coaches at the Metropolitan Opera during the early 1960s, allowed me to sit in his studio day after day while the stars of the opera world came to him for repertoire preparation. The list of singers who came to him during those years included every artist who was responsible for a leading role in the Italian and French operas at the Met. My education about how to produce the best possible sounds in a particular voice developed in that studio. It was truly a miraculous opportunity. I owe Victor Trucco more than I can ever express, as I owe so much to the great singers who permitted me to sit through their coachings for several years.

Pamela knew about all of this exposure and never stopped encouraging me to write it down for posterity. I owe to her the fact that I have actually composed the technical aspects of singing into a book. She never relented in her determination that I would write a book that would uniquely describe the differences and commonalities that the greatest singers recommended and practiced in their long, fantastically successful careers. Thank you, Pamela, dearest friend and believer.

Once the book was written, how could I hope to get it published? Fate seemed to step in at exactly this point and presented a new/old factor into the process. A former student of mine, Richard di Renzi, just happened to contact me. He was interested in getting his voice in shape and wanted to submit himself to my gentle persuasion. Of course, the first thing I did was to send some of my writings to him in order to help him with his efforts to review what he had learned from me.

The fact that we were 3,000 miles apart contributed to a mail-order solution to the distance problem. He is a marvelous tenor and only needed to be reminded of technical concepts he hadn't heard for many years. Richard liked the book so much that he recommended it to his famous friend, Christopher Arneson. These two high-powered professionals have since become my compilers and editors and supporters for which I am grateful beyond my ability to express. Without them and their enthusiastic support, the book would be sitting on my desk, gathering dust, and lost to the community of singers and teachers who are seeking information concerning usages and applications of vocal knowledge employed by some of the greatest singers in history.

In his book, *The Library of Babel*, Jorge Luis Borges wrote:

> *On some shelf, in some hexagon, it was argued, there must be a book that is a cipher and a compendium of all other books.*

As seekers of knowledge and artistic practices, we are all involved in the search for truth. Hopefully, this book will prove to be worthy of the efforts of those open-minded fellow travelers who have given of their time and enthusiasm to make it available.

Michael Trimble, 2013

Praise for Trimble's Work

"...A *Bel Canto* specialist, he has combined the best of Manuel Garcia's and Giovanni Batista Lamperti's schools of singing to serve the divine art of song. He has an encyclopedic knowledge of all things vocal and has my complete confidence. I recommend him without reservation to anyone who is serious about pursuing the ideal vocal technique for a lifetime of singing."

Kim Josephson
Metropolitan Opera Baritone
Professor of Voice, University of Oklahoma

"...Mr. Trimble works diligently with each individual student encouraging the study of a variety of repertoire, focusing on that wonderful combination of artistry and musicality with an optimum vocal approach. This is truly the joy of singing."

Joanna Porackova
Internationally Acclaimed Soprano

Fundamentals of Great Vocal Technique:
The Teachings of Michael Trimble

Table of Contents

Publisher's Forward

I believe that Michael Trimble's *Fundamentals of Great Vocal Technique* is a significant contribution to the pedagogic literature. It is also a big departure from previous works published by Inside View Press. Our other titles, especially *Your Voice: An Inside View* (Scott McCoy), *Resonance in Singing* (Donald Gray Miller), and *Sing Into Your Sixties... and Beyond!* (Sangeetha Rayapati), present singing and voice pedagogy through the lens of science. In each case, accepted principles of anatomy, physiology, acoustics, and resonance are used to explain how the human voice functions as a biomechanical, acoustic instrument. Science is employed to describe voice function, not as a method for learning to sing.

This new volume takes a much different approach. If we examine the historic record of great singers, we find few—if any—artists who were truly educated in contemporary singing science. Many people consider Pavarotti and Caruso to be the greatest tenors in the history of singing, but it is doubtful that either realistically understood the anatomy of breathing and phonation, or had the faintest notion about the scientific basis of resonance. Clearly, one can sing at an extraordinarily high level without this information, just as one can be a winning racecar driver and not know how to change a flat tire.

Instead of science, this book is based on practical experience, common sense, and the physical sensations one experiences while singing. Often, these sensations run contrary to what is now accepted as scientific fact. This is not unusual, nor does it in any way detract from the significance of the work. For example, prominent researchers have shown that "professional singers' descriptions of how they thought they breathed during singing bore little correspondence to how they actually breathed;"[1] nonetheless, each breathed well enough to sustain a successful career on the opera stage!

We have highlighted a few of the more important deviations from settled science in the body of the text. For example, the discussion of resonance makes statements about the chest being the most important resonator of the voice, and that like a drum, a larger size is required to produce a bigger sound (e.g., a bongo versus bass drum). Science shows us that the chest does indeed function as a resonator, but its effects are experienced only by the singer, not the audience. Imagine what that bass drum would sound like if it were filled with wet, soggy sponges, which are the acoustic equivalent of the lungs inside the chest.

You will find statements in this text that are explicitly *anti-science*. As publisher, I find many of these to be valid. Science cannot teach anyone how to sing. But it can explain why the techniques we use to create beautiful sound are successful. I believe there is room for both of these pedagogic viewpoints to coexist, each supporting the other.

Scott McCoy, publisher and editor-in-chief, 2013

---

[1] Watson, Peter J. and Thomas J. Hixon (1985). "Respiratory Kinematics in Classical (Opera) Singers." *Journal of Speech and Hearing Research,* volume 28, pages 104-122.

Introduction

When I was asked to compile and edit the various essays on vocal technique by Michael Trimble, I jumped at the chance. I have been a student of vocal pedagogy for many years, and I knew of Trimble's work, but never had the opportunity to meet him. In 2011, my colleague Richard di Renzi, Trimble's long-time student, asked me to be involved. I had no idea at the time that I would be reading a 4,000 page manuscript. Trimble had been writing down his method for a number of years with the help of his wife, Pamela. The material was organized in essays, covering any number of topics including the major areas of vocal pedagogy (breathing, support, registration, etc.) and some more specific material such as *How To Teach a Tenor* (which may be published separately, sometime in 2014). Each essay is detailed and comprehensive. What I realized is that Trimble is a link to the pedagogy of the 19th century (his teachers were the great Mack Harrell—who studied with the Anna Schoen-René, a student of one of Manuel Garcia's pupils—and Olga Ryss). Many of Trimble's affiliations were with the great singers of the middle twentieth century. Trimble reintroduces many of the "lost" methods of the nineteenth century, assimilating them with ideas imparted to him by these excellent singers and with various systems of movement such as yoga, to create a unique and highly effective method of voice instruction. While some of the concepts are not couched in scientific jargon (in fact, Trimble creates a colorful vocabulary of his own), they are absolutely based in sound pedagogic principles. In the area of breathing, for instance, Trimble uses the term "contrary motion" to describe the *appoggio* method of breathing utilized by nineteenth century singing teachers.

We decided to maintain the general format of the essays, and since it is impossible to completely separate the components of voice pedagogy, there is some redundancy. It is my hope that these will serve to underscore the importance of the specific points Trimble is making. Happily, Mr. Trimble has agreed to make DVD recordings in which he gives thorough explanations of his method. These recordings will be available in the near future and will serve as a valuable tool for teachers and singers.

It is an honor for me to present this material. Like many great pedagogues who preceded and will follow him, including Oren Brown, Richard Miller, Cornelius Reid and many others, Michael Trimble leaves a wealth of essential information which when used effectively, will sustain the legacy of excellent singing.

Christopher Arneson, co-editor, 2013

I first met Michael Trimble while I was a student at the Aspen Music Festival. Michael was a member of the voice faculty at the Festival for many years, and founder and director of the Aspen Vocal Institute. Paul Sperry, with whom I had gone to Aspen to study, introduced us. Michael had the reputation of being a "vocal guru" of sorts, and an air of mystery surrounded him. As a young tenor, I was both in awe of and intimidated by his knowledge and presence. These many years later, I do not believe there is a teacher who has the depth and diversity of knowledge that Michael possesses. It is for this very reason that I am so thrilled to have helped bring to future generations of singers and students of the vocal arts a sampling of Michael's encyclopedic knowledge.

It is a sad reality that, as time progresses, we lose the last vestiges and connections with the two "Golden Ages" of singing. The more generations that separate us from the original teachings, the more diluted the teaching becomes. It is unrealistic to believe that any one teacher has the ability to teach a student everything they know or everything there is to know. So as each generation moves forward, less and less of the whole is passed on. There are teachers I have known who base their entire philosophy of teaching solely on one aspect they may have learned from a great teacher, not realizing it was but a fraction of the whole method.

Trimble's vast knowledge of singing comes from not just the written word, but from firsthand experience as both a leading international tenor and as a teacher active for more than fifty years. As a student of singing, Michael had the opportunity to study with important teachers associated with the first Golden Age of singing, as well as study and work with singers of the second Golden Age. His curious mind drove him to question the many singers he met on their individual vocal techniques while still managing a very successful international career. All this information has formed an amazing database of knowledge that Michael shares with his students. His teaching incorporates methods from both the Garcia and Lamperti schools of singing, but has grown to also include the information culled from a lifetime of learning. I feel it is of great importance to preserve and disseminate as much of this information as possible.

Confident and willing to express his opinion, Michael possesses a rare gift in that he is able to convey a technique or an idea to his students by drawing from an endless variety of approaches, persisting until the desired result is achieved.

In my own teaching, I use many of the methods and techniques I have learned from Michael. I consider myself very fortunate to know him, to have worked with him and to have reaped the benefits of his knowledge as a singer, a teacher and, dare I say, friend.

Richard di Renzi, co-editor 2013

Forward

"Faulty singing is caused by awkward respiration. In fact, all bad habits of the throat are merely efforts of protection against clumsy management of the breath. The foundation of all vocal study lies in the control of the breath."

Giovanni Battista Lamperti

The Premise of this Book

We need a method of singing that is based upon a repetitive sequence of correct thoughts and exercises, one that will allow us to be reasonably secure and dependable, while fulfilling the criteria of good singing under all normal conditions.

During the Golden Age of Bel Canto (approx. 1810-1930), the greatest singers and teachers who wrote books about singing repeatedly emphasized the importance of the relaxed, totally free throat and a breathing method that prepares and sustains that freedom of the throat for singing.

Of course, there is no guarantee that we will be able to execute every note perfectly with every emission of the voice, no matter how correctly we learn the proper preparation and approach to the art of singing. The greatest archers do not hit the bull's eye with every arrow, and the pitcher does not throw a perfect strike with every pitch. Even the great tenor Enrico Caruso sang tones that were not his best at times; indeed, in the beginning of his career he was known as the "glass tenor" because he cracked so often. However, a certain degree of expectation must be fulfilled if we are to become professional at anything. We must be able to stand and deliver over and over again, on a regular, dependable basis. There must be a methodical approach, developed through repetitive thought and action (right thinking, right doing), which allows us to fulfill the criteria of our profession (right being) under many different conditions. We do not always feel our best, physically or mentally, and we do not hit the bull's eye with every note. But we must, in order to perform at the professional level, hit the target. The more firmly our technique is established, the less we need to preoccupy our minds with technique during a performance. It is on the bad days that we need every tidbit of technical know-how we have learned and practiced over many years to help us make it through a difficult performance.

Scientific knowledge does not help us *sing* better. It is useless for us to think scientifically while singing or while learning to sing. Enrico Caruso and his colleagues had never heard of a style of singing based on the scientific names of throat parts. Before Manuel Garcia II invented the laryngoscope in 1854, everyone thought the voice came from the stomach, because eating a big meal would interfere with the production of the tone. How was it possible for the greatest singers in history to learn to sing the way they did without knowing an arytenoid from a hemorrhoid?

The truth is that the knowledge we call scientific and the knowledge great singers put into practice to produce great singing are two distinct kinds of knowledge. One kind lies in the cognitive part of the brain and the other lies in the psychomotor system. The psychomotor system is programmed through desire and repetition, like learning to play golf or tennis or a musical instrument. The intellect, or cognitive side of the mind, is applied to learning languages and music and, in the case of instrumentalists, where to place the fingers. The psychomotor system is then programmed through repetition to learn to execute the coordinated functions necessary to master the instrument or to learn to speak a language fluently. Singers need to practice the biomechanical processes that create breath control, phonation, and all the many criteria of singing. The voice scientists can neither learn to sing themselves nor teach anyone else to sing by informing the cognitive mind of the correct names of the various parts of the throat that act/react when great singers sing. The greatest singers of the past did not know the names of their throat parts, but they had acquired the knowledge of how to use them.

How do we use our talents for singing to our best advantage? Sitting in judgment of the sounds we make is a hopeless business. It utilizes the cognitive side of the mind. We need to avail ourselves of the miraculous powers of the psychomotor system in order to sing well. Imagine the mind is made up of many different chambers, each dedicated to its own primary function. In a house, we cook in the kitchen and sleep in the bedroom. We should not cook in the bedroom or sleep in the kitchen. The cognitive mind decides it wants to sing. This message is sent to the psychomotor corner of the mind. It is there that the actual singing is organized. We must coordinate the proper commands and the proper activity with the appropriate, designated space in the mind. The tone will find itself through correct cognitive commands to the psychomotor system.

The opinions and/or interference of others who constantly give us advice can be completely wrong, although they may mean well. The most famous teachers can be wrong, especially if the advice is general and not specifically tailored to the problems of the individual student. We need a secure method that separates ease from strain, freedom from constriction, cognitive command from psychomotor response, and neutralizes non-essential actions in the entire body while singing. In essence, we need a system for separating the good from the bad.

But what is good and what is bad? The only criterion that is foolproof is to identify resistance in the throat while singing, either through the sense of touch or through the sense of sight, as described above. Resistance always has to do with muscular action/reaction. It can be identified by the responses of the nerves in the throat, either through sensation or through visual recognition. According to Dame Eva Turner, one should never feel the throat at all! When asked what she did in her throat when she sang, she answered, "I don't know. I never felt anything in my throat when I sang!" She had been taught the vocal philosophy of the invisible throat, the invisible tongue, the invisible jaw, and the invisible muscles under the jaw and under the chin. Her warnings to young singers had to do with minute actions in the throat being unacceptable in singing. She expressed it by saying, "Even the weight of one grain of salt or sugar would still be too much action in the throat." You can imagine how horrified she was when she heard that young singers were being taught to open their mouths vertically, spreading the tone with the jaw pressing downward! Other young singers would dip their heads downward with the chin held against the chest, creating tracheal resonance! Caruso warned against this specifically in his book. It has long been considered one of the most dangerous vocal techniques, because it seems to be successful for a time, until it causes irreparable damage to the vocal folds! Dame Eva thought that the vertical pulling down of the jaw was the worst technique she had seen in a lifetime of being internationally associated with the highest artistic level of great singing. The other action she hated was to see any movement in the middle or back of the tongue. She believed that only the front of the tongue should move vertically to articulate the dental consonants against the upper front teeth. Otherwise, the tongue was left absolutely flat in a dead state, as if invisible, and on every vowel.

One summer, during my many years on the voice faculty of the Aspen Musical Festival, a nineteen-year-old soprano came to audition for me. She sang an Italian song and asked for my opinion of her voice. I explained to her that before I would offer any opinion, I would like for her to breathe deeply into her lower back, try to relax her jaw and tongue, and sing some easy scales. She agreed to give it a try. We proceeded in this manner and she did very well, finding that she could sing very high into the soprano range without effort. Suddenly she stopped with a quizzical look on her face, and began to rub her throat. I asked her what was happening. She said, "I don't understand. I have no pain in my throat. I always have pain in my throat when I sing. My teacher in California said it is normal for the throat to hurt when we try to sing classical music." As a member of the voice faculty in Aspen, I heard students from all parts of the U.S. This was the first and only time I had ever heard that pain in the throat was acceptable when singing classical music!

This young lady was a perfect candidate for the "posture" system I've been teaching to professional singers for many years. If she had been doing the following series of postures described in this book, the same ones I use with professional singers, she would have recognized immediately that tension (resistance) was causing conflict in her throat. Her attempts to focus the sound in her sinus cavities, after breathing into the front of her body and swelling her belly outward, was causing the pillars of the fauces to partially close, narrowing the throat and causing a whole series of action/reaction responses in her throat, forcing the voice into the nasal cavity. The faulty method of breathing (the sleeping baby who is silent, not crying or making sound), and focusing the resonance in the nasal-cavity, set off a chain reaction of tension in the muscles under the jaw, causing first a tugging upward of the larynx, followed by muscular reactions in the trachea and spasms in the epiglottis. She had been able to relieve the effects of the contraction of the muscles under the jaw by pulling the jaw extremely downward, which made her look grotesque and eliminated any possibility of smiling or making any expression except the one in the famous painting by Munch called *The*

Scream. The pain went away immediately, along with the unnecessary scream expression, as soon as she breathed deeply into her lower back while drawing the abdomen inward and released the belly outward while singing (the natural crying baby breathing), thus releasing the muscular tension in her throat that was causing the pain. This was not exactly rocket science or any kind of miracle, although it seemed miraculous to her! The muscles in the throat want to relax when we breathe into the lower rear quadrant of the lungs, exactly as recommended by Luisa Tetrazzini in her book. Lilli Lehmann recommended the same and added the condition of the breath jerk, which required a sudden jerking in of the abdomen the instant before beginning the inhalation into the lower back. Caruso described the action of the lower back while breathing as being like a bellows, saying "the lower ribs in the back open like a bellows when inhaling and squeeze together when singing."

The best way to gain control and awareness of incorrect resistance in the body and throat is to perform a routine of postures and breathing exercises that vanquish all muscular action unnecessary to the free production of the tone.

Michael Trimble, 2013

Fundamentals of Great Vocal Technique

Getting Started

On my seventy-first birthday, March 15, 2009, I decided to write down for posterity an in-depth record of the biomechanical and psychomotor processes I have studied, compiled, tested and implemented over a fifty-year period as a professional singer, voice teacher and coach. This long experience has given me many opportunities to learn the essentials of breath development, beauty of tone, stamina, health and vocal longevity. I have given this project a great deal of thought since the first serious opportunity arose to have a book published on this subject in 1980.

Train the body and the mind will follow

One of the problems in writing down all of this information has been to sort out the useful knowledge from the useless. In order to do this, I have had to find out, objectively, what I have learned that is useful to someone else and what is useful to me in my capacity as teacher, advisor, and mentor. Some of what I learned was useful to me as a singer and only to me, because every voice is unique and every singer is unique. Each singer is made up of a particular combination of anatomy, conditioning, chemistry, strength, natural breath capacity (as opposed to developed breath capacity), musicality, psychological health, and physical health. A teacher must be aware of this dynamic and be able to approach each student on an individual basis. Singing is a talent and cannot be learned or taught. It is important to understand, however, that the singer who possesses the ability to match pitches with the voice, and obviously has a natural talent, must still strive to learn the criteria that are required of professional singing.

> Train the body and the mind will follow.
> *The Buddha*

Down to Basics

The essential blocks that are integral to my teaching are a result of many influences, including the encounters and friendships I nurtured with great singers during my developmental and professional years as an operatic tenor. From 1960 through 1975, I met, sang for, and took lessons and coachings with a number of renowned singers. My great friend, Lawrence Shadur[2], a wonderful baritone with the Metropolitan Opera, was Lauritz Melchior's godson. Through Larry I had the opportunity to meet Melchior and the great Richard Tucker. Trying to find out the technical secrets from these singers was like studying with the Zen master described in Eugen Herrigel's book, *Zen in the Art of Archery*[3]. I was young and full of enthusiasm, and the advice given by these legendary singers seemed so vague and undefined. The management and/or use of the breath, however, was the root of all discussion. When I sang for Mr. Tucker for the first time, the first words out of his mouth were "get a good breath un-

---

[2]Please see Appendix I for birth and death dates of all people cited within this text.
[3]Eugen Herrigel. *Zen in the Art of Archery* (New York: Vintage Spiritual Classics), 1989

der that." "How?" I asked, "What should I do?" Richard Tucker was a master technician, a tenor's tenor who could sing everything from Mozart to Verdi beautifully.

At a later coaching, Mr. Tucker said: "I've only got two things to tell you, kid. Breathe behind you and sing in front of you, like this." He then proceeded to demonstrate a gigantic, thrilling, free high note that seemed to threaten the layers of paint on the walls. I was sure the rafters would come down from the incredible vibrations bouncing off the walls and off my head. When the tone ended, Mr. Tucker said, "See what I mean? Always keep it light. It is all done by stopping the breath and not with the vocal cords." I'll never forget that day! It was 1962 and I was a twenty-four-year-old lyric tenor with great promise. After a few months of study, Mr. Tucker said: "Too bad Paul Althouse [his only teacher] died. He could have helped you."

Mr. Tucker repeatedly said: "Breathe in your lower back and don't let the belly wall or the chest move at all, especially on the attack." This was the same approach to breath control I received in conversations with Cantor Charles Bloch in New York and with Cantor Irving Bushman in Cleveland when I was Chairman of Vocal Studies at the Cleveland Institute of Music where Bushman taught. Both men were beautiful singers who had very long careers.

Great singers echo again and again the same approach to breath control. The following quotations are taken from the writings of Enrico Caruso, Luisa Tetrazzini and Lilli Lehmann:

> To take a full breath properly the chest must be raised at the moment that the abdomen sinks in. Then with a gradual expulsion of the breath, a contrary movement takes place. It is this ability to take in an adequate supply of breath and to retain it until required that makes or, by contrary, mars all singing... this art of respiration, once acquired, the student has gone a considerable step on the road to Parnassus.[4]

> In order to ensure proper breathing capacity it is understood that the clothing must be absolutely loose around the chest and also across the lower part of the back, for one should breathe with the back of the lungs as well as with the front, upper part of the lungs... In learning to breathe it is well to think of the lungs as empty sacks, into which the air is dropping like a weight, so that you think first of filling the bottom of your lungs, then the middle part, and so on until no more air can be inhaled.[5]

---

[4] Enrico Caruso. *The Art of Singing* (New York: Dover edition), 1975: 53-54
First Publication by The Metropolitan Co. 1909

[5] Luisa Tetrazzini. *The Art of Singing* (New York: Dover edition) 1975: 11-12
First Publication by The Metropolitan Co. 1909

> In order to have the throat perfectly open it is necessary to have the jaw absolutely relaxed.[6]

> This feeling of singing against the chest with the weight of air pressing up against it is known as breath support. In Italian we have even a better word, *appoggio,* which is the breath prop or lean... Never for a moment sing without this *appoggio,* this breath prop. Its development and its constant use mean the restoration of sick or fatigued voices and the prolonging of all one's vocal powers.[7]

> I learned this: To draw in the abdomen, raise the chest and hold the breath in it by the aid of the ribs; in letting out the breath gradually to relax the abdomen... A horn player in Berlin with the power of holding a very long breath, once told me, in answer to a question, that he drew in his abdomen very strongly, but immediately relaxed his abdomen again as soon as he began to play. I tried the same thing with the best results.[8]

> The breath pressure, which includes abdomen, diaphragm and chest muscles, is often named *Atemstauen* (breath stop) or *appoggio,* the breath lean or breath prop.[9]

We really need to discuss the singing methods that have been successful for singers who have had long careers without vocal problems. Giovanni Lamperti said that all success and all vocal problems are a result of either the correct management or mismanagement, respectively, of the breath. Lilli Lehmann called her control concept the "breath stop." Breathiness is considered bad in classical singing and can lead to many vocal problems, including hoarseness and nodules. It should be understood that any excess of breath, especially under pressure, can be disastrous for the vocal folds.

I met the great tenor Giovanni Martinelli at the Metropolitan Opera in 1961. He was seventy-seven years old at the time and still singing! I asked him what his ideas were about how to sing. He answered very energetically, "*primo respirare* (first breathe), *poi appoggiare* (then lean)." I asked, "How should I breathe?" He grabbed my lower ribs in the back and said: "*Qui, qui e profondo* (here, here and deeply)."

I heard Lauritz Melchior sing a concert when he was seventy years old. His voice was still clear, strong and remarkably youthful. When I asked him to describe his singing technique, he began to explain how he breathed. It is always the same story. Breathe into the lower back, lean on the diaphragm, never sing into the nose. Let the breath open the throat. No action in the throat, only reaction to low back breathing.

---

[6] Ibid. p. 23
[7] Ibid. p. 15-16
[8] Lilli Lehmann. *How to Sing* (New York: MacMillan), 1949:14
[9] Ibid. p. 23

George London, with whom I had a wonderful working relationship, said to me: "the ribcage should not move independently. The ribs move only if the breath moves them." He called the process "the machine" and said to me many times, "Mike, make the students work the machine. Open the back, close the back, repeatedly!" Cesare Siepi and Cornell MacNeil would not say a word about technique. Jan Peerce said "don't move anything in the front of your body when you breathe or sing."

Dame Eva Turner was the only singer I ever met who used the term "psychomotor system." In 1962, we sat down together and talked about vocal technique. She said, "The mind must be programmed through repetition to do the right thing as a habit, thus training the psychomotor system to sing for you." "How and what must I repeat over and over, Dame Eva?" I asked. Again I heard those magic words; "breathe, breathe, breathe and no action in the throat!" The next thing she said has stayed with me for decades; "even a grain of salt or sugar dropped in the throat would be too much action."

Leave your voice alone, and train your breath.[10]

Moving the Mind

Memory Location

If someone suddenly steps on your toe, ***your mind moves instantly to your toe***. This mental process of identifying specific locations in the body is common to all of us. We can use this ability to guide and organize the mind/body connection for singing. The ability to repeat the thought or memory of an activity in the body can guarantee the accuracy of a predetermined location or function.

We Call It Talent

The mind can move effortlessly from one location in the body to another, simply by thinking specific thoughts. The mind doesn't always need to specify location, but it is a precious gift to be able to choose exactly the desired point of activity. The ability to move the mind from one location to another in the body is a mental activity, and, in some cases, an extraordinary talent. It can be organized to function as an instigator, triggering a coordinated, complicated process into a preconceived, predictable, conceptual process. The mind/body connection must be correct, powerful, relentless and reliable. Great athletes have this ability, and there is a definite athleticism required in singing. The flexible, agile, instigating thought, based on desire or mental conception, can be repeated at will once it has been sufficiently practiced and programmed into the psychomotor system. This conceptual process can consistently produce a predictable physical result, and it has a name: *The Moveable Mind.*

A Precious Gift

Great singers have often described the mental approach to voice production as the ability to move the mind to an area where the inhalation for singing occurs or to lean the pressure of the breath against the chest while singing. Zinka Milanov put her hand

---

[10] G.B. Lamperti. *Vocal Wisdom* (New York: Taplinger), 1931: 142

on her chest and said "put the breath on the voice and sing." All we have to do as singers is identify what she meant by voice. Did she think her chest was her voice? That was what she indicated to the listeners, and that is what we saw her doing when she sang. Remember that the advice she gave us applied to what she was feeling *inside the body*. Except for the position of the chest as a constantly maintained sternal arch, her singing was invisible. One thing is certain: she was physically calm and still, had great breath control, and was the best singer I ever heard in my life.

General or Dispersed Response

The mind also will respond to general sensations. A gentle breeze against the skin can be very pleasant, just as the general sensation of a hot bath or a cold shower can be exactly what we desire at times. In such a case, the mind will lose focus, and a general awareness of sensations will be dispersed over the area of the entire body. However, singers need to be able to concentrate the mind in a specific direction, toward a specific location, that will organize the rest of the body to fulfill the criteria for beautiful, free singing.

In order for the singer to repeatedly execute the particular mind/body connection and coordination that we call artistic singing, negative influences, either emotional or physical, must not be allowed to invade the mind. Conflicting physical, mental, or emotional concerns may disperse the mental focus away from singing and disrupt the coordinated process needed to produce the voice. Emotional or intellectual conflict must be avoided as much as possible.

Deleterious Effects of Wrong Ideas

The rub, of course, is that we must think the correct things in order to achieve the correct results. Buddha said, "Right thinking, right doing, right being." The ability of the mind to move with deliberation to a specific place can have deleterious effects on the voice if the mental commands are wrong. Modern teachers urge singers to move the mind into the nose by asking for focus. The psychomotor response to this request is invariably the narrowing of the pillars of the fauces in order to accomplish a nasal, artificially concentrated sound. We know that such a command is in direct conflict with Enrico Caruso's command to: "Never sing into the nasal cavity. It is against all the rules of song." Therefore, we must learn to move the mind to those specific locations, recommended by the greatest singers in history, which are beneficial to the art of singing. We want to practice the organic methods of breathing and controlling the breath that promote stamina, vocal longevity, range, volume, and beauty of tone.

Moving the mind from a singer's perspective

The Inhalation: first movement of the mind

The first movement of the mind as described by the previously mentioned singers dictates the location of the place (target) for *inhalation*. When I asked Giovanni Martinelli what he taught his students, his first response was to put his hands on his lower back and say "breathe here." Next, he put his hands on his lower chest and said to "sing here." Finally, he indicated the place on his chest and said *"il posto, il posto, il posto"* (the place).

According to the recommendations written in the books of the greatest singers in history, inhalation is directed by the mind to settle deep into the lower back. Luisa Tetrazzini said, "The first drop of inhaled air should go into the lower rear quadrant of the lungs." One needs only to think of the exact spot where the activity of the inhalation should take place and draw the breath silently through the nostrils (Tetrazzini said, "like smelling a flower") down to that location. The singer can choose the tip of the tailbone as a target for the inhalation (as recommended by Jerome Hines and Robert Merrill), move the mind there, and breathe in silently through the nose with energy and determination while maintaining the thought of the target of the inhalation.

Another way of telling the mind the exact location for the inhalation is to imagine that "the buttocks are balloons and must be filled with breath before singing any sound." This advice was given to me by the Danish tenor, Helge Roswänge, who was an advanced yoga practitioner as well as an amazing singer. The direction and target he chose for moving the mind while inhaling were very clear! Joan Sutherland shocked a group of young singers when she responded to a question about her breathing method by saying, "I breathe up my rectum."

Support: second movement of the mind

The abdomen has no function in the act of actual singing. The abdomen is useful only if drawn inward while inhaling. This inward movement of the abdomen should occur with each inhalation before singing, and never while singing. Once the emission of the tone begins, the abdomen must be completely relaxed outward and downward. It must be out of the picture, having completed its mission of eliminating one of the three possibilities of breath placement (the belly, the chest, and the back) before singing. The only area of the body that should open and expand for the purpose of inhaling is the lower back. That crucial expansion should not be accomplished as an independent process. The ribs must not move unless the breath moves them! Never expand the ribs independently.

Drawing the abdomen inward, while inhaling, prevents the filling of the belly with breath and aids the expansion of the ribs in the lower back. The drawing in of the abdomen while inhaling can be a secret weapon in the war with the breath. If the abdomen moves inward while singing, the war is lost!

Breath will rise toward the throat if the abdomen is drawn inward while singing. The muscles of the throat and neck will have to compensate and try to control the emission. There must never be a pressure of the breath against the throat or any form of muscular action in the throat. There must never be a release of unutilized breath upward toward the throat. The chest must not move, and the abdomen, when not assisting with the inhalation, must remain totally

> relaxed downward and outward. The controlling pressure of the breath, sent from the squeezing, lower ribs in the back, is maintained against the chest, and never allowed to rise upward against the throat! The abdomen, once singing has begun, has no function. It must relax outward and downward while singing.
>
> Dame Eva Turner

> The abdomen should be drawn in while inhaling and a contrary motion should occur while singing.
>
> Enrico Caruso

> At the instant before the breath is inhaled, jerk the abdomen in, thereby creating the maximum opening of the lower back! As the singing begins, do the opposite and let the abdomen relax downward and outward.
>
> Lilli Lehmann

Thinking Makes It So

One of the most difficult concepts to explain, and one of the easiest to demonstrate, is that we can make ourselves heavier simply by thinking. Again, we are touching on a very odd way to move the mind. A quote from Shakespeare's *Hamlet* has the hero saying, "Nothing is good or bad, but thinking makes it so." By thinking we are suddenly very heavy, we can tap into a mysterious source of energy that is common to all soft style systems of martial arts.

When exploited in singing, the energy resulting from the soft style[11] approach can create more volume and intensity in the voice if the singer suddenly thinks that she or he wants to be heavier. A good example of how to use this common but strange ability is to imagine that we don't want to be pushed aside (perhaps in the subway) or picked up off the floor. If someone asks you to help him reach up and change a light bulb in the ceiling, you automatically make yourself lighter in order to elevate your body toward the light. The desire to become as light as a feather is a basic requirement of ballerinas, who make themselves as light as possible when lifted repeatedly by their male partners. However, if you do not want to be lifted off the floor to change the light bulb, you resist the efforts of your friend by making yourself heavier.

As an exercise, try lifting a friend off the floor. Have him or her stand up straight without bending his/her knees. During the first lift, the person being lifted should try to help achieve as much height as possible by reaching upward to touch the ceiling (or to change a light bulb). On the second lift, the person being lifted, still with unbent knees, must resist being picked up without changing any aspect of the posture of the body. The only resistance should be mental. The person being lifted must definitely *not* want to be picked up off the floor. You will immediately feel that your friend has suddenly taken on a lot of weight and is dramatically heavier.

---

[11] In martial arts, the term 'soft style' is used to describe movements and responses that are based on the energy provided by gravity and not by muscles. When muscles and effort are used to accomplish something, the term 'hard style' is used.

Tito Schipa's sighing method worked for him, although his gravity lean was diagonal, because the reaction in his throat was benign. He was limited to singing very light, lyric music, which was correct for his voice. The demands for volume and declamation in dramatic music were not expected of him. He very cleverly sang only the roles that suited his light voice and his gentle, passive lean of the breath.

A true dropping technique can be a wonderful vocal technique if all the singer has to do is stand in one place and deliver huge tones. The singing is usually full of power and color because letting go of the breath downward with a vertical, relaxed feeling of weight in the lower body lengthens and broadens the air column and causes no stiffening reaction in the throat. The bigger the amount of air in the drum (chest), the bigger and richer the sound is from the voice. It must be made clear that when I advise against a vertical lean, I mean that no degree of pushing downward can be allowed. A dropping relaxation of the inside of the body is not really *appoggio*. Actually pressing downward with energy and effort into the pelvic area as if trying to move recalcitrant bowels could be called an active or hard style vertical lean. However, the reaction to the vertical angle of such a lean causes paralyzing pressure against the throat. The dead-drop of the breath into the deepest point of the pelvic floor, using no downward pressure, could be called a soft-style vertical lean. Personally, I prefer to distinguish the word lean (*appoggio*) by implying a pressure of the breath against the diaphragm whenever lean is used. The word *appoggio*, as used in singer parlance in Europe, means that the active pressure of the breath against the diaphragm is being applied in a way and in a place that does not cause a reaction in the throat, but, instead, does the opposite. It guarantees that, by deliberately creating pressure (hard-styling) against the chest, the throat remains free.

I asked George London about many of the singers with whom he sang. His favorite vocal technicians were Zinka Milanov and Richard Tucker. Jerome Hines agreed with these selections. Hines considered Milanov the greatest singer he heard in fifty years of singing with the Metropolitan Opera. Aside from her incredible voice, she was also the most dependable singer. Milanov maintained a level of performance that has been equaled by only a few singers in history. She never had a bad performance; every performance was steady, reliable, phenomenal, and an example for everyone of how to sing.

Flagstad, according to London, was in a category by herself because there was no one like her. She, like Caruso, Ponselle, and Titta Ruffo, could not be compared to other singers. Her voice was so tremendous that he could not find words to describe it. He tried to remember everything she had told him about her concept of voice production. As great as she was, she had limitations in terms of what she could or could not sing. In spite of her phenomenal, lustrous voice of gigantic proportions, her extraordinary dropping technique did not provide her with the ability to fulfill the criteria of the great Italian operatic roles. On the other hand, Zinka Milanov, the very best Verdi soprano in the world during her era, who could sing anything without apparent effort, refused to sing any Wagner. Her *appoggio* technique, placed against the middle of her chest, which produced a huge voice with a golden, metallic glow and ultimate ease, was not the best vocal technique for the long, sustained roles of Isolde or Brünnhilde, and she knew it. Although she received offers to sing those roles, she refused to perform them. She also turned down Puccini's Turandot. No one could understand why these two ladies, the greatest sopranos of their time, refused to attempt to expand their repertoires into each other's vocal categories. The dropping method is limited in its ability to allow the singer to create special effects, like staccati, sforzandi, high pianissimi, martellati, fast coloratura singing, etc. Flagstad did not attempt to make the vocal effects required in the Italian repertoire. She was satisfied to be the best in the world at what she did, and her level of performance granted her a position among the greatest singers in history.

Thinking, Doing, Being

In her book *The Pursuit of Perfection,* Maggie Teyte allows that some singers don't have to worry or analyze or have a psychological construct that brings order to the myriad possibilities of the vocal organ. Cognitive planning and execution are not necessary in the minds of a chosen few singers; when repeatedly asked by colleagues and admirers, they seem to have no idea how they sing. The usual analytical process that brings mind and body to obedient coordination seems to be unnecessary for the chosen few. Sadly, they, the perfect ones, either don't attempt to teach at all, or they become very bad teachers.

Essential to our pursuit of perfection is learning to move the mind in the right way to the right places at the right times. We must appreciate the order in which this advice has been given to us. We must think the right thoughts (move the mind to the lower back and inhale), in order to do the right things (move the mind to the chest and press the breath against it while singing) in order to be good singers. It is what we think about during our pursuit that will decide if we become good singers or not.

Beneficial Thoughts

Caruso's breathing method agreed with Lilli Lehmann's when he said to "draw the abdomen in when you inhale and do a contrary motion when you sing." This breathing method relaxes the throat, tongue, and jaw, opens the epiglottis, raises the soft palate, lowers the larynx, and creates the *stai*[12] form in the back of the throat (as described by Lamperti), causing no reaction in the *appoggio* that will interfere with the control of the breath and the emission of the voice. The voice remains free because the throat, tongue and jaw are free. The essential parts of the vocal puzzle responsible for phonation of the vowel and the free passage of the resonance through the throat and into the head are unencumbered by muscular action or reaction. It is obvious that Caruso was thinking specific thoughts at all times while singing, and everything was based on his breathing method. In his small book, he mentions breathing sixty times!

---

[12] As in the bright [a] sound found in the Italian word *stai*

Insights into the Biomechanics of Great Singing

Chi sa respirare, sa cantare.

"Who knows how to breathe, knows how to sing."

Traditional Italian Maxim
Attributed to Maria Celloni, 1810

Introduction

Picking Brains

During the past fifty years I have been fortunate to be around great singers, as a fan, student, or colleague, and in some cases, a teacher or advisor. It was my own insatiable curiosity that drove me to ask questions, to pick the brains of those who could stand and deliver great singing in the most difficult operatic roles, and do it for years. I wanted to know what they thought about technically while singing. Every singer with whom I spoke, (Giovanni Martinelli, Lauritz Melchoir, Dame Eva Turner, Mack Harrell, Jenny Tourel, Richard Tucker, Lucine Amara, Jan Peerce, Jussi Björling, Birgit Nilsson, Helge Roswänge, Elizabeth Schwarzkopf, Gottlob Frick, Maureen Forrester, Frederick Dalberg, Joan Sutherland, Mario del Monaco, Jerome Hines, Hilde Konetzni, George London, and dozens of others) mentioned breathing as the first consideration when discussing singing and vocal technique. The inhalation was always described as placed into the lower back, with the support point of the breath while singing being described as against the chest.

Visual Clues and Invisibility

There were two inhaling methods consistently mentioned as the proper way to prepare the basis of the *appoggio*. Some of the great singers could be seen pulling their abdomens in while inhaling. Some of them would hold the abdomen perfectly still while inhaling. The stillest ones gave the impression that they did nothing while singing. The voice would appear from inside their bodies as if by magic. Not one of them advised swelling the belly outward while inhaling. In nearly every case, the chest was kept as still as possible while inhaling or exhaling. If the chest did rise slightly during the inhalation, it was held as still as possible while singing.

Breathing and Support

Inhalation

Two Methods of Abdominal Control While Inhaling

- *Pulling the abdomen in while inhaling*
- *Holding the abdominal wall perfectly still while inhaling*

If the posture of the chest is established and the sternal arch is firm, the back is left as the only part of the body ready to expand when inhaling. Pulling in the abdomen during inhalation will cause more extreme expansion of the lower ribs in the back than just holding the abdomen still. If the breath cannot go into the belly because expanding the belly outward while inhaling is not permitted, and the chest is already raised in the form of the sternal arch, it must go into the back. The lower the breath is inhaled into the back, and the greater the expansion of the lower ribs, the deeper and richer the sound of the voice will be.

Caruso and Lilli Lehmann very clearly describe the function of the abdomen in their approaches to breathing and support in their books. Caruso said to "draw the abdomen in while inhaling" and Lehmann said to "jerk the abdomen in an instant before inhaling." There is a long list of great singers who used the "pulling in the abdomen while inhaling" method. Some singers, like Amelita Galli-Curci, apparently pulled the abdomen in when she inhaled and kept it there ("glued it to the spine"). Lauritz Melchior and Helge Roswänge followed Caruso's methodology. Other great singers held the abdomen still while inhaling and singing. The idea was to not allow it or the chest to move at all. Richard Tucker, George London, Lucine Amara, Joan Sutherland, and Luciano Pavarotti used this method.

One thing is common to these approaches to body and breath control: not one of the fabulous singers mentioned above pushed the belly outward to inhale or pulled the belly inward while singing. The sleeping baby function of the breath does not exist as a method used among great singers. They all use the laughing/crying baby function of breathing and support. This is a critical difference in the success or failure of singers as they attempt to make professional careers.

Rediscovery: breath jerk

The implementation of the inward pull of the abdominal wall while inhaling into the lower back causes the back half of the diaphragm to descend as a result of extreme contraction. This function, if practiced correctly over time, can give singers the feeling that they can increase their breath capacity (creating a bigger drum) compared to inhaling with the belly going outward. Lilli Lehmann called the sudden, inward movement of the abdomen before inhaling, the breath jerk (Der Atemzug). The abdomen was to be jerked in suddenly and vigorously every time the singer inhaled.

Geraldine Ferrar and Olive Fremstad were students of Lilli Lehmann, and it is reasonable to assume that they both employed her breathing method. They were both renowned singers, and, like their teacher, had very long careers without vocal problems. The technique of pulling the abdomen inward while inhaling, as employed by Lehmann, Ferrar, Fremstad, and many of the greatest singers of the Golden Age of Singing, was the basis for the most advantageous breathing/support method ever developed. I hope that singers who truly desire to release the potential greatness of their own voices will return to the same method. Perhaps, if we are to have a Caruso or Tetrazzini or Ponselle or Battistini in the future, teachers will begin to insist that their students learn the way of breathing that creates the perfectly open, free, relaxed throat.

Der Atemzug **(the breath jerk): placement of the inhalation**
The ribs in the lower back will expand as a reaction to the inhalation. The ribs should never move unless the inhalation moves them.[13] Expansion of the ribs or chest as an action independent of breathing, especially the expansion of the ribcage outward and sideways, creates stiffness and artificiality. Any action of the ribcage not instigated by the deep, silent inhalation through the nose and into the ribs in the lower back can cause tension in the upper ribs and throat. Action in the upper ribcage, based on stretching or opening the ribcage independently of the inhalation, will prevent the activation of the lowest ribs in the back.

Reiteration of the Process: placement of the inhalation
The steady, controlled closing of the floating ribs in the lower back (the closing of the bellows) was tested and practiced for several generations of great singing and has proven itself to be the most efficient method for providing a steady stream of breath to the larynx. By sending the breath against the chest and leaning or pressing it there, the *appoggio* is established. The breath stop is crucial if all tensions in the throat are to be avoided.

Breathing Method: Bel Canto

The Bel Canto style of Italian singing: Emission and Division
Tetrazzini said that in the bel canto style, the breath was drawn into the "lower rear quadrant of the lungs," which elongated the lower spine and contracted the diaphragm downward to its maximum extent. Caruso added that at the instigation of tone, the breath, "squeezed by the lower ribs in the back, like squeezing a bellows" was leaned (pressed) against the perfectly still, contracted diaphragm (the lower chest). The front of the diaphragm and the chest were pressed outward and forward, creating the sternal arch. By closing the lower ribs in the back while singing, pressure was created against the chest. This exaggerated action created more compression and increased the energy available to the voice.

Breathing Makes the Voice
The young singers of today must realize that the placement of the voice will be absolutely correct if the breathing is absolutely correct. Most teachers don't know how to develop the breathing of their students. They choose, instead, to accept the inadequate breathing methods their students use at the moment. Unfortunately, many teachers themselves breathe incorrectly and cannot help. Breathing into the lower back and leaning the breath against the lower chest while singing was common knowledge among professional singers and teachers of previous generations. A contemporary role model is found in Luciano Pavarotti, who recommended the same breathing method that was used in the early 1900s.

---

[13] This statement reflects sensations experienced by singers and does not represent accurate physiology. During respiration, movement of the thorax, back, and abdomen *cause* inhalation and exhalation [publisher].

Big and Beautiful: breath capacity

The amount of air in the lungs decides the richness and amplitude of the voice. The largest drum makes the biggest sound. Larger people have larger lungs and more capacity for air. We generally associate large voices with large people.

When Pavarotti appeared on *The Tonight Show with Johnny Carson,* Carson asked him what it was like to be such a large person:

> Carson: *Opera singers seem to be larger people than non-singers. For instance, I'm a small man and could never have a big voice. You are a large man and have a great voice. How do you feel about being so big?*
> Pavarotti: (answered with a sweet smile) *I don't know about the outside, but, on the inside, I feel very beautiful.*

Method, Non-Method, and Modern Method

The breathing method described above was taught in Italy by the Lampertis and quickly spread to the far reaches of the world by their protégés. The method they taught has passed down to following generations and is still being used by a limited number of singers.

One amazing result of Garcia's teaching in London, although not directly attributable to him, was the development of an approach to singing that was psychologically different from what had gone on before. Garcia had taught a biomechanical approach to singing: breathe in a certain way, hold the mouth a certain way, use the abdomen a certain way, etc. Frederick Dalberg, who studied with a student of Manuel Garcia II, used the same approach, and taught a process of sequentially applied biomechanical actions that had predictable results.

Somehow, in England, around 1912, this approach changed into a "do nothing in the voice approach to singing." The idea was to allow the resulting response in the respiration to find itself. Instead of telling the student to actively inhale in a way that would relax the throat, students were told to imagine the invisible throat. In other words, the singer should achieve a perfect state of nothingness in the jaw, tongue, neck and head, while breathing and singing. This psychological approach to singing was most successful for two of the greatest singers in history, Dame Clara Butt, a student of Belgian bass Jacques Bouhy, and Dame Eva Turner. It is interesting to note that both Dames studied for a time with the same teacher, Daniel Rootham when they were still very young (Dame Eva studied with Rootham between the ages of eleven and fourteen). According to Dame Eva, the two women discussed the invisible approach to singing somewhere around 1932, and they were in complete agreement that the approach had always worked for them. It was not clear to me at the time where the concept originated. I assumed it was with Rootham, but I am not certain. Dame Clara was twenty years older than Dame Eva, and it is unclear if their paths crossed in a common voice studio at some point. By the time I met Dame Eva in1962, she was seventy years old and her magnificent career was behind her. She was concentrating on teaching young singers the secrets of her fabulous vocal technique.

The basis of her approach was typical in some ways, agreeing with the advice of the great singers of her era ("Shape the mouth like an oval lying on its side." "Breathe into the lower back if you need more air." "Keep the pressure of the breath against the chest."), but was different psychologically from any approach I had ever experienced. The idea was to imagine a state of invisibility in the entire area of the body above the middle of the chest while singing. A total lack of sensation was created by using the imagination, described by Dame Eva as a "combination of invisible parts" of the vocal apparatus (throat, tongue, jaw, head). Invisible was the term used to try to stir in the imagination the possibility of singing with a total lack of sensory stimulation or perception in the vital areas of the muscles and resonators above the chest that produce the singing voice. It should be as if you could pass a hand through your throat and feel nothing there. Even the arms were supposed to float without the need to lift them by muscular action. The approach was close enough to the total stillness of the breath demanded in my lessons with Olga Ryss to allow me to attempt to win Dame Eva's approval. I was already accustomed to being very still and sensitive to movement in the throat. Needless to say, it was not a vocal method that could be learned overnight. However, I have tried to use the invisible approach as much as possible during my own singing life. Some students and colleagues respond to it, especially when trying to teach young singers to relax the jaw. Some think I'm crazy if I suggest such a thing! It is very difficult to learn to ignore the sensations caused by the vibrations of the voice in the mask and in the head. Theoretically, it is possible and very efficient, and at least two of the greatest singers in history proved that it worked for them.

Touching the Bell

In the old Italian school of singing, the breath would never have been allowed to enter the throat in excess of what could be utilized by the vocal folds. Singing was dependent on, and defined by, breath control. Only the smallest amount of breath necessary for the creation of the desired tone was allowed to pass upward into the throat. The superabundance of the breath had to be restrained until it was needed. Modern singers need some form of breath control below the throat, before the air arrives at the larynx. It must be developed in order to allow the vocal folds to vibrate freely. Any vibrating string, on the violin or in the throat, will cease to vibrate at its fullest if unnecessary action influences it. A bell must be allowed to ring freely with no impediment to its vibrations. Touch a vibrating string or bell and the sound will instantly diminish or cease. If the vocal folds are touched by exaggerated pressure of the breath or by muscular tension, either as action or as reaction, the efficiency of the vibrations of the voice will be diminished.

Propping the Superabundance

There is a way to breathe that will create a free, invisible zone in the throat and neck, including the tongue, jaw, muscles under the jaw and behind the chin, upper pharynx and lower pharynx, and epiglottis. Faulty breathing methods create tensions, which cause nasality, a shaking jaw, and—very often—a visible and disturbing quiver of the tongue. Muscles and ligaments of the entire inner and outer neck and throat will become tense as a result of faulty breathing. Lamperti said, "All problems in singing arise because of mismanagement of the breath."

The Italian term to describe the pressure of the breath against the chest is *appoggio*. Translated literally, it means lean or leaning, as in propping a ladder against a wall or leaning against anything that can take the whole weight of a person or thing. In German it is *sich hinstützen* (to lean oneself or itself against something). "Keep the pressure of the breath against the sternum at all times," Tetrazzini advised. Lehmann called for "constant pressure against the chest while singing," which she referred to as stopping the breath (the German word is *Atemstauen*, but *sich hinstützen* is closer to the Italian meaning of *appoggio*).

Propping the breath against the sternum or the chest was the ultimate method for controlling the accumulated breath held in the lungs that could not be utilized by the vocal folds, called the superabundance of the breath by Manuel Garcia II in his book *Hints on Singing*. Any breath not required to produce the desired tone must be restrained while emitting only the amount of air necessary.

Verhaltungsmethode (restraining method): singing is inhaling

Some singers have sung successfully with an exaggerated, continuous breathing-in technique (the sensation of inhaling while exhaling). The drawing inward of the abdomen continues while singing, and the control of the diaphragm depends on the sustaining strength of the inhalation. However, the efficacy of this method of breath control, maintaining the diaphragm in a drawing-in mode while singing, is limited almost exclusively to the German repertoire. Elizabeth Schwarzkopf was the most famous singer who used this vocal method, called in German, "*Verhaltungsmethode*." She had a radiant, beautiful voice, but had international success only in the German repertoire, including, of course, roles in operas by Mozart. Her technique was perfect for singing the German language. Singing German requires that each word that begins with a vowel must be separated from the preceding word and enunciated anew. The inhaling technique is perfect for this vocal style. It sustains diaphragmatic control in the silences between words, and allows for an evenness of the required, repeated attacks on each new vowel.

Don't Make Bubbles: Verhaltungsmethode

In the *Verhalten* German vocal style, breath control is achieved by continuing the inhaling process of the diaphragm and the lower ribs in the back, which Lilli Lehmann described as a breath-stop. In German, it is *Atemstauen*, which is accomplished by maintaining the inhalation pressure of the breath against the expanded ribcage. This type of support method is a variation of the candle flame exercise. Ernst Kozub described it as trying to sing underwater without making bubbles!

The exercise of singing with a candle flame in front of the lips without disturbing the steadiness of the flame is good for both German and Italian vocal styles. Instead of sending out the right amount of breath to produce tone, the German vocal stylist restrains the excess by maintaining the inhalation command, and allows just enough breath to escape to make tone.

The difference between the two methods is much more than just psychological. The constant restraining of the breath prevents emotional, and, especially, sentimental singing. Beniamino Gigli's sobbing method would have been impossible if he had used a restrained breath method of support. However, the *Verhaltungsmethode* is perfect for singing music that requires more of an instrumental approach; i.e. Mozart, Bach, Lieder of the greatest German and Austrian composers. The most effective Liedersänger (singers who specialize in the performance of songs composed by major classical composers) often use the *Verhaltensmethode*. Dietrich Fischer-Dieskau and Hermann Prey successfully used this method, combined with a variation of the pre-sneeze technique that created a particular formation in the throat and trachea. The action/reaction process that resulted caused a holding reaction in the breath, which they sustained by keeping the upper ribs expanded. The result was extraordinary control. Fischer-Dieskau, especially, developed the ability to sing very quietly with expressive colors and very clear diction. It is interesting that Prey's best friend, Fritz Wunderlich, tried to change the baritone's restraining method to a leaning method. The effort was not successful.

Modern breathing method: Limited Vibrations

In contrast to the breathing method discussed above, the modern breathing convention is to swell the belly outward while inhaling and to pull the abdomen inward and upward while singing (the sleeping baby). This is exactly the opposite of the recommendations of the greatest singers and teachers of the past. Many of today's singers are taught to pull the abdomen inward while singing, which forces breath up against the larynx. In this approach, there is no breath stop below the area of the throat and the breath is pressed upward directly against the throat. Breath that is pressed upward by the collapsing abdomen overloads the function of the free vibrations of the vocal folds. Various muscles in and about the throat must be activated in order to neutralize this pressure. The equalization of pressures against the throat and the neutralization process of flexing muscles to counteract muscles limits the vibrations of the vocal folds. One sad result of this approach is that sound enhancement systems are becoming more common in theaters in the United States. Voices no longer project as well as they did in the past. Unfortunately, as if deadening the vibrations of the vocal folds were not bad enough, the constant pressure of the breath against the throat will eventually cause physical damage. Nodules and bowed vocal folds, chronic hoarseness, vocal fatigue, inadequate stamina, and a host of other problems plague singers today. Air that is released or pushed upward, especially in the passaggio, will have to be controlled by muscles in the throat. Breath must not be allowed to overwhelm the vibrations of the edges of the vocal folds if rich, vibrant tones are to be achieved. Singing, even the worst kind of singing, becomes impossible if the vocal folds cannot vibrate due to unutilized breath being pushed up against them. The only control method available, if a stream of air is forced upward into the throat by the abdomen, is to use the very muscles in the throat that interfere with the freedom of the voice. Remember the rule: *No action in the throat.*

Squish, squish, squish: faulty breathing method

Allowing the belly to expand outward while inhaling does not cause the soft palate to lift upward as a reaction. This faulty breathing method, because of the lack of response in the soft palate, directs the path of the voice straight into the nose, exacerbating any nasal tendency, and generally causing incorrect actions and reactions in the throat. Franco Corelli said in a master class, "The American singers all sound like they are singing through a straw!" He indicated a pinching motion in the throat with his fingers, and said, "The American throat goes squish, squish, squish!"

Baby Breathing: Two Perspectives

Babies, considered to be examples of natural breathing, utilize the breath in two different ways. Many teachers advise their students to observe and imitate the breathing of a sleeping baby. The problem I have with this idea is that, when we are singing, we are not asleep! Perhaps we should find out how a baby breathes when it is awake and laughing or crying.

If we are going to apply the concept of natural breathing, how should we inhale, and how should we control the breath while making sounds? Which breathing function of a baby will achieve the best results? Which way will allow the jaw, the muscles under the jaw and the tongue to be free, relieving the many muscular contractions that cause the tongue and jaw to shake and quiver and damage the voice? The quivering tongue, the shaking jaw, and contracted muscles under the jaw and behind the chin, must be eliminated in order to sing the full-throated, ringing, *chiaroscuro* (clear/dark) tones that are the hallmark of great singing. Freedom of the muscles in the neck, throat, tongue, jaw, those behind the chin, along with a total lack of resistance inside the larynx, should be the goals we seek.

Natural Breathing: a repeat of perspective

For the sake of those singers who believe that breathing like a sleeping baby is the only correct way to breathe, because it is obviously natural, let us examine the breathing processes of babies from two perspectives:

1. The function of the belly when the baby is silent:
   Babies inhale and exhale a certain way when they are sleeping (or are awake but silent). The belly goes outward when inhaling and goes back inward when exhaling. This is nature's method, and it is, therefore, perfect. It is the way of breathing we should all practice if we want to be perfectly silent.

2. The function of the belly when the baby is crying, laughing or making sounds: Babies inhale the opposite way before they cry or laugh or coo. When the sound making occurs, whatever the sound may be, the movement of the belly reverses, as compared to the method used by a baby when it is sleeping. The belly is drawn inward when inhaling and moves outward when sound is made. This is nature's method, and is, therefore, perfect. It is the way we should breathe if we want to make perfect sounds.

Observations

Sometimes these movements of the belly are small if the sounds being made are small, and sometimes vigorous if the sounds being made are vigorous. These observations are easy to confirm if a crying baby is nearby. I've had four of my own babies to observe, two beautiful girls and two beautiful boys, and I agree with Luciano Pavarotti, who had three of his own to observe while still a young tenor. He explained in his master class at the Juilliard School, when asked by a student how he supported his voice, that he imitated the support method of his children when they cried. Babies definitely move their bellies outward when they make sounds. Pavarotti went on to describe the correct function of his belly when singing. To quote him as accurately as possible, he said he supported his voice while singing "like a crying baby. It is here like a baby! Push, push, push!" As he gave this advice, he demonstrated by putting his hands against his lower chest and pressing his belly outward. He relaxed his belly inward to inhale, and then pushed his lower chest slowly outward while giving an example of an airplane taking off. "It is like the airplane. The motor goes whoosh while the plane is flying. If the motor stops, the airplane falls down."

After this master class, I asked Pavarotti if he had meant to use the English equivalent of the Italian word *spingere* (to push) when he recommended that singers "Push, push, push" the breath against the lower chest. He laughed when he realized that he had used the wrong word. He said, "Oh, no! I meant to use the same in English as *appoggiare*. I had forgotten this difference in the English. I should have said lean, lean, lean!"

Pavarotti, considered a wonderful vocal technician, and the best example of bel canto singing since Dame Joan Sutherland, definitely moved his chest and belly outward while singing. This technique follows the crying baby model and is exactly the same function of the belly/chest as described in the books written by Caruso, Tetrazzini and Lehmann.

Crying or Sleeping

The famous tenor Georges Thill, tried to teach the bel canto breathing method at the Paris Conservatoire, but the students rejected it. Thill had learned it from Fernando De Lucia, the greatest male exponent of the bel canto vocal style in history. De Lucia was known as La Gloria d'Italia (The Glory of Italy), because of his ability to demonstrate the perfection of vocal art. However, by the time Thill retired from his performance career and began to teach, the insidious, reversed-breathing technique of a sleeping baby had become well known as a so-called natural short-cut to breathing and support. None of the students wanted to learn the old bel canto breathing and support technique of the crying baby. They would have to wait too long to learn to sing!

Illogical Acceptance: wrong breathing

Many singers and teachers have inherited this belief that the best approach to breathing and support is to imitate a sleeping baby. They generally have no idea that this theory was conceived in 1883 in the mind of a non-singer! It is amazing that intelligent people don't question the illogic of this concept, especially considering the fact that it conflicts with the breathing and support method that has produced the greatest singers in history!

Support: *Appoggio* or The Lean (the lean of the breath)

Appoggio is the word used in Italy since the Golden Age of *Bel Canto* to describe the biomechanical process that controls the breath while singing. In the German language the word *Atemstauen* is translated by Lilli Lehmann into English as breath stop. Another common term used by German singers of the past generations to describe a support method is *Staumethode* (stopping or jamming method). Modern terminology used in Germany includes *Stützmethode* (support method) and *Verhaltungsmethode* (restraint method).

Definitions and terminology

Lean, Lean, Lean!

When I taught in Munich and Vienna, I used the terms *sich hinlehnen* (lean itself against) to describe the lean of the breath against the diaphragm. Unfortunately, there is no clear equivalent in common use in English that describes the breath control method used by professional singers in Italy or Germany. Most English speaking singers and voice teachers, unless they have been trained in the Italian or German vocal style, use the terms *support* or *breath support*.

The Inadequacy of Words

Words are very important in the way we communicate ideas, but words cannot explain everything. If they could, singers would learn to sing by reading books. All we can do is use information written in books or passed down to us as quotes by great singers to let us know if we are on the right path or not. Caruso said, at the beginning of his book, "I have my own way of singing, but I will try to give a few pointers."

What's in a Name? The Point of Leaning

The point of the leaning of the breath had the name *il punto d'appoggio* in the Italian language, *el punto de apoyo* in Spanish, and *der Punkt des Atemstauens* in German. The modern French singers use the word, *soutenir*, which means to support or lift the breath. However, when Manuel Garcia II, Mathilde Marchesi, and Blanche Marchesi taught in Paris, *appuyer* (to lean) was the French word used to describe the correct function of the breath while singing. George Thill, having learned the concept from

Fernando De Lucia, tried to teach De Lucia's method of the *appoggio* in Paris after his retirement from performing in 1953.

The point of leaning, and the more general term, *appoggio*, was defined and described in the past, as "the pressure of the breath against the chest (or sternum) while singing." This support technique has proven to be the most successful example of the mental approach to breath control ever discovered and applied in the entire history of singing.

The Flower of the Throat: explanation of the term "Support"

Support means to hold something up. This is the opposite concept of what the Italians mean when they use the word *appoggio*. The difference in meaning between these two words is crucial if the throat is to open vertically downward and remain loose and free. The great Italian voice teachers of the past often referred to the flower of the throat (*il fiore della gola*). The flower of the throat opened as part of the vertical reaction to deep inhalations into the lower back. The throat and its soft flower were kept "open and invisible, as if a hand could pass through it and find nothing there" (Dame Eva Turner). Caruso talked about the "massive respiration required for great singing" and "the open throat maintained by the power of the respiration." According to Tetrazzini, the "weight of the breath would be leaned (propped like a ladder against the wall) against the sternum at all times while singing." The amount of pressure used against the chest was always as little as possible, but sufficient to maintain the vertically opened throat, to maintain the *fiore della gola*, to equalize the resistance of the vocal folds according to their length and thickness, and to permit the freedom of the voice to achieve the vocal range and dynamics demanded by the composer.

A Ladder Against a Wall: use of the terminology in the United States and Britain

In the U.S. and U.K., the terms support and breath support have become standard terms in singing. Singers should stop for a moment and consider the differences between the terms used in the past—lean the breath, breath prop, breath stop, press the chest with the breath, press the breath against the chest, sigh against the chest—and the terms commonly used today in the English speaking countries: support and breath support. As previously stated, support means to hold something up from underneath. Breath support suggests that the breath must be held up from underneath while singing. A more efficient term would be the reflexive form of support: to have the breath support itself against the diaphragm. *Appoggio* means to lean something against a solid resistant structure, without pushing or grunting, allowing gravity to do the work. The breath should lean itself against the diaphragm. If I lean my weight against a wall, I am not pushing the wall. I am not holding up my weight or the wall. The wall is passively holding my weight, not actively lifting me. In the great school of Italian singing, the breath is leaned against the diaphragm. Tetrazzini, in her desire to explain and describe the *appoggio*, used the image of a ladder leaning against a wall.

The Superabundance of the Breath: the crucial factor

It is obvious that the total amount of breath accumulated in the lungs must not be suddenly released and allowed to gush against the vocal folds at the instant of attack. We must control both the emission of the breath that produces the singing voice, and the superabundance of the residual breath that remains in the lungs until it is needed. Manuel Garcia coined this term—the superabundance of breath—to identify and describe the air that fills the lungs that cannot be utilized by the vocal folds at the beginning of a phrase. This is the same concept as the *Atemstauen* that Lilli Lehmann used with her students. It is obvious that the massive inhalation recommended by Caruso must not be allowed to suddenly pour out of the lungs all at once when a singer begins to sing a note. The breath stop must be applied with sufficient energy and determination to balance the resistance of the vocal folds. Equalization to the degree of resistance of the vocal folds is necessary with each note or phrase being sung. The emission of air to the larynx is a perfectly controlled, slender stream of breath that does not exceed that flow which can be utilized by the vocal folds at the moment of initiating and sustaining the sung tone. Any amount of breath left in the lungs and not needed at that moment is retained and controlled by the *appoggio*. Lamperti said, "The problem for the singer is to give the breath and restrain the breath at the same time."

Moving the mind to the center of the chest and leaning the breath there will cause the ribs in the lower back to close. They will create sufficient breath pressure against the chest to ensure that the slender emission necessary to create the singing voice is predictable and uninterrupted. Franco Corelli called this continuous pressure the portamento. He carried the tone from one to the next by continuing the pressure of the breath during an uninterrupted emission. This has also been called singing legato. The exact location of the *appoggio* has been referenced by numerous singers with the following descriptions: against the center of the sternum (Luisa Tetrazzini); against the general area of the chest (Lilli Lehmann and Mattia Battistini); against the lower chest (Pavarotti, Paul Schöffler, Gottlob Frick); leaned against the chest at a forward and downward angle (Caruso, Roswänge, Richard Tucker, and Eleanor Steber).

Close observation of the silent film of Caruso actually singing does not reveal the slightest movement of his chest while he is inhaling or singing. His chest remains in a fixed position, even during the most dramatic moments of "Vesti la giubba" from Leoncavallo's *I Pagliacci*. We will discuss the constant position of the chest, called the sternal arch, shortly.

Angles of support

Degree of Angle

A singer must ask himself/herself the following questions: What degree of angle shall I employ while inhaling, relative to the vertical, and toward what target shall I direct the angle of the inhalation?

What degree of angle shall I employ for leaning the breath while singing (relative to the vertical), in order to exploit the space behind my sternal arch? If I thrust my chest outward while inhaling into my lower back, with my abdomen simultaneously moving inward, at what angle (relative to vertical) do I lean the breath while singing?

The Ideal Angle

The ideal angle of the *appoggio* or *Atemstauen* should be established as a directed line of breath that is propelled from the lower back to the center of the chest. It is the angle described by the great singers of the past as a leaning of the breath against the chest while singing.

A vertical angle of *appoggio* will act (or react) directly against the larynx and limit the vibrations of the vocal folds in direct proportion to the degree of the intensity of the vertical pressure being applied. In order to prevent a reaction in the vocal folds, the mind must be moved to the front of the diaphragm immediately after inhaling into the lower back, and the breath must be sent from the lower back against the chest under sufficient pressure to ensure that the breath will not leak or gush into the throat while singing.

A Vertical Angle of *Appoggio*

Any steeper angle of lean than those described above becomes a vertical lean, and is not recommended for singers of the Italian repertoire because of the Third Law of Motion (every action has an opposite and equal reaction). *Appoggio,* as a method of support in the Italian school of singing, is always based on the pressure of the breath against the chest as a breath control method. However, there is a kind of successful support system that is not based on the pressure of the breath; rather, it is based on the lack of pressure. It is possible to use a vertical lean successfully if the pressure of the breath is removed from the equation, and dropping or relaxing the breath downward into the deepest part of the body becomes the key concept.

We have tried to describe the ladder leaned against the wall and the weight of the breath falling into the lowest part of the lungs during the inhalation, as suggested by Tetrazzini. These ideas may sound benign, but, once the breath has been leaned against the chest, some systematic method must be activated to sustain its placement. We have discussed how the mind moves to specific locations to perform specific actions. The greatest Italian vocal method in history, as described by Caruso, Tetrazzini, Mattia Battistini, Giuseppe De Luca, and Zinka Milanov, was based on maintaining the pressure of the breath against the chest at all times.

As previously noted, the martial arts employ concepts of hard style and soft style. The difference between these two methods can be illustrated as follows: Throw (the hard style) a stone straight down off a bridge or drop (the soft style) a stone straight down off a bridge into a deep ravine. Both stones will have energy when they arrive at the bottom of the ravine. The question is, why throw the stone when dropping it will achieve the same result? The answer is determined by the desired effect when it reaches bottom. If dropping it and depending on gravity are sufficient to the task at hand, why expend energy throwing it? The same principle applies to singing and breath support.

Types of Lean

The Dead Lean and the Live Lean

There are two identifiable possibilities that a singer can use to create a lean against the wall that will provide a secure, free posture and a free throat. One is called a dead lean. Stretch the arms out with elbows straight and stiff, and, placing the open hands against a wall with the legs straight, lean the weight of the body forward at a forty-five degree angle or until completely committed. The body is now secure but without any flowing circle of energy. Singing in this posture will be dead, without expression or performance energy. It will cause the diaphragm to produce straight or still tones that are completely lifeless and boring. Singers who sing a lot of straight tones use a dead lean of the breath against the chest. It is common among singers who specialize in Baroque music or barbershop quartets, and should be taught to those who want to sing without vibrato for some reason. The most famous dead leaner in the recorded history of opera was Nellie Melba. When Rosa Ponselle was asked her opinion of Melba, she replied, "Melba had a fabulous voice, but she sang too many still tones."

Another possibility is to lean the weight of the body against a wall using the hands as before and the legs straight, but with the arms bent at the elbows at a medium angle, as if halfway through a push-up. Some practitioners of yoga do the Cobra position with the elbows bent. Straight elbows are not to be used in this type of lean, called a live lean. It is live because the energy flowing through the bent arms, coming from the entire body, creates a circle of energy that will influence the production of the voice and the many possible expressions to be used in the repertoire we sing. Singing based on a live lean will be full of excitement and color. The idea is to transfer the concept of the live lean against the wall to a live lean of the breath against the chest.

In the discussion above, the immovable wall represents the perfectly still chest, thrust forward and outward, creating the immovable sternal arch. The weight of the body, leaned against the wall, represents the weight of the breath, leaned against the chest. The dead lean represents the type of inactive diaphragmatic non-action that, although leaned, produces straight or still tones. This method is necessarily taught to certain singers in order to deliberately prevent wobbles and/or tremolos in the tone.

The live lean, also totally learned and committed, represents the type of active diaphragmatic action that produces expression, color, and vibrancy in the voice. Laughing and crying are good examples of the activated lean. The breath should be leaned (pressed) against the immovable, forward-thrusting chest (the sternal arch), as if the breath were alive and had weight, and not pushed as if trying to move the wall itself (the chest) with dead force.

The Resistance of the Vocal Folds: Live lean

The degree of intensity required by a live lean will depend very much on the resistance of the vocal folds. Huge voices require more intense (heavier) leans than small voices in order to equalize the resistance created by thicker, longer vocal folds. A large person doing push-ups will have to expend more energy than a small person, and will require more muscle development. Perhaps this explains why singers with huge voices often have huge bodies. Lauritz Melchior was 6′6″ and weighed 350 lbs. Clara Butt was 6′2″ and had a full figure. Leo Slezak was 6′9″ and weighed 390 lbs. Marti Talvela was 6′9″ and probably weighed much more than those others!

On the other hand, very light voices tend to come in smaller people. Tito Schipa, whose gorgeous voice was very light in color and weight, was a small man. Because of the lack of resistance in his small, short vocal folds while singing, he was able to use his concept of "sighing against the chest" as a breath control technique. His vocal folds were delicate and slender, and could not have functioned if they had been loaded with exaggerated breath pressure. Leaning heavily against his delicate voice would have ruined it in a short period of time. Thank goodness his teacher understood how to train his voice with tenderness and exquisite balance instead of overreaching the capability of the voice. Beniamino Gigli said about Schipa's singing, "We must all bow down to the art of Tito Schipa."

The Only Successful Vertical Lean

Dropping the breath has not been a successful support method for singing the great operas of the Italian repertoire. Tito Schipa said that he used a dropping method when he sang, which he called the sighing technique, but his angle of lean was directed against the chest and was not vertical. The very lack of activity in the vertical breathing method has limited its efficacy to roles written by Richard Wagner for powerful female voices. Turandot could be included with the Wagner roles, because of its particular vocal demands. Although some of the requirements are the same in Wagner's and Verdi's music, there are differences that require more diaphragmatic action in the vocal writing of the latter. For instance, Verdi demands more coloratura, staccati, martellati, sforzandi, crescendi and decrescendi, and sustained, exposed, high pianissimo effects. However, his sopranos must also fulfill the vocal demands that are similar to those made on Wagner's heroines, including: volume, sustaining ability, powerful declamation, incredible stamina, lyrical amplitude in the middle range of the voice, perfect diction, and erotic expression. In order to be able to fulfill the vocal demands of the Italian composers, a way to sing had to be found to accomplish all of the effects mentioned above. Throwing rocks instead of just dropping them became necessary because the targets became different and required varying degrees of intensity and accuracy of the breath stop. *Appoggio* became the ideal solution to the problems presented by all composers, including Wagner, who was quoted as saying that he wanted "bel canto specialists" to sing his music. Richard Tucker said to me in 1962, "Sing Verdi! Sing Verdi! If you can sing Verdi, you can sing anything!" He was right, and he proved it to an appreciative world.

Grunt and action in the throat: The Valsalva Maneuver

Audible grunting or squeezing of the sound produced by the slightest upward or downward pressure of the breath is a clear indication that a reaction to an active vertical lean is taking place in the larynx and against the vocal folds. One manifestation of leaning the breath vertically is known as the glottal attack (or glottal onset). This kind of misdirected attack must never be allowed. When used in excess, it is destructive to the edges of the vocal folds and, if not corrected, might ruin the voice in a relatively short period of time.

It is possible and desirable to press the breath against the chest with sufficient intensity to balance the resistance of the vocal folds. Although the biomechanical procedure of *appoggio* resembles what is called in the field of medicine a Valsalva maneuver, there is a crucial difference. The true Valsalva maneuver, originally designed by an Italian anatomist to help clear stopped up ears by exerting breath pressure against a closed glottis, requires a vertically pressed lean. A reaction against the glottis under these conditions may be considered medically normal, but it is vocally terrible. The resulting grunting sound, especially if sustained and coming from the throat, is a sure sign that the pressure of the breath is functioning in a vertical fashion, which is common in heavy lifting, or pushing downward against a constipated bowel.

The Diaphragmatic Cut-off: *good grunt* versus *bad grunt*

Although it can be confused with the damaging stroke of the glottis, there is a good grunt that is audible if the cut-off of a note is founded in the diaphragm. It happens when words end with a vowel, and, therefore, is more often heard among Italian singers. In some great singers, both male and female, it is very audible on recordings. The ultimate grunter was Caruso; however, both Rosa Ponselle and Luisa Tetrazzini were often guilty of allowing some unladylike grunts to be audible. The great difference between a bad grunt and a good grunt is determined by the evidence of activity in the throat. Bad grunts always are directed vertically or are exaggerated to the extreme, as when lifting heavy weights, which cause the vocal folds to cease their vibrations and begin to communicate effort and strain. Bad grunts always show the work in the throat, and the pressure of breath is generalized in the body.

Good grunts invariably are directed in a non-vertical direction, away from the throat and against the chest, which leaves the vocal folds entirely free to vibrate at their maximum level of performance. There is no evidence of tension or strain in the throat or neck while singing and the tiny grunt is really not a grunt at all, but the sound of a diaphragmatic cut-off. The sound of the mini-grunt is deliberately incorporated into the vocal methods of some teachers in Italy. If it can be used without causing any action or reaction in the throat or neck, does not exceed the volume or intensity of the music, and is produced by the lean of the breath against the chest, it is not only acceptable—it is to be desired. Some teachers teach it in order to acquaint the student with the correct mini-grunt, and to help them identify the bad vertical grunt that can make a singer turn completely red in the face! Perhaps it is a good thing to be acquainted with the bad one in order to avoid it in the future, in case some bad technical singing should creep into the singer's life.

Singers and teachers who are curious can listen to Caruso, Gigli (the sobbing grunt), Carlo Galeffi (another sobbing grunt), Rosa Ponselle (who sometimes would grunt between the syllables of a word), Maria Callas (who used it as an acting tool), and Tetrazzini (who was obviously pressing her breath against her sternum and the release of the pressure is sometimes audible). Once the listener becomes aware of what to look for, he/she will be amazed to hear how common the audible mini-grunt was and how easily identifiable it is among the greatest singers on recordings.

Push Down and Grunt: abdominal muscles

The muscles of the lower abdomen must never flex or harden while inhaling or singing. Ideally, the abdominal wall (muscles) should remain soft while being drawn in during inhalation, and should be released outward while singing (Caruso's "contrary motion" to the act of drawing the abdomen inward while inhaling). The abdomen must never become hard like a brick wall. In fact, Amelita Galli-Curci said that one reason to pull it in against the spine is to totally neutralize the possibility that the muscles might flex. Pulling the abdomen inward while inhaling and relaxing it outward while singing guarantees that it (the abdominal wall) cannot be involved in the production of sound. I've heard teachers say "Push down as if constipated," and "Pretend you are lifting heavy weights." One must understand how wrong these ideas are: pushing the breath down vertically while singing will cause a reactive pressure of the breath upward against the vocal folds, restricting their vibrations and reducing the sound to a strained grunt.

If we desire to enjoy the benefits of a free and loose throat while singing, we must not push the breath downward, instigating reactive pressure upward into the throat, or pull the abdomen inward, which will force the breath upward, creating active pressure in the throat. Vertical actions or reactions, other than absolute non-reactive gravity leans (dead drops, successfully used by some severely obese singers), are not to be recommended. Breath control must be accomplished by utilizing diagonal leans, with the base of the breath column situated in the lower back, and the top of the breath column placed against the front of the diaphragm (the sternum).

Abdominal Effects on the Attack

As we already have observed, the action of swelling the abdomen outward while inhaling causes an opposite and equal reaction in the body. When this reaction is allowed to rise up into the throat, it interferes with the relaxed, low position of the larynx by pressing it upward. This pressure displaces the entire throat, including the phonation of the vowels and the vertical opening of the epiglottis. It leads to tensions that must be neutralized by other muscular actions in order to allow the edges of the vocal folds to approximate pitch.

Freedom of the throat and larynx is created by the relaxation of the throat muscles and the muscles under the jaw and chin as a response to deep breathing into the lower back. The throat opens vertically, and the back of the soft tongue moves downward in a relaxed manner, allowing the epiglottis to open to its utmost possibility. The upper pharynx, being completely open, allows the sound made by the vibration of the vocal folds to pass directly into the head, over the soft palate, over the hard palate, and into the upper half of the face, known in Europe as the true mask. *Chantez dans la masque* (sing into the mask) is one of the oldest dictums in the history of operatic singing. It is still commonly used in theaters all over Europe.

Contrary Motion: Every Action Has an Equal and Opposite Reaction

The key word here is equal. If I push my breath downward into the body, I will feel a push upward of the breath in my throat. Therefore, since no action in the throat is the first rule of the bel canto style of singing, pushing downward into the body is wrong because it causes an upward pressure in the throat. However, if I drop my breath vertically while singing, as if it has weight, into the pelvic floor, relaxing every muscle inside my body while maintaining the open chest cavity provided by the posture of the sternal arch, the opposite and equal reaction will be to relax every muscle in the area of the throat and neck. It is a support technique called the dead drop method. It depends on doing nothing in the body while singing, based on relaxation and stillness of the breath. The voice floats low in the body on a calm ocean of air, kept under control by gravity, balance, and perfect stillness of the chest. The result is a vocal expression that is benign and soft-throated, and as full as the size of the air. The biggest voice I ever heard in the old Met was that of Paul Schöffler, the great German *Heldenbariton* (heroic baritone). When I asked him how he sang, he described a dual approach, depending on the role he was singing at the moment. I heard him sing the bass role of The Grand Inquisitor in Verdi's *Don Carlo*. He explained that when he sang a bass role, especially a very low role like Sarastro in Mozart's *Zauberflöte*, he used the dead drop method; however, when he sang heroic baritone roles like Wagner's Flying Dutchman or Wotan, he would "press the breath against his chest."

A similar discussion took place in 1971 in Toronto with the famous concert contralto, Maureen Forrester. She was singing Fricka in *Die Walküre* for the first time. Her performance was fantastic and everyone was raving about it. She was definitely the best Fricka I have ever heard. Her voice sounded completely different in a dramatic mezzo role from the contralto voice I had heard many times in concerts. As a matter of fact, she was the definitive contralto on the concert circuit at that time. When I asked her about the differences between her usual contralto repertoire and such a dramatic, high mezzo role, she explained her technical approaches to the demands of the two vocal categories by explaining her use of the breath. The contralto music required a more relaxed, deeper, full-bodied use of the breath than the mezzo music. She demonstrated a complete dead drop inhalation and said, "See. If I need the wider, darker, voice to fulfill the requirements of very low music, I breathe this way and do nothing inside my body; however," she went on, "if I want to sing higher and more dramatically, with more metal in the voice, I breathe like this." She then demonstrated a perfect *appoggio* technique by breathing into her lower back and leaning against her chest. Both of her voices were gorgeous and full of power. She was the best I heard in both categories, and was the living example of how two completely different psychological approaches to voice production can be successful.

Appoggio and the Sternal Arch

The position of the chest must be pre-established and fixed in space by the posture of the singer, before breathing and singing begin. This is the source of the concept of the permanent sternal arch in singing, which is the wall against which a singer leans the breath.

The sternal arch is created by thrusting the sternum out and forward, using the back muscles, which create a curved (arched) chest wall against which the singer must lean the breath. It is sometimes created by pre-leaning the chest outward, which is a posture that is independent of the inhalation, or sometimes as a result of deep breathing into the chest while drawing the abdomen inward, which creates the ultimate expansion of the breath-box. The same extreme opening of the chest can be accomplished over time by posturing as in the practice of yoga. This position of the chest is often called the correct posture for singing (Lamperti said to "stand up like a soldier"). No additional outward movement of the chest wall is necessary if it can remain fixed in space in spite of the collapsing (squeezing) of the ribs in the lower back. The chest must never be allowed to collapse inward or downward while singing. The pressure of the breath against the chest is often referred to inaccurately as breath support, as if the breath itself holds the chest up in its position. The breath does not support the chest, just as we do not support the wall we lean against. Rather the chest is exploited in singing by taking advantage of its pre-set, fixed position. It is the solid wall against which we lean the breath. A singer can establish the posture of the chest independently and maintain it separately at all times by the muscles in the lower back, whether singing or not.

The sway-back or curved back is often used to support the chest in its arched outward position. However, it is not necessary to sing with a swayback if the lower spine is elongated with every inhalation into the lower back. The elongation of the lower spine when inhaling will prevent the curved appearance of the back while singing, and still allow the muscles that support the posture of the sternal arch to function.

Types of support

Passive or Active Support

The controlling pressure of the breath against the chest (the *appoggio*) is created by closing (squeezing) the expanded bellows in the lower back. The resulting movement of the air/breath is then propelled against the front of the diaphragm. However, there is another way to support the voice that is completely passive. The ribs in the lower back can also collapse while singing against the chest as a reaction to the power of gravity. This is passive support, called a sighing technique by Tito Schipa, or a gravity technique by Alexander Kipnis.

Passive Support
Passive support can be the best approach if the role is very long and the orchestration is very heavy. It requires the singer to drop the breath as low in the body as possible without allowing any muscular action. In Europe one hears old recommendations, such as "Sing like you are fourteen months pregnant with triplets." Gravity alone is used to create the effect of the breath stop. The muscles of the back are left slack in order to allow them to respond to the loss of breath as it is used by the voice. The secret is to use gravity to drop the superabundance of the breath down against the diaphragm instead of actively, muscularly pressing it against the chest.

Active Support
An active support method is based on muscular action in the ribs of the lower back. They must squeeze the breath against the chest to establish control. The squeezing propels the breath against the front of the diaphragm in order to achieve a continuous connection. Dropping the breath, as if dropping a heavy weight into the body, causes the ribs in the back to collapse. As long as the breath remains dropped, the sound can be sustained without muscular action. This way of singing is usually practiced by obese women or very pregnant women who sing long, sustained roles that do not require coloratura, staccato, accents or the many other vocal effects required by Italian composers. Some singers lean the body forward at an exaggerated angle with the chest thrust exaggeratedly out, in order to assist the gravity type of breath control. If a true gravity drop is achieved, the chest is held up and immobile, and the abdomen will completely hang out, completely loose, and without any action in the chest except posture. The collapsing ribs in the back will automatically send the right amount of breath to the voice to fulfill the demands of sustained vocal music.

To Collapse or Not to Collapse: Something Has to Give
Good singing, and the fulfillment of professional criteria in singing, require that the emission of the breath that creates the singing tone be sent from somewhere in the body. From where should the breath be sent to the chest and larynx? Which wall of the drum should be allowed to collapse when singing is begun and sustained?

The lungs are surrounded by the ribcage. As the lungs lose air, some part of the ribcage, or the belly under the ribcage, must yield to the loss. George London made an issue of the ribs in his master classes.

> The ribs should not move unless the inhalation moves them, and then, only in the lower back. They should close in the lower back as the breath is used for sustaining a tone. The chest and the belly should never move, whether inhaling or exhaling. The chest should be held in an up and open posture and remain perfectly still while either inhaling or singing. The idea of opening the upper ribcage and holding it open in a sideways posture while singing has never been recommended by a great singer from the past. The breath must be allowed to flow freely and directly from the lower back,

through the throat, without any change of emission or resistance to the emission.

The Collapsing Balloon

One of my colleagues used a support technique that gradually collapsed all three sections of the air box as evenly as possible at the same time, like a balloon that has sprung a leak. Of course, this approach was learned from a repertoire coach, and not from a famous singer. Unfortunately, her dynamic range and her vocal range were extremely limited. She couldn't sing louder than a mezzo forte without getting hoarse, because the pressure of the breath against the larynx, although comparatively mild, was leaned directly against the only possible mechanism left for control of the emission: the vocal folds themselves.

The Collapsing Chest

The vibrations of the air in the upper lungs are reduced if the chest collapses downward or inward while singing. In spite of this obvious fact, some singers allow the chest to collapse while singing, and try to control what is left of the superabundance of the breath by flexing muscles elsewhere in the body. They try to compensate for the loss of the breath prop against the chest by leaning into the big belly (abdomen), or against the upper back, or sideways and outward against the upper ribs. The big belly leaning method is most commonly used by men with big bellies, especially basso buffos (male singers with low voices who specialize in comic roles). Usually, they are limited to playing the funny men, in spite of possessing natural voices that are of good quality in terms of range and volume. The collapsing chest and the loss of the vibrating air in the upper part of the air box leave the singer with a generic sound that lacks the possibility of noble expression. Imagine the effect on a drum if it were slowly collapsing and losing air while being played. The sound would gradually become less resonant and have a dead quality. A slight adjustment of the sternal arch would stretch the front part of the diaphragm.

The greatest practitioner of the belly-leaning method I ever heard was Salvatore Baccaloni, who was generally considered the greatest basso buffo in history. The quality of his natural voice was definitely beautiful enough to have been a leading character in any kind of bass repertoire. However, his vocal method, dominated by letting the chest collapse and pressing the breath into his large belly, responded to an exaggerated Santa Claus "Ho-Ho-Ho" way of delivering the vocal lines. Although his method gave him the freedom of the throat he needed to fulfill the requirements of the comic characters he portrayed, his sound was always comical and without nobility. There were no subtle changes of color and emotion. His diction was clear and facile, and his high notes were secure. A higher placement of the point of leaning would have made the voice more slender and adaptable to the expression of delicate emotions. A higher placement of the *appoggio* would have prevented the unsteady, slow vibrato that dominated his sustained singing at times.

The Collapsing Belly

The belly can be pulled inward or allowed to collapse inward while singing, forcing or allowing breath to escape upward against the throat. If the abdomen is pulled inward, the pressure of the breath being pushed upward will land directly on the larynx, creating havoc with the vibrations of the vocal folds. The muscles of the throat, tongue, jaw and the muscles under the jaw and behind the chin get involved in trying to control breath that is being pushed from underneath. This method is simply a vocal disaster in action. It is a method that collapses the lower section of the breath-box and provides no lean in the body at all. It is the most damaging method of releasing or sending air against the throat of all of the many possible ways to misuse the breath. If breath is pushed up by pulling the abdomen or middle belly inward and/or upward while singing, the muscles in and around the throat will have to compensate for the pressure from underneath.

The Collapsing Ribs

The ribs in the lower back should collapse (close, squeeze together) in order to send and sustain the pressure of the breath against the lower chest. However, it goes without saying that there must be sufficient breath in the lower back before the squeezing begins. It is the breath control method every singer should strive to master. This will require that the chest remain thrust forward in the position of the sternal arch, and must remain still and full of breath while singing. The abdomen will have no function at all in this method of breath control. After breathing into the lower back becomes a habit, pulling the abdomen inward while inhaling can be left out of the breathing method completely. For instance, pregnant ladies can't breathe into the belly—the space is already occupied—and they certainly cannot pull their abdomens inward while singing. The inhalation of a pregnant singer has to go into her back. She has no choice. This is the reason some ladies seem to sing better and better as the fetus develops and the belly gets larger. By eliminating the belly as a possible breathing space and maintaining a full, still chest, we allow the ribs in the lower back to open when inhaling and close when singing. This process coordinates the various processes of the breathing system to produce the loosest, softest, most open throat, the smoothest emission of the breath, and the guaranteed longevity of the vocal organ. It also results in the most resonant sounds we can make with the voice, due to the perfect freedom of the vibrations of the vocal folds.

POSTURE

Back/Spine

Elongation of the Spine: Sway-back posture

The elongation of the lower spine was a concept that helped to prevent curving the lower back extremely forward while leaning (pressing) the breath from the lower ribs in the back to the area at the center of the chest. The most successful singers—who were willing to discuss their breathing and support techniques, especially those I met in Europe—generally followed the rules of inhaling the breath into the lower back while drawing the abdomen inward. However, some of them added an extra downward movement in their lower backs. While inhaling, the lower spine was elongated downward which caused the pelvis to tip under and forward, thereby preventing the noticeable tendency of certain singers to appear to be arching their backs extremely while singing. The sway-back posture, although not necessarily wrong in terms of the diaphragmatic function that controls the emission of the breath for singing, looked bizarre in some cases, especially among male singers. Elongation of the lower spine while inhaling developed into a successful concept for helping to place the breath into the lower back while preventing the tendency to stand with sway-back posture while singing. A separate action of elongating the lower spine will not be necessary to expand the lower ribs in the back if the breath is drawn into the lower back silently through the nose and with sufficient strength. Elongation of the spine is not detrimental to the bellows, and can actually help some singers, just as drawing the abdomen inward while inhaling can assist the lower ribs in the back to open extremely by causing the inhalation to go down even deeper into the lower rear quadrant of the lungs.

Posture of the Chest

The Sternal Arch

If a singer notices that the chest is sinking while singing and rising with each inhalation, it means that the fixed position of the chest, which should be thrust forward and slightly upward and totally without movement while singing, has not been perfectly established. The position often recommended by some of the older singers and teachers in Europe is called the sternal arch, as was earlier noted in the discussion of breathing and breath support.

It is important to make clear the difference between the depression at the base of the throat called the sternal notch (the junction of the interior ends of the clavicles), and the sternal arch, which is centered in the middle of the sternum and shaped horizontally and vertically into an outward arch by lifting the sternum outward and slightly upward using the back muscles. The notch is used as a phonation base and a point of leaning by some singers. Although it is a functional choice of *appoggio* in terms of producing great sounds—it was used very successfully by Mario Del Monaco, Franco Corelli, and George London—it creates the most dangerous of all points of breath pressure (leans). If the pressure of the breath suddenly releases against the vocal folds, there is no time to recover before the pressure has done its damage. The damage, unfortunately, is usually severe.

The exaggerated, outward and forward arching of the sternum is a method for stretching the front of the diaphragm as part of the basis of diaphragmatic breath control. The front of the diaphragm should ideally be stretched at all times while singing. The sternum should be arched both vertically and horizontally. As I've previously stated, information gleaned from over fifty years of observations and question and answer sessions with great singers has taught me that singers who sing the great operas of the Italian repertoire never lean the breath vertically. Leans, which always imply that pressure of the breath against some part of the chest is the basis of the control of the emission of the voice, are horizontal or diagonal, and they happen on the inside of the body. They are usually not visible from the outside, because the open chest cavity provided by the sternal arch provides plenty of space inside the body for the various angles of lean to function unseen. The sternal arch, against which the breath is pressed, is created by posturing.

Head posture

The posture of the head should be maintained in a position that faces the second balcony. Tetrazzini said, "The head should be tilted back in order to open the cavities of the head." This angle of the head offers room for the jaw to hang/drop downward and open in a completely relaxed position. Allowing gravity to unhinge the jaw, with the corners of the mouth pulled back, while keeping the posture of the head facing the second balcony, guarantees that the jaw will not be muscularly pressed downward against the top of the larynx. Historically, singers who have exaggerated the head-tilted-back posture have enjoyed very long careers. Of course, it makes sense, because tension in the throat and jaw is not possible if the head is thrown extremely back. There is left only the possibility of supporting in the body and not in the throat.

The Open Head

Maintaining the position of the head in a posture tilted up and back, facing the second balcony, was considered the most efficient use of the megaphone in the throat. Singers should study photographs of the great singers caught in the act of producing tones. Every picture we have of Caruso singing shows him with his head up facing the second balcony.

Shape of the Throat

The Open Throat

The open throat is a very misunderstood and dangerous concept. How to achieve it correctly was explained by the greatest singer of them all, when, after describing his method of inhaling and controlling the breath, he added that "massive respiration is required for great singing." He also explained how to keep the throat open while singing. "The open throat is maintained by the power of the respiration." These are the words of Enrico Caruso.

The throat is never to be opened by muscular action, such as yawning or raising the soft palate independently, or by spreading the upper or lower pharynx. Although the mouth in the Italian School is open horizontally, with the corners of the mouth always pulled back (the gentle smile), the throat is to be opened only vertically and only by the power of the inhalation. The open throat refers specifically to the opening action of the epiglottis during the massive respiration described above. It should be breathed open, which can only be accomplished by deeply inhaling into the lower back. Any action in the throat that is not a direct result of the power of the respiration is wrong and can cause tension and spreading of the upper and lower pharynx. Muscular action in the throat (yawning, raising the soft palate in any direction but up and forward, covering, hooking) can easily be misidentified as opening the throat by those who have never based their singing on correct respiration. Sadly, they insist on giving bad advice to vulnerable young singers, recommending muscular actions in their throats to achieve that which only deep breathing can accomplish. It should be stated here very clearly. Young singers who take bad advice will never have singing careers. Robert Merrill, when asked to describe the most important thing a singer needs in order to make a big career said:

> *You have to have the talent or intelligence to know what is good for you and to avoid bad advice. Everyone thinks he or she is a genius and will give you advice. You must be able to distinguish between good advice and bad advice or you will not survive as a singer.*

ARTICULATION

Jawbone

Some singers have jaws that could kill 10,000 Philistines! The old rule of the invisible jaw, which demanded that the completely loose jaw hang down without flexing while singing, seems to have been forgotten.

Pac-Man®

This section is about the jaw and the freedom thereof, because it is, by its looseness or its rigidity, an indicator of tension, or lack thereof, in the throat. It can also be the cause of tension in the throat, if it is not kept in a totally relaxed state while singing. A relaxed jaw, unhinged at the back, can be a major contributor to a healthy voice and beautiful singing. Faulty support and sleeping baby breathing cause tension in muscles that normally have nothing to do with the production of the voice. The jaw, because of its sympathetic reactions to muscle contractions in the throat, can begin to shake, quiver, extend vertically downward, jut forward, or "Pac-Man" in a chewing function while singing text. To watch singers singing today, one would think that many have never heard of anything as radical as a loose jaw! In the old days, singers would work constantly on nothing but the loosening of the jaw. Tetrazzini said she spent hours in front of a mirror learning to use her eyebrows, in order to portray the emotions of the characters in the many operas she sang—without flexing her jaw. She considered the looseness and the unhinging of the jaw to be essential to the open throat, and thus to good singing. At one point in her book, she said, "Never get upset and try to sing. It will stiffen the jaw, and you will not be able to sing." So, whatever her definition of singing was, she couldn't do it if she flexed the muscles in or around her jaw. How many singers today demonstrate a totally loose jaw while singing?

Obsession Recommended: invisible jaw

In summation, the relaxed, unhinged jaw is essential to good singing. It should be accorded the importance it requires by all who desire to sing well. The jaw is important because it affects so many parts of vocalization. The best way to learn to sing with the invisible jaw is to develop a breathing method that will relax the jaw instead of causing tension in the throat. The dedication necessary on the part of the singer for the total looseness of the jaw cannot be exaggerated if freedom of the jaw is to be achieved. The alternative is a tight, flexing set of muscles around the jaw that will prevent the throat from opening, and have only negative effects on the sound of the voice. Obsession is, in this case, to be recommended. For some singers, the only way to get the jaw to relax will require an obsession with the freedom and invisibility of the muscles that surround the jaw.

The jaw is correctly positioned by using gravity to drop the mouth open the width of one finger, and by pulling the corners of the mouth back. The open smile was once considered one of the most important characteristics of the bel canto style of singing. The resulting shape of the mouth and throat was the open smile or the oval lying on its side. It caused the jaw to unhinge at the back which, when combined with a deep inhalation into the lower back, had a profound influence on the overall opening of the throat all the way down to the lungs.

Tongue

The invisible front of the tongue

The front of the soft, flat, wide, and loose tongue is kept in contact with the lower lip from corner to corner of the mouth on all vowels, allowed to activate only when the articulation of the dental consonants required the tip of tongue to flip up and down, from the lower lip to behind the upper front teeth and back, without closing the teeth together.

The invisible back of the tongue

The loose back of the tongue is drawn downward as a response to deep, silent inhalation through the nose and into the lower back, without allowing the front of the tongue to leave the lower lip. Enrico Caruso said, "The open throat is maintained by the power of the respiration." The back of the tongue and the unhinged jaw contribute to the opening of the throat if the power of the inhalation is sufficient to draw the tongue down and out of the way of the tone. Luisa Tetrazzini said, "The tongue can literally be a stumbling block to the voice." The tongue should never be shaped, pointed, cupped, lifted or curled, and the front of the tongue should never be pulled backward into the throat. Cupping the middle of the tongue or creating a ski slope with the front half of the tongue are inventions thought up by bad teachers who never sang over big orchestras. There is only one rule that applies to all situations where the tongue is concerned. It should be completely loose and soft at all times, except when the tip is activated up and down to articulate dental consonants. Ideally, the tip of the tongue will separate from the relaxed lower jaw and move up and down while the teeth stay separated.

Mouth

A horizontal opening of the mouth (the gentle smile or the open smile)

Marcella Sembrich called the correct form of the mouth the "oval lying on its side." Caruso told Rosa Ponselle to "keep a rectangle in the back of her throat at all times." Helga Roswänge called the position of the mouth best suited for the projection of the voice the "open smile." Tetrazzini said, "The correct shape of the mouth is formed by smiling. The mouth must not change shape while singing."

The hinges of the jaw open if the corners of the mouth are pulled back. Some singers take this to the extreme, regardless of the words or the emotions to be expressed. Text is sung through the soft, oval-shaped opening of the mouth without changing the form, just as a ventriloquist can pronounce words clearly without any distortion of the vowels or tension in the throat. Many Italians speak through one horizontal mouth form (the laterally shaped mouth, or the oval). Interested singers need only to observe an Italian TV announcer and watch the corners of his/her mouth, which will remain pulled back. The interior form of the throat will retain its horizontal, open shape, regardless of the vowels being pronounced. Or, even better, find the silent film of Caruso singing "Vesti la giubba" from Leoncavallo's *I Pagliacci*. Every singer and singing teacher should study that film closely and observe the shape of the mouth. The corners of his mouth were never brought forward (Figure 1).

The natural mouth shape of babies: Truth and Nature

Singers, who are seeking the truth about natural singing, will observe the mouths of babies while they are laughing or crying, which always open sideways, with the corners pulled extremely back. The clever student or teacher will compare the shapes of babies' mouths to the mouth shapes demonstrated by Caruso in the book *Caruso's Method of Voice Production*, written by his otolaryngologist, Dr. P. Mario Marafiotti. The photograph of Caruso, demonstrating the proper mouth shape for the Italian [a] vowel, shows the exact same shape as a crying or laughing baby's mouth.

The Shape of the Mouth While Singing

The corners of the mouth are pulled extremely back. This action creates curved grooves just outside the corners of the mouth where the cheeks and the corners of the mouth connect. Tetrazzini and Nicolai Gedda described this function as "opening the throat." Lamperti said, "The open throat is the same shape as the bright [a] in the Italian word *stai.*"

The upper lip is pulled down to cover the front teeth (or in our small baby, to cover the gums!) In all of the photographs of Caruso performing or demonstrating the correct way to pronounce vowels, he never shows his teeth. Franco Corelli also was known to have repeatedly pulled down on his upper lip during performances. The critics in the New York newspapers did not approve and mentioned his private behavior during performances as being distracting.

Hiding the upper front teeth, by pulling the upper lip down while singing, is easily observed in films of Richard Tucker, Lauritz Melchior, Zinka Milanov, and many of the greatest singers. It is a fairly common technique among active singers in Germany. One only needs to observe Elizabeth Schwarzkopf's upper lip while she sings, which is repeatedly pulled down for every syllable and sustained vowel. In her master classes, she taught young singers to pull the upper lip down exaggeratedly while singing, calling it "pulling down the elephant's trunk."

The upper lip is pulled down while singing to prevent *white* sounds, which will be made if the vowel is formed in the front of the mouth instead of being inhaled into the pharynx. Some teachers mistakenly believe that the bright sound that is the result of lifting the middle of the tongue is frontal resonance. Actually, it is a sound dominated by low facial resonance that, since it is below the true mask, is lacking overtones. This is the worst effect caused by humping the tongue or forming a ski-slope in the middle of the tongue. Raising the tongue, or pulling it back into the pharynx, is like stuffing a hamburger into a megaphone! The sound that manages to escape the tongue trap is

[a]

[e]

[i]

[o]

[u]

Figure 1: Caruso's Mouth Shapes for the Cardinal Vowels

weak and pale, with no depth. If the teeth are shown while singing, shallow sounding vowels will be created. Caruso considered it a technical fault to "show beautiful teeth while singing." Pulling the upper lip down over the teeth assists the proper phonation of the vowel. The *stai* formation of the throat creates the *chiaro* (bright or clear) effect. Deep inhalations into the lower back provide the *oscuro* (dark or mellow) effect.

The front of the tongue should be in contact with the lower lip, from one corner of the mouth to the other corner of the mouth. The lower lip protrudes slightly, with the corners of the mouth pulled back. This will create a horizontal groove under the lower lip (on the outside and visible), in order to create the labial consonants [m, v, p, b, f].

The corners of the mouth are kept back, even on the [u] vowel. Again, study the photograph of Caruso demonstrating the [u] vowel, as shown in Figure 1. Notice that the greatest singer of all protrudes his lower lip. The corners of the mouth are kept in a pulled back formation, and the jaw unhinges and moves slightly forward. This is called the Italian [u], the lateral [u], or the ventriloquist's [u], as opposed to the French [u], which is pronounced with the corners of the mouth puckered forward. Puckering the lips forward causes the jaw to drop slightly downward instead of forward, and it deadens the resonance by trapping sound in the mouth and in the flesh of the lips and cheeks. Puckering the lips while singing is to be avoided at all times. The Italian formation, with the corners of the mouth pulled back, should be practiced on all vowels at all times, and every labial consonant has as its basis, the same shape of the mouth. The Italian [u] is to be substituted for an [u] that occurs at any time, in any language. Of course, French people smile sometimes when they say *l'amour*. A smiling [u] will allow the resonance to go above the mouth and nasal cavity, and find its way into the mask. It should not get trapped inside the mouth.

Tugging at the Larynx: position of the mouth

The positions of the corners of the mouth are crucial if the jaw is to be unhinged, and if the area surrounding the jaw is to be kept totally free at all times while singing. Tension under the jaw can exert a pulling force on the muscles attached to the hyoid bone, causing the larynx to be pulled upward while singing. All contracted muscles shorten their length. The contraction of the muscles under the jaw should never occur. Muscle contractions in the jaw and the throat must be relaxed back to a normal position. Unfortunately, if they are not relaxed, a compromise must be made. The only compromise available to the singer, if the larynx is not to be pulled upward, will be to press the jaw downward, thus distorting the phonation of the vowels and lowering the resonance from the mask downward into the mouth cavity and the insides of the cheeks. Peter Glossup said, "If you open the barn door, the cow will get out!" (If you pull the jaw down and open it extremely, the resonance will escape through the mouth and flow out under the mask.) He was known as a singer who, like Christa Ludwig, sang with the mouth almost closed.

Try to speak on the telephone to a friend with the jaw pulled downward and see how ridiculous it sounds. This ugly process, amplified by the compression of the breath while singing, makes for a distorted sound, bad diction, severe reactive tensions in the throat, and loss of resonance in the true mask.

Soft Palate: True Mask

The True Mask

The true mask is across the upper face, where we wear glasses (Helge Roswänge said, "Sing through the eyes and the eyebrows, not into the cheeks"). The true mask is above the nose and never in or through the nose, and is above the [ng] resonance line. As Caruso said: "Never sing into the nasal cavity. It is against all the rules of song." Other great singers spoke to this issue in similar ways:

> The true mask has nothing to do with the nose or nasal resonance. The nose must be closed and tightly sealed shut while singing. This is achieved by using the pre-sneeze formation, or vocalizing by using the consonant [b] or [d] in front of every sound. Never vocalize using [m] or [n].
>
> (George London)

> The true mask resonance is the result of "the flow of the vibrations of the vocal folds. They proceed as follows:
>
> - They pass up from the larynx through the open epiglottis.
> - They continue through the lower pharynx and the upper pharynx.
> - They pass up the back wall of the throat.
> - The vibrations (the sound) pass behind and over the forward lifted soft palate.
> - They follow the natural, open path that passes over the hard palate.
> - They continue until they strike the hard surfaces of the upper half of the front of the skull, well above the bridge of the nose."
>
> (Lilli Lehmann)

> *La maschera nel canto* (the mask in singing) has nothing to do with the sinus cavities in the cheek bones. They are too low in the face. We must sing from low in the back of the neck, and allow the resonance to angle upward and pass over the soft palate, until it arrives above the level of the cheeks and the bridge of the nose. The sound must resonate into the eye sockets, the eyebrows, and the forehead.
>
> (Mario del Monaco)

The resonance of the true mask is the result of vibrating air in the nasopharyngeal chamber, which must be sealed completely by lifting the soft palate. This action can be achieved by a mechanical command (Lilli Lehmann's "move the back wall of the nose forward"), either by creating the pre-sneeze formation of the interior of the nose (George London and Leonard Warren), or by trying to sustain the consonants [b] or [d]. Of course, neither can be sustained, because the palate lifts and seals the nose.

The best way to achieve the lifting of the soft palate up is by breathing deeply into the lower rear quadrant of the lungs (ideally, with the abdomen moving inward to increase the drawing in response of the lower ribs in the back), causing an opposite and equal reaction of the soft palate. The nose will be sealed reactively, and no separate, mechanical command to lift the soft palate is necessary. Singing with the resonance of the voice placed too low in the face, below the true mask (nasally), will be impossible.

The Misdirected Soft Palate: true versus false mask

Many singers try to lift the palate straight up or up and back to avoid a nasal sound. Raising the palate in this manner will cut off the passage to beautiful head resonance. Inefficient solutions to achieve facial resonance cause one bad technique to build upon another. This approach leads invariably to some form of muscular chain reaction in the throat. Compensation techniques become necessary to help maintain the artificially created space in the throat. The strain on the voice of both artificially created space in the throat and the complicated muscular process required to neutralize tensions around the larynx must be alleviated by exaggerating the activity of the support system. Unfortunately, this exaggerated activity is evident in many singers today. Tremolo (an abnormally fast vibrato) has become almost the standard concept of vibrato. It is a direct result of compensating for the artificially created space in the throat caused by lifting the soft palate up or up and back, and breathing into the belly or chest instead of into the lower back.

The Free Larynx: The Invisible Goal

The goal is to sing without flexing the muscles behind the chin or under the jaw. The tendency to pull the hyoid bone upward (for all practical purposes, the singer is more likely to feel that the larynx, not hyoid, is being pulled upward), caused by flexing muscles under the jaw, will be resisted by other muscles in the throat, especially if the breathing is too shallow. Tensions and reactions in the throat will reduce the vibrations of the vocal folds. The sounds become thin, nasal and weaker in most cases, and, sometimes, chestier and darker, than the true potential and capabilities of the voice. Remember the old dictum: "The invisible jaw, the invisible tongue, the invisible throat, and the invisible face." We also must establish criteria for ourselves that include as a priority the invisible muscles under the jaw and the invisible muscles behind the chin. Our ultimate goal is total freedom of the vocal organ in all its complexities.

Phonation and Resonance

Creation of Tone

An Acoustical Principle: DRUM

John Phillip Souza said, "The bigger the drum the bigger the sound." This saying applies to the singing voice perfectly. The more we can develop our breathing, the greater the expansion of our drum (the chest capacity), and the bigger and richer the voice will become if we sing in a way that allows the vibrations of the vocal folds to affect the air in the lungs. Caruso said, "The tone should vibrate the air down inside the body."

Vibrating Cavities[14]

Playing a drum will reveal that the volume of the sound is directly related to the volume of air set into vibration. A snare drum is a skin stretched over a frame. It is open underneath and, when struck, makes the "rata-tat-tat sound." Take the same skin (head) and stretch it over the head of a large Conga drum and strike it. The sound is not only louder, it is deeper and richer, with many more overtones, and will carry great distances. A marching band often has many snare drums, but only one bass drum. The air in the larger drum disturbs the air more, and is, therefore, more efficient acoustically.

The air in the lungs of the singer works the same way: The larger the air box, the greater the sound. Therefore, any air not needed to vibrate the vocal folds is held in reserve, like a drum full of air. The air is set into vibration when the vocal folds begin to vibrate if the throat is vertically open and the air in the lungs is accessible. Caruso said to "feel the tone vibrating down into the body," and Rosa Ponselle said to "sing deeper and deeper and deeper into the body."

Developing a large breath capacity will make the voice more beautiful and more powerful. Pushing more air through the vocal folds to try to increase volume will only damage the voice and should be avoided at all times! Everyone knows that yelling at a football game will make the voice hoarse. Remember, a large drum can be played very softly, and it is still makes a large sound at a less voluminous level. Striking it with more energy will make it louder only to a certain extent. Too much force can split the head and ruin the drum. Yelling and screaming will eventually ruin the most beautiful voice. If the singer wants the voice to have sustaining power, ease of delivery, fullness, color, and adequate volume relative to the repertoire to be sung, the breath capacity must be in ample supply. Some singers naturally have plenty of breath capacity; the rest must develop their capacity (their drum) to make the voice competitive in large theaters.

---

[14] Almost all of this discussion is based on sensation and is not supported by current research in voice acoustics. This fact, however, does not diminish its value to singers in terms of sensation and perception [publisher].

Onset

To Strike a Note Clearly: attack/onset

Singers do not need all of the air in the lungs to initiate a sound. However, we will need the breath that remains in the lungs after the attack if we sustain a tone or sing a long phrase. How should we control that excess air until it is needed? How do we instigate a note without releasing more air than the tone requires or can utilize? Many old books written by teachers of singing in Italy during the nineteenth-century devote whole chapters to the attack of the tone. The choice of the word *attaccare* or *l'attacco* in Italian leaves room for interpretation. It can mean attack, as in a battle; however, its several other definitions, and the ones we are looking for, are to attach, to bind to, and in music, to strike a note clearly. A small difference in interpretation can have a devastating effect on the voice. Any strike or stroke of the breath against the vocal folds is dangerous. The sense of the word attack in common usage in English does not suggest a gentle movement of the breath against the vocal folds! In German, the word *Angriff* (attack, based on the verb, *angreifen* (to grasp or grab at something), is never used in singing. The word used among singers in Germany for the beginning of a tone is *Ansatz* (at set), from *ansetzen* (based on the verb, *setzen*, set or place it, as in "to set it against" something).

In Italian, it is better to use the first translation given in the dictionary: to attach. Italian teachers and coaches I worked with would not allow a sharp attack. Every note had to be calmly and steadily attached to the diaphragm without accent or a perceivable, sudden release of energy. In singer parlance in Italy, *attaccare* meant to attach or to bind the breath to the diaphragm by way of gentle, steady pressure of the breath (the *appoggio* or lean) against the lower chest. Even with a clear understanding of the word *attaccare*, it is still not as safe as the word *appoggiare*. *Appoggio* has been used in the Italian vocal literature for generations as the concept of how to control the breath for the attachment of the breath to the diaphragm.

Another important word for a singer to understand is legato, which is created by a continuous leaning of the breath, and describes a process that creates an uninterrupted emission of the voice. It allows the tones to be tied together or bound together, with no space between musical, psychological, or physical entities (two notes in a phrase or a word).

The Correct Attack Functions

A correct movement of air through the open vocal folds will cause an area of lighter pressure (a decrease) to occur along their edges. Singers should become acquainted with Bernoulli's Principle: *A decrease in pressure occurs simultaneously as the velocity of a fluid is increased.* This decrease in pressure, at the instant the breath passes by the edges of the vocal folds, causes their edges to be drawn together until they begin to vibrate. It is advisable to utilize the smallest emission of the breath to produce the voice while restraining the rest of the air in the lungs. Both Caruso and Zinka Milanov advised singers to develop total command of their soft singing before developing the power of the voice. It is crucial for singers to understand that a delicate movement of a tiny stream of air across the edges of the vocal folds is all that is needed to draw them together until they begin to vibrate.

Resonance and Voice Placement

Nasality and Sound Enhancement

The concept of focus has become the rage in New York. In some circles, nasal resonance is actively taught and sought! Singers who have performed often with big orchestras know this: nasal focus will make the resulting tone sound thin, especially at a distance and over an orchestra. Tones placed into the nasal cavity will be without color or amplitude. That is why Caruso said, "Never sing into the nasal cavity. It is against all the rules of song." He did not have the benefits of artificial amplification or sound enhancement!

Experienced singers, coaches, conductors, and managers know that nasal voices are always small in the theater. It was common knowledge as recently as the end of the Bing era (1950-1972) at the Metropolitan Opera. Part of the legend surrounding Sir Rudolf Bing was that he would wander from place to place in the back of the auditorium of the old Met during auditions and performances, to find out if the voice of a new singer was projecting over the orchestra or not. As far as I know, no one does that anymore.

Nasal focus has become acceptable since the invention of electronic sound amplification. At last, nasal singers can be made audible, although many of them sound terrible! Many theaters in the U.S. have installed built-in, so-called, "invisible" sound enhancement systems. Microphones are not seen and the loudspeakers are blended in with the proscenium in a way that the audience often has no idea that the sound is being artificially enhanced. This provides artificial volume to small, nasal, unattractive voices, and allows small-voiced singers to perform in large venues. It is a tragedy for the continuance of vocal art, and, in a way, for the singers who have been taught to place the voice into the nose. They will never develop into great vocal artists. When they perform without the assistance of amplification, which is very rare indeed, everyone realizes that the voices are completely inadequate in every way: thin, colorless, and generally inaudible. No one seems to understand that the voice can be made to sound inadequate in a large venue by singing with a faulty technique! It is obvious that, if I speak to someone through my nose, my voice will sound narrow, thin, and nasal. Yet, singers study with teachers who teach their students to place the voice into the nasal cavity. These teachers have never sung major roles in large theaters with huge orchestras. Many voice teachers were never singers at all.

Over or Under: hung line

In the case of a singer who is taught to be a practitioner of nasal placement, often disguised psychologically as focus, he or she must either accept the nasal sound, or lift the soft palate up and forward in a separate, mechanical action, to achieve as much of the resonance of the upper half of the face as possible (the true mask). The sound must go over and above the [ng] or [m] resonance line, which can be sensed across the bridge of the nose, to achieve the true mask. Never sing into the [ng] line or the [m] line or under it. Lifting the soft palate straight up or up and back can cause the passage to the head resonance to close, causing the sounds made by the vibrating vocal folds to pass under the hard palate instead of over it.

This path the voice should follow, as described by Lilli Lehmann, avoids the nose all together, placing the resonance above the nose and into the true mask, thus conforming to Caruso's admonition: "Never sing into the nasal cavity."

Vibrato

Vibrato in the voice while singing, in all its incorrect manifestations, whether too wide and/or too slow (a wobble), or too fast (a tremolo), is caused by tension in the muscles surrounding the throat and the lungs of a singer. The secret to finding the ideal vibrato for an individual voice depends on absolute relaxation of the throat, a method of inhalation that relaxes the throat before singing, and the placement of the *punto d'appoggio* against the lower chest, which controls the breath and allows the throat to remain relaxed while singing.

Vibrato imbalances are a necessary evil if the thickest sections of the vocal folds are activated by a desire to make a bigger sound instead of utilizing only the edges of the folds and depending on overtones to produce the beautiful singing tone we all love. This tendency is most common among singers with low voices as they try to sound darker and deeper. If they are able to sing the high notes required by the repertoire they sing, the notes usually wobble. I once asked Gottlob Frick, the famous German *basso profondo,* how he approached his marvelous voice. It was so black in color and huge in volume that I assumed he must do something in his body or throat to be able to make such enormous sounds. He answered, *"Ich versuche die Stimme von meinem Kollegen, Fritz Wunderlich, nachzumachen. Alles so leicht und schlank wie möglich, genau wie er"* (I try to imitate the voice of my colleague, Fritz Wunderlich. Everything as light and slender as possible, exactly like him).

The correct approach to the production of tone has always been to sing as lightly as possible in terms of the basic quality of the voice. Only the edges of the vocal folds should vibrate while singing, and the quality and volume of the voice should emanate from the amount of retained, vibrating breath in the lungs.

Wobble

The exaggerated type of vibrato known as a wobble is the result of a basic misunderstanding of how the voice functions. The resistance of the vocal folds should not be felt or noticed by the singer, and the breath-box should be as large and as full of breath as possible. This approach will eliminate the terrible wobble that comes from singing with too heavy a tone. All singers should include staccati and coloratura phrases in their warm-ups to keep the voice light and slender. This is especially important for singers who tend to have a vibrato that is too slow or too wide.

It is obvious that to avoid a wobble—usually based on deep, frontal belly-breathing that causes muscular reactions in the larynx—the breath for singing must be inhaled in a way that relaxes, rather than activates the throat. In order to avoid all muscular tension in the throat caused by either action or reaction when inhaling or singing, the breath should be inhaled as deeply as possible into the lower back. Once the breath has been placed into the lower reaches of the rear quadrant of the lungs, laughing gently (giggling or chuckling) or crying gently (sobbing, resorted to by some singers, is definitely not necessary) while singing will incorporate the correct muscles in the body for singing and create a correctly produced vibrant tone. It can be easily observed that laughing or crying will cause pressure against the lower chest. The solar plexus will protrude as the laughing or crying begins.

Straight tone

Straight tones are sung tones with no vibrato. This type of dead tone is produced by leaning the pressure of the breath against the chest, but without any hint of emotion or expression. The most famous singer in history to use the straight tone consistently was Nellie Melba. She was exemplary as to the correct use of her breath, and was considered the greatest soprano during her career. However, she was also an example of a cold singer who never allowed any emotion to disturb her voice. Known as the Blue Diamond because of her exquisite voice and ice-cold presentation, Melba sang with an utter lack of emotion or any expression. The result was that she sang with straight tones exclusively. Rosa Ponselle, when asked what she thought of Melba, said, "She has an indescribably beautiful voice, but she uses too many still tones. In New York the public demands passion in the voice on every note." Of course, that may be why Ponselle's voice was full of vibrato and passion. She was the darling of New York audiences and known for her incredible, heart-rending performances.

Straight tones, sought deliberately by male singers who specialize in music written for barbershop quartets and by some singers who believe madrigals and Baroque vocal music should be sung without any vibrato in the tone, can be easily produced using the same method of inhalation and support, but any vestige of laughter or expression must be eliminated. The tiniest chuckle or tear in the voice will instantly produce vibrato in the sound, and it will be the correct vibrato for the individual voice.

Tremolo

A vibrato that is too fast, called a tremolo, results when intense involvement of the upper muscles of the chest squeeze breath that has been inhaled into the upper areas of the lungs only. The deepest parts of the lungs have not been included in the inhalation. A tremolo cannot be produced if the breath before singing has been inhaled deeply enough into the lower rear quadrant of the lungs. It is the easiest of all vibrato problems to correct. Shallow breathing into the chest or upper ribs, usually caused by expanding the upper ribs to the sides without breathing deeply into the lower back, leaves the singer with no other possibility to support the voice except to squeeze the muscles around the upper torso and to pull the abdomen inward while singing.

Correct vibrato

Correct vibrato is most easily demonstrated by first inhaling deeply into the lower back and then instigating the activity that emulates gentle laughing or crying. The muscles that respond to laughter are generally distributed around the entire ribcage and are immediately responsive to the desire to express joy or pleasure. An understanding of the complete process of respiration (inhaling into the lower back and leaning, pressing or, to quote Lilli Lehmann, stopping the breath against the lower chest), is the all-important factor in the regulation and sustaining of a correct vibrato.

As we have seen, tremolo and wobble are caused by faulty respiration and the desire to enliven the tone artificially without applying genuine emotional stimulation to the diaphragm. The worst examples of vibratos that are quivery, wobbly or overly intense are often heard in opera because of the extreme emotions required by the characterizations of leading roles. In order to assure the correct degree of vibrato in any particular voice, it is necessary to establish limitations as to the activation of muscles, which is achieved by using only a limited amount of the emotional expression inspired by the text and music. Exaggerated breathing, which Caruso called massive respiration, can only be good if the inhalation is correctly placed into the lower back and the controlling pressure of the breath is established against the lower chest. However, it is to be noted that Caruso recommended exaggerated breathing, not exaggerated emotional outbursts. Exaggerated expressions are to be avoided if they cause any action or reaction in the throat. This is the great danger of singing heavy, dramatic roles over huge orchestras. The amount of intense emotion demanded by some roles can cause the singer to become vocally *überfordert* (over-demanded). Usually a gentle laughing or crying stimulation of the diaphragm is sufficient to express any degree of vibrato necessary for the production of the overtones required for beautiful singing. Heavy dramatic roles should not be attempted until years of correct singing have safely passed without vocal problems. The correct processes of healthy vocalism must become both habitual and strengthened to the degree that there is no danger of demanding more from the voice and the strength of the respiration than they can safely and consistently produce. Giving less volume and intensity with the voice is never dangerous. Giving more volume and intensity is always putting the voice at risk.

Vibrato exercise

Here is a simple exercise for finding the natural vibrato in an individual voice:

1. Inhale into the lower back, bending over forward (touching the toes) if necessary to get the feeling of where the breath should be placed.
2. Sustain a straight tone by pressing the breath gently against the middle of the chest and relax the abdomen outward. This is the easiest and safest way to produce a dead tone.
3. Gradually allow yourself to feel happiness or sadness as you hold the tone. You will notice that vibrato begins instantly.
4. Any emotion will stimulate the diaphragm and the muscles surrounding the lungs. The singer can experiment with different emotions to become acquaint-

ed with the correct muscular process. After some practice, it will not be necessary to emote all the time while singing.

The induced or manufactured vibrato is not a disturbance of the tone caused by emotional stimulation of the *appoggio*; it is rather an artificially produced, rhythmically sub-divided movement of a tone accomplished by easing the pressure of the breath against the chest. The loose lean, which is not a true lean at all, requires that the pressure of the breath back off away from the true point of leaning just enough to allow the breath to lose its focal point. A generalized, compensated state of expanding energy will occur in the lungs. This state of outward pressure of the breath, usually created by pulling the abdomen inward while singing, controls the emission of the breath while at the same time providing wiggle room for the regulated disturbance of the emission. The singer is forced to resort to nasality to achieve even an imitation of a correctly placed tone.

This set of explanations can be very useful to singers who are aware they have a wobble or a tremolo, or that they sing too many straight tones. Simply follow the breakdown of the parts of the breathing system and utilize those parts in a manner that is applicable to you. The principles are the same for every voice type, from highest soprano and tenor to lowest contralto and deepest bass. Giovanni Lamperti said, "All problems in singing are caused by the mismanagement of the breath." And I believe Caruso when he said, "Whoever masters this method of breathing will have taken a giant step toward Paradise."

Vowels

Soft purity of the vowels, formed by thinking them

When singing, we attempt to create our vowels simply by thinking them, using as little muscular action or tension in the tongue, lips, jaw, and throat as possible. There is no need to form vowel shapes with the lips or the cheeks, which will deaden the resonance of the voice. Vowel modification, the action that causes a change of the shape of the throat, causes a reactive change in emission of the breath. Changing the shape of a vowel in the throat by separate action breaks important rules of the bel canto style of singing:

The first rule of phonation is:
The vowels must be pure and undistorted when sung.

The first rule of the bel canto vocal style is:
No action in the throat may occur while singing. Only reactions to deep breathing are permitted. Inhaling the vowel is a common approach to creating vowels without separate action in the throat.

The second rule of the bel canto vocal style is:
There must be no change of the emission of the voice once a phrase has begun, unless to satisfy the demands of the composer.

Every action of any kind causes an opposite and equal reaction somewhere. Modifying vowels will definitely cause an action/reaction sequence to occur in the throat. The result will be a change in the emission of the voice. The acoustical modification, that occurs when the vowel is sung correctly, is of the sound itself, as it passes from the middle register to the upper register, and not of the phonation of the vowel. The modification is purely acoustical, as the resonance moves from the chest into the head. It is not caused by physical action in the throat. Action in the throat is not needed to pass the voice from register to register if the inhalation is placed deep in the lower back, and the *appoggio* is firmly and evenly maintained. This acoustical phenomenon is very easy to demonstrate if the teacher is knowledgeable.

Timbre

Sound Quality

It is important to understand the distinction between the quality of the voice and the color or timbre a singer uses to express an idea. Quality is the word used to describe the basic sound of a voice that makes it unique and identifiable. The quality of a voice remains the same whether or not it is expressing joy, nostalgia, wistfulness, wonder or sadness. Every voice on the planet has its own quality. Various law-enforcement agencies use technologies that can absolutely identify any individual by voice-print (the basic quality of a voice), just as readily as if they were using fingerprints. However, each person is capable of many emotions and expressions, which are reflected in the color of the voice as individual timbres. In singing, if the breathing has prepared a free throat, the sound of the voice can reflect thoughts that inspire a constant change of emotional colors. The opportunities for expression are limited only by the artist's imagination, or lack thereof. Every voice, from deep bass to high soprano, can express a full range of emotions simply by thinking, as long as the throat is relaxed and not locked into a predetermined shape that can produce only one timbre.

Timbres and Nasality

Singing with nasality because of incorrect breathing, or by deliberately placing the voice into the [m] or [ng] position, will eliminate the spectrum of possible colors in the voice. The singer becomes limited to one color of expression (a nasal one!). The choice of vocal color, easily changeable if the voice is not placed in the nose, can be sad, happy, wistful, yearning, or nostalgic. Practice saying, "I love you" or "I hate you" or "I'm happy" or "I'm sad" with the voice placed in the nose. It becomes impossible to make a clear distinction between the emotional colors demanded by a composer, including composers of art songs. Everything sounds the same, in spite of the words, which may be suggesting opposing sentiments. In real conversation, we must allow the expression generated by thought and feeling to influence the timbre of a sound. Otherwise, we cannot convince anyone that we mean what we say. "I love you" should not sound the same in its timbre as "I hate you." How do we express colors without words? How many timbres can you successfully sing while singing a sustained [a] vowel? A laugh can sound happy or sarcastic, depending on our intention of expression. Nasal placement negates differences between expressions and interpretations. We may want to send a happy message, but sarcasm may be the color communicated due to nasality. Singers should practice exercises using various vowels and expressions. Try to change the colors of expressions without words—by imagination only.

Sound Amplification

Synchronization is to be Expected

Sound enhancement systems now make it possible for vocal music by great composers to be sung by singers using the tricks of pop artists. Will synchronization (lip sync) on stage be next? The art of singing already has suffered the loss of criteria established long ago by singers who had to deal with the problems of projection of sound and text over an orchestra and into a huge theater. They had to project characterization and emotional coloring of the voice so that every member of the audience could hear the story line and appreciate the interpretation of the role. There was no sound amplification other than the phenomenon of the resonance of the true mask. Imagine hearing a brand new opera or musical today without amplification. We wouldn't be able to hear the vocal music, the text, the emotional coloring of the voices, or be able to follow the story line.

Good Singers Don't Need Help

Of course, there are still a few singers who sing in the true mask. Luciano Pavarotti was an example of a singer who did not need any form of amplification. His voice was placed correctly. He proved that a well-placed voice needs no amplification, and in those instances when he did use amplification, he sounded better than anyone who sang with him.

It was amazing how well his voice projected over the orchestra and streamed out into the auditorium. He was the living proof that the use of the *appoggio* provides everything that is necessary for great singing. When asked about vocal technique, he never mentioned the nose, or focus, or covering, or lifting the soft palate, or vowel modification, or any kind of action in the throat. All he talked about was breathing and pushing his lower chest outward while singing. Of course, his observations were, for the most part, ignored by the singing teachers who heard his comments. One teacher remarked disdainfully, after hearing Pavarotti in a master class at the Juilliard School describe his support method: "He doesn't understand how he sings. He is just a natural singer." Well? Isn't that the idea? Are singers stupid and ignorant if they sing in a way that makes it sound natural instead of labored and nasal?

It has become obvious that singers no longer have to sing correctly to be heard by an audience. The magic of electronic enhancement technology can easily make the weakest voice sound like it is full of overtones and power. Any nasal singer can stand next to Pavarotti in any theater that has a sound enhancement system and sound as powerful as the greatest singer in the world. Amplification allows singers to sing in a nasal placement of the voice that is "against all the rules of song" (Caruso) and get away with it!

Alas, poor great singers! I knew some of their voices well.

Just Speak the Sounds: The resonant speaking voice

Most Americans speak nasally to a certain degree, depending on where they grew up and from whom they learned to speak. The experts say we speak a mother tongue, learned, literally, from our mothers. That means we learn a mother accent, and a mother placement of the voice. If Mom spoke nasally, the children will speak nasally. Those singers and teachers, who believe that it is necessary to only sing as if speaking, forget that most people do not speak correctly! Country singers and pop singers may be able to rely on the concept of simply speech-based singing. They also have a major advantage in live performance situations because they use state-of-the-art amplification systems. Opera singers have to contend with huge theaters, thick orchestrations, and sing in several different languages. They have to learn to speak correctly if they don't want to sound like pop singers or country singers trying to sing opera!

Just as an aspiring Shakespearian actor must learn to speak correctly (can you imagine performing the role of King Lear with a New York or South Carolina accent?), a singer must learn to phonate vowels and control the breath in order to use a speaking method while singing. In other words, the speech method and placement of the voice must be based on the same principles of vocal health and the necessity of projection into large theaters that singers are supposed to learn when studying singing: correct breathing which relaxes the throat, phonation of vowels in different languages, and a method for controlling the emission of the breath while singing or speaking. Many singers are required to speak dialogue in performance. Their natural way of speaking will not always project into the auditorium without pushing or forcing the voice, and they may sound provincial. Projection of the voice, in a theater without sound enhancement, depends on the placement of the voice in the true mask, and a correct method of breathing and breath control. Many singers and actors sing and speak into the nasal cavity instead of above the bridge of the nose, which causes the voice to lack clarity and projection in a large space.

It does occur that some people speak beautifully without training, but it is very rare. Most actors with great speaking voices, such as Gregory Peck, Olivia de Haviland, Basil Rathbone, Walter Pidgeon, Lawrence Olivier, Peter O'Toole, Richard Burton, and Albert Finney were all taught how to speak correctly (Singers and actors who have not seen the movie, *Beckett*, should rent it immediately and listen to Burton and O'Toole speak!). The best speaking technique today is to be heard in Michael Gambon. Gambon does everything correctly; his tone is magnificent, his diction is flawless, and his breath supply is endless. Perhaps these great actors could have become opera singers if their incredible talents had included musicality and the desire to sing. The speaking on pitch technique would work in such cases.

Methods and Techniques of Famous Singers

The Power of Observation: Trimble's observation of great singers

I had, by my third year in New York, developed my own style of physical analysis of technical singing, which was based on observation and physical, aural, and when available, intellectual confirmation. The information upon which I based my system of analysis has been gathered from every source available to me, and especially from the very best singers who sang in New York from 1959 to 1964 and in Europe from 1963 to 1972. My curiosity continued when I returned to the U.S. and again had access to the greatest singers in the world. The following points and questions were already a part of my method for acquiring technical knowledge about great singing, and I did my best to apply them to my search for understanding of the vocal process.

Moveable Parts

First, observe the posture of great singers. It is possible to actually see some of the greatest singers performing live on YouTube. Do they stand up perfectly straight with the weight on the front leg, or do they lean the body in one direction or another? Aspiring singers should observe the physical movements of the bodies of great singers while they are singing, and especially when they breathe. The main areas to be observed are the abdomen, the chest, the back, the mouth, the throat, the jaw, and the angle of the head. Milanov was as still as a statue in the chest and the belly. Of course, her belly was held in by a corset! She could not have used the sleeping baby method of breathing if she had tried! Lauritz Melchior wore a corset that covered his body from his mid-thighs to his armpits! He couldn't push his belly out to breathe, either! It was obvious that both singers did not, indeed could not breathe into their bellies. They had no choice. And, since there was no movement in their chests, they had to be back-breathers! This was confirmed in 1962 when I had lessons with Melchior. In one session with him, which resembled an interview, he described his breathing and support method to be the crying/laughing baby method described by Caruso in his book and Pavarotti years later at Juilliard.

Observations of Milanov: Always Save a Leg

After I applied my system of analysis to the singing of Zinka Milanov, who was only one of the many great singers I have studied during my fifty years of involvement in the vocal arts, I was left with the following observations and notes. The dates were spread out over the Met season of 1962-1963.

Posture and Breathing

The Milanov posture while singing was definitely old school, with her weight on one front foot or the other at all times and the chest thrown outward and forward with the elbows pulled back. I want to mention here that I was admonished by every great singer for whom I auditioned never to stand on two feet while singing. "Always save a leg," advised Mario Del Monaco, "You may need it later!" Melchior said, "The balance and coordination needed for great singing is crucial in the very long roles. Never stand on both feet. It spreads your balance and is much more tiring. Standing on one foot makes you balance and saves your energy for singing. You can shift back and forth, but never stand on two feet at the same time if it is avoidable."

I never saw Milanov stand on both feet while singing. The perfect stillness of her chest seemed to be an extension of her balance. The whole body was leaned slightly forward, but not as extremely as Dame Joan Sutherland, Luciano Pavarotti, or Jan Kiepura. She would change back and forth from one foot to the other in order to change direction, or, perhaps, to rest one leg while the other worked. The shoulders were kept back, dropped down, and relaxed.

Her belly and chest did not move when she breathed. What space in her body was left for breath? It was certain that she had to have breath to be able to sing. I realized that I would have to observe her back to see any action when she breathed.

Her chest did not move. It was held high and formed the sternal arch that is still a common concept in Eastern Europe today. Helge Roswänge described the chest as being:

> Like a shield made of iron. It should be maintained in an arched position, solid like the Rock of Gibraltar, filled with breath from the bottom of the lungs to the top of the lungs. The chest must be impenetrable, immovable, and unshakable by any outside influence. The *King of Dancers* posture in yoga creates the perfect shape of the chest for singing.

Milanov's lower back was her secret weapon. It filled with air when she inhaled, with the lower ribs expanding. The lower ribs would close together when she sang, exactly like Caruso's description of the bellows in the lower back. Her pelvis was turned under, in the old-fashioned posture of the elongation of the lower spine.

Articulation

Her mouth was not kept in the typical Italian *stai* shape, or in the shape of an oval lying on its side. She was not an Italian by nationality, and her accent was not as exemplary as it could have been. She definitely pulled the corners of her mouth back when she sang high notes, but did not use the open smile at all times in her middle voice. Observe, on YouTube, her high b-flat at the end of "Vissi d'arte" from Puccini's *Tosca*; she pulled the corners of her mouth back extremely for every high note, regardless of the volume level she chose at the moment. I heard her Tosca many times. That note, "Signor," was gigantic in its fullness and ringing power. Although Milanov was nearly a perfect singer, the looseness of her jaw affected the way she sang the Italian language, and marked her as a trainee of the Eastern European school of singing.

Her throat was breathed downward so extremely that her larynx almost disappeared from view. Its movement downward, when she inhaled, was the only visible movement in the front of her body. There was not a hint of visible tension or strain in her throat, no visible tendons or blood vessels, no quivering or shaking. I was reminded of Dame Eva Turner's description of the invisible throat. Milanov was living proof that such a criterion could be fulfilled.

Her jaw opening seemed to generally follow the rule of one finger wide in the middle range, two fingers wide in the upper range. Although she did not always use the *stai* form in her middle range when she had a lot of text to sing, her jaw was never pulled down into the "baby-bird-ready-for-worm" opening that is so common today among singers of every category.

Another technical plus in her singing was that she did not chew consonants by moving her chin up and down to enunciate dental consonants. Ideally, the teeth should not come together to enunciate dental consonants (d, l, n, s, t, z). She used the tip of her tongue to pronounce those consonants, without moving the chin up and down while singing. This particular approach to articulation was very old school. The modern Italian singers sometimes chew their consonants, although it is not as efficient as leaving the jaw invisible. Flexing the jaw to enunciate consonants used to be considered a flaw in a singer's technique.

Her neck was loose and free, and provided a relaxed support column for the position of her head, which was always tilted back and up, facing the balconies. There was no visible tension in her neck. Her head seemed to be balanced of top of her spine like a ball balanced on top of a pole. Because of the lack of tension in her neck, she could move her head in any direction while singing, including all the way back, without the tone being affected. Desdemona's death scene in Verdi's *Otello* was staged at the Met in the 1960s with the soprano hanging her head back and down off the side of the bed while lying on her back. She was the only soprano I ever heard who sang Desdemona's last, pitiful notes with such freedom of the throat and such floating beauty.

An Inspired List

I had noticed for a long time, that the greater the singer, the less movement there was to observe in the chest. Another member of the invisible gang was Richard Tucker. He was one of the stillest singers I have ever seen, especially in the lyric sections of his most dramatic roles. Only his back could be seen moving, opening and closing, with the chest perfectly still. Gestures as part of acting were freely made, but never allowed to disturb the perfect stillness of his chest. No exaggerated actions were obvious when he pronounced words.

I also have found this list to be very useful in teaching actors. Olympia Dukakis said that one of the old rules of the theater is to *never show the work*! Being dead-still, with the chest in a high, open posture while singing or speaking, not only helps control the vocal requirements of a difficult role, but also negates superfluous movement, and contributes to the success of the interpretation of a role. Singers need to practice never showing the work if they want to become good actors.

Fritz Wunderlich: The Natural Singer

I would include Fritz Wunderlich on the list of great singers. He was a fabulous vocalist with a marvelous, free, and sympathetic vocal delivery. His entire approach to singing seemed to rely on a psychomotor response to his desire to sing. In other words, he fulfilled the definition of a pure, natural singer. Although his voice was pure silver, and as sweet as candy, and his vocalism was in every way extraordinary, he did not want to discuss his mental approach to singing. When I asked him how he sang, he said, "like everybody else." Well, that certainly wasn't true! He was, without a doubt, the very best Mozart tenor in recorded history. Tucker was astounding to hear in Mozart because he had such a big, ringing, multi-colored voice in such light music. However, those of us who were fortunate enough to have heard Wunderlich in a live performance knew we were in the presence of a vocal and stylistic phenomenon. There was no need to compare him with anyone, and certainly not with the power tenors. He was able to stand alone as a great, unique singer who could please all people all of the time. There was no evidence that he was analytical about his vocal method, or that he had a process of sequential thinking to keep him organized. Most of the singers who worked with him regarded him as a natural singer. He just opened his mouth and out came flawless singing.

Like Cornell MacNeil and Cesare Siepi, perhaps Wunderlich simply didn't want to discuss vocal technique. There are singers who keep their secrets to themselves, for whatever reason, and there are singers who really don't know how they sing. They don't seem to think a series of thoughts that dictate predictable responses in the body. Tito Ruffo comes to mind as the greatest example of a historical singer who couldn't explain how he sang or what he thought about while singing. When asked why he didn't teach to provide an income for himself after his retirement, he said that he "had no idea what to tell a student about how to sing." He "opened his mouth and the voice came out." One day he opened his mouth and his voice did not come out and he didn't know why. He had to retire from singing. Ebe Stignani and Eileen Farrell were the same way. They never discussed technical singing. They just punched their mental buttons that called forth perfect singing and they did it for years.

During an engagement when I sang a series of performances of Dvorak's *Rusalka* in Munich, I decided to observe Wunderlich closely in performances on my days off, and try to discern the actions of the key elements of the vocal puzzle when he sang, just as I had done while a student at the old Metropolitan Opera when the best singers performed.

I concentrated my observations on a list of observable body functions while Wunderlich was actually singing:

- The chest (sinking or still)
- The belly (moving inward or outward while singing or inhaling)
- The nose (open like and [m] or closed like [b] or [d])
- The corners of the mouth (puckered forward or pulled back)

- The hinge of the jaw (showing a separation from the skull or not)
- The angle of the head (held level, lifted upward, or facing downward)
- The upper lip (covering the upper teeth or lifted to show the teeth)
- The tongue (pulled back away from the teeth or placed against the lower teeth or the lower lip), the teeth (showing or hidden?)
- The movements of the lower back during the alternating functions of inhaling and singing

Needless to say, he used all of the parts of the vocal puzzle like a fabulous tenor from the Golden Age of Bel Canto. As far as I could tell, everything functioned when he sang exactly like the technical, physical responses of Richard Tucker, Jussi Björling, and Helge Roswänge! No wonder his voice was so exquisitely beautiful and full of tenderness and velvet. He could have written the Caruso book!

I never knew if he was actually moving his mind when he inhaled or if he thought about the *Atemstauen* when he sang, but he definitely achieved what can only be described as perfect singing, while fulfilling every criterion desired in a world-class tenor. What was he thinking about when he sang? Was he thinking at all in order to achieve the physical movements in the back and the posture of the chest we observed while he sang? Was it all natural and automatic? According to the German baritone, Herman Prey, Wunderlich's best friend, Fritz was a pure, natural singer who couldn't tell even his closest friend (Prey) how to become a better vocalist. All he told him was that he "dropped everything when he had to sing." "God and Nature," to quote Lilli Lehmann's praise of Adelina Patti, provided Wunderlich with everything a singer can possibly possess in terms of vocal beauty, volume, ease, and range, along with a touching, charismatic quality that thrilled the public.

Jon Vickers: An Exception to the Rule

Jon Vickers was the only successful singer I have known who had a great career by pretending to move his bowels while singing. I know for a fact that he supported with this concept because I asked him in Mexico City in 1962, during a run of performances of Verdi's *Aida*. He explained it very carefully. He opened his throat in the biggest yawn possible and pressed down like he was constipated and trying to move his bowels.

Vickers was a lumberjack in his youth and had the physical strength of ten men. He was able to produce huge tones in his middle voice, and the color of the voice was magnificent, in spite of the enormous efforts demanded to neutralize the vertical pressures against his larynx. Extraordinary physical strength, superior to any professional singer I have known, was not sufficient to overcome the reactions in his throat on his high notes. Although he could reach the highest notes in his repertoire through sheer effort and muscle, they did not ring or project like his massive notes in the middle range of his voice (and certainly not like those of Mario Del Monaco, Richard Tucker, Franco Corelli, Lauritz Melchior, or the most powerful tenor I ever heard, Helge Roswänge).

Helge Roswänge: A Vocal and Technical Phenomenon

There have been a few singers who have had long, successful careers, basing their vocal techniques on the writings of great singers and teachers of the past. Helge Roswänge never had a voice lesson, and was, in the minds of many fans, the world's greatest tenor for fifty-five years. He depended on the technical approach described in Caruso's book as the best way to organize his own vocal method. He especially practiced the breathing and support functions and the mouth shape as described by the great Italian artist. Although he was Danish, Roswänge was called the *The German Caruso* because of his enormous, thrilling voice and the fact that he made his career mainly in Germany and Austria. Critics, colleagues, and fans in the German speaking countries who heard Roswänge in his prime referred to him as a *Stimmphänomen* (voice phenomenon). Many of Caruso's fans who heard Roswänge in the 1930s found no reason to consider one voice better than the other. There has probably never been a better voice that Roswänge's. It would have to be a matter of personal taste, especially among the Italian fans, to prefer Caruso or Roswänge. In any case, it is certain that the voice of *The Great Dane* was indescribably beautiful and powerful, with a scintillating *mezza voce* that could effortlessly fill every theater. He could sing the complete range of highest (including high D) to lowest notes at any volume level he desired. Even at the age of seventy, when I heard him live at the *Gärtnerplatztheater* in Munich, the voice was still one of the wonders of the world! When I asked him about vocal technique, he immediately said that I should read Caruso's book.

Roswänge was a scientist by training and mentality, and he had a clearly defined, sequential mental and physical procedure that he practiced and applied to his singing. He followed the advice in Caruso's book to the letter, which provided him with the ability to exploit one of the greatest vocal gifts in history. He was an extremely advanced practitioner of yoga and had the most prodigious breathing capacity I have personally observed. His application of the principles of the bel canto vocal style learned from Caruso's book, plus the enormous breath capacity at his command, gave him the ability to astound the world with his phenomenal voice.

I studied singing with Roswänge for one winter in Munich. One approach to teaching and vocal technique he used was demonstrated by letting me observe his own singing. As did so many of the great masters, he pulled his abdomen inward while inhaling into his lower back; at the same time, he smiled and raised his chest. The intensity and depth of the inhalation was extremely exaggerated, and because of his life-long practice of yoga, his breath capacity was enormous. During the warm-up period, the inhalation was especially long and sustained. His inhalations certainly fulfilled Caruso's demand for massive respiration.

He would demonstrate the open throat by breathing deeply with the corners of his mouth pulled back exaggeratedly in the shape of an open smile. No teeth were allowed to show. The upper lip was pulled down to cover the upper front teeth, and the tongue across the lower lip covered the lower teeth. Each vocalise began with movement of the chest outward and forward in coordination with an outward and forward movement of the abdomen. He would then begin to sing a series of staccati on different vowels in the middle range, bouncing them on his downward moving diaphragm while relaxing his abdomen outward.

After locating the two responses to the activity of the staccato function—one on his chest and one in his lower pharynx—he would sustain a tone on each point provided by the staccato, alternating from the chest to the throat and back. The sounds he made from the point on his chest sounded exactly like the sounds emanating from the tones based on the staccato point in his throat. I would not have been able to tell the tones apart if he had not clearly demonstrated with his hands and pointing fingers the source of each tone. At the instant of the attack of any sustained sound, he would press the breath from his lower back against the corresponding staccato point on his chest.

He would demonstrate the open throat by not allowing the mouth to change shape from low note to high note while singing octave leaps on different vowels with the corners of the mouth pulled back as far as possible. No covering or vowel modification was allowed as an action, although a definite change of acoustical quality occurred automatically as he passed through the passaggio.

The front of the tongue was kept in contact with the lower lip from corner to corner of the smiling mouth, while the back of the tongue was inhaled downward. The corners of the mouth were kept pulled back at all times as a contribution to the open throat, just as demonstrated by Caruso in the photographs in Dr. Marifiotti's book on every vowel, including [u].

These few ideas, sequentially applied to his breathing and his phonation, comprised the totality of his vocal method, and it was learned from a book!

Breathing Methods of Master Singers

Common Aspects

How did the greatest singers in history describe their sequential thinking processes that produced the most fantastic voices in history? How did they describe the way they inhaled and the way they controlled the breath while singing?

It is noteworthy that the inhaling and breath control methods described have aspects in common with each other. The most striking criterion they shared is inhaling into the lower back and the contrary motion of the breath at the instant of attack of the tone. Caruso said, "never try to sing while still breathing in." The suspension or restraining technique, so popular among *Liedersänger* (singers who specialize in songs written by composers who attempt to create a work of art as opposed to a piece designed to entertain), requires a continuation of the inhalation process while singing. The *Verhaltungsmethode,* which was described earlier in this book, requires a lateral (sideways) pressure against the upper ribs to prevent the release (dropping) of the breath while singing, instead of a leaning of the breath and steady pressure of the breath against the lower chest. The restraining method or the suspension method would not have met with approval from Caruso, as it functions like a continuation of an inhalation that is high in the ribcage, with the drawing in action directed against the inside of the upper ribs, which are flexed outward to the sides. Caruso's method, according to his own words, functions like a "stopped exhalation." The *appoggio* was the concept common to many great Italian singers of the past, and to some of the greatest German and French singers who studied and sang during the Golden Age of Bel Canto. Frieda Hempel was an example of a fabulous German singer who used the *appoggio* method. Her approach to singing is described in her book, *My Golden Age of Singing,* which detailed an Italian vocal style based on exaggerated inhalations and the *appoggio.*

Caruso's massive respiration

The "massive respiration required for great singing," as described by Caruso, is an aspect of vocal technique that often stirs curiosity among young singers. The question often arises: "Why worry about extreme inhalation and an ever increasing volume of air in the lungs, if only a small amount is needed to sing a phrase?" It should be enough for us to realize that the greatest singers in history recommended inhaling as much air as possible at all times. Montserrat Caballé said, "You should be able to inhale for, at least, eighty seconds, before you have a voice lesson." When asked what a singer should do who does not have such extreme breath capacity, she answered, "Find another line of work!" There must have been a reason why the greatest singers recommended such extreme development of the breath capacity and strength. It is up to us to figure out why, because we know their approach was the most successful method in the history of singing.

Nothing Moves Unless the Breath Moves It: George London's breathing method

One important rule that should be scrupulously observed is as follows: *The ribs should not move unless the impetus of the inhalation moves them.* George London would point at the lower back of the young singers and say, "make the singers work the machine (the lower back) when they breathe, both inhaling and exhaling. And remember, nothing should move back there unless the breathing moves it." According to him, elongation of the spine should be coordinated with the inhalation and not be an independent motion. He went on to explain that powerful respiration should be the only source of energy that causes movement of any part of the vocal tract. That includes the lower back, the throat, the back of the tongue, and the larynx. The entire area of the throat, and especially the back of the tongue, must be kept soft and relaxed, without any flexing of the muscles in the throat, the jaw, the tongue and the neck. The back of the tongue and the larynx descend only as far as the strength of the inhalation can lower them. The larynx must never be depressed downward independently by muscular action. It should descend only as a response to the strength of the inhalation.

Medical Opinions: Levi Mandl's breathing method

Almost every voice teacher in every conservatory today teaches the breathing method recommended by Dr. Levi Mandl in 1883. The famous medical scientist discovered what he called a "new and more efficient method of breathing," Based on the breathing patterns of a sleeping baby, this method would shorten the developmental period of time required by famous voice teachers of the Bel Canto era. Dr. Mandl suggested that the abdomen be pushed outward while inhaling, and pulled inward while singing. This was, of course, the opposite way of breathing that was practiced and recommended by the greatest singers and teachers in the world at that time. However, the old and proven vocal method, breathing like a crying baby, was incredibly reliable and efficient if thoroughly learned and applied. It allowed singers to do everything required by composers while producing fantastic sounds, but had one major drawback.

Learning the bel canto method of breathing and breath control was a very slow, tedious process, but the benefits of mastering the old method were amazing. The method handed down by the castrati, who had developed it from childhood as a true natural way of singing, was based on a baby's cry. Everyone admitted that the proven way of singing, up to that point, was wonderful. However, every singer and teacher wanted a faster way to get voices under control. The sooner a singer could get the voice under control, the sooner the career could begin and money could be earned, both for the singer and for the teacher.[15]

Dr. Mandl's method was based on scientific discoveries that came from his study of cadavers. It seemed to work, with very few negatives, and often sped up the learning process. The drawbacks were:

- Nasality, which dominated the sound and still does today among adherents of the Mandl method.
- Pushing the breath upward into the larynx by pulling the abdomen inward while singing.
- Actions in the throat, necessary to accommodate the pressure of the breath against the vocal folds caused by the pulling in of the abdomen while singing.
- A much smaller amount of breath in the lungs. The capacity of the lungs was half of that achieved by the old breathing method.
- Loss of volume and projection of the voice over an orchestra, caused by nasality and the drastic reduction in the capacity of the drum.
- Loss of overtones, reducing the beauty in the voice drastically.

---

[15] Teachers in those days received a percentage of their students' earnings. Leo Slezak paid 15% of his earnings for life to his teacher, and Caruso paid 25% for years. He finally broke the contract by taking his teacher to court. It turns out that Caruso had signed a contract that required him to pay 25% of earnings for five years of actual singing! The old man still managed to get a huge chunk of change from his star student.

Push! Push! Push! Pavarotti's breathing method

According to Pavarotti, there is a constant outward and forward motion of the lower chest required for correct singing. As we noted earlier in this book, in his master class at the Juilliard School of Music in 1982, he insisted that the diaphragm must go outward and forward while singing. He kept repeating, "It is like a baby here: push, push, push!" (but as we know, he actually meant "lean, lean, lean!").

Succinct and Simple: Caruso's breathing method

I've already said a great deal about Caruso's breathing method. As a reminder, he talked about inhaling into the bellows (the ribs in the lower back) and squeezing them together while singing.

The Happy Surprise: Tebaldi's breathing method

Renata Tebaldi would take small, audible mini-gasps between phrases during her most beautifully sung lyric sections of music, which she found to be "helpful with creating the correct shape of her throat for singing." I asked her why she did it. Her answer surprised me: "Melis (Carmen Melis, Tebaldi's voice teacher) made me do it before every scale. It felt good, so I never asked her why. I know it opened my throat, especially for the high notes. All I had to do was stay *chiaro* (clear or bright) when I used it."

All Tebaldi had to say about her breathing was that her breath capacity never matched the size of her voice. Her voice continued to grow more powerful during her career, but her breath capacity seemed more and more inadequate. She had been taught the happy surprise and the mini-gasp as methods of preparing the correct position of the throat, but had never learned how to expand the capacity of the lungs.

- Tebaldi didn't swim, like Caruso, Melba and Sutherland, who were all ocean swimmers.
- She didn't play a wind instrument, like Beniamino Gigli, who played saxophone.
- She didn't practice yoga, like Robert Merrill and Helge Roswänge.
- She hadn't been a competitive cyclist like Ezio Pinza. She was not obese or huge in her ribcage.
- She didn't know any deep, developmental breathing exercises.

Tebaldi was living proof that development of the breath capacity is necessary for great singing. Although her voice was incredible in its beauty and power, she was always struggling to reach the extreme high notes. She often sang under pitch, especially in the passaggio. The complaint did not come from me. I loved her! The complaint came from *her* when she began to sing the big, dramatic roles. She wished for more air and sustaining ability, especially in Verdi's *Aida* and Ponchielli's *La Gioconda*. Of course, those of us who heard her worshipped her sound. We felt that we should all have such problems!

Dr. Sheetz's breathing method

My wife and I interviewed Dr. Maurice Sheetz when he was a Pulmonary and Critical Care Medicine Fellow at St Luke's/Roosevelt Hospital in New York City. I asked him what he thought about the type of breathing technique that Caruso, Tetrazzini and Lehmann describe in their books. Why would these great historical singers develop a breathing technique in a manner opposite to what is being taught to our young singers in universities and music conservatories of today? His response amazed me in its directness. He said that it was obvious that Caruso, Tetrazzini and Lehmann wanted to force the back half of the diaphragm down, thus increasing the breath capacity compared to the amount that is achieved by letting the belly go out while inhaling. Dr. Sheetz went on to say:

> It is like saying that at one end of your body you've this tremendous pressure of breath against your sternum, but at the same time you are learning to relax the muscles from the neck up. There are these little muscles that surround the vocal cords; the ones in the back that change the length and tension of your cords are called the arytenoids.[16] What happens is that you build up pressure against your sternum, and then you have to learn how to relax the muscles surrounding the vocal cords so that you can open your throat and at the same time slowly release some of the pressure, not all of the expiration, directly against your vocal cords. It is analogous to banking a pool ball off a side cushion instead of going directly through; you divert that air so that it goes through in a controlled amount, as little as possible.[17]

I asked him about so-called natural breathing—the so-called sleeping baby breathing—for instance. He said that babies breathe one way when they sleep and the opposite way when crying or laughing. So, I asked why Tetrazzini said she kept the pressure against the chest at all times. Again the pulmonologist said it was very obvious that the continuation of sound required a continuation of control of the diaphragmatic tension in order to prevent the breath from coming into the throat and flooding the vocal folds with more air than can be utilized while singing or speaking. He described this function as "a controlled expiration of the breath against a closed glottis." Apparently, the front of the diaphragm must remain still while the back of the diaphragm gradually relaxes. This allows the amount of air that can be utilized by the vibration of

---

[16] Anatomically, the two arytenoid cartilages are located in the posterior of the larynx. Formerly, muscles that connect to these two cartilages were generically labeled "arytenoid muscles." In current voice science literature, they are differentiated by function and attachment points as: *thyroarytenoid* (thyroid to arytenoid cartilage / the body of the vocal fold); *interarytenoid* (between the two cartilages / closing the glottis); *lateral cricoarytenoid* (cricoid to arytenoid cartilage / closing the glottis); and *posterior cricoarytenoid* (cricoid to arytenoid / opening the glottis) [publisher].

[17] This analogy represents sensations perceived by many singers, but does not reflect the physics of respiration. According to Boyle's Law, which is universally accepted, pressure of a gas within a container must be uniform; it is impossible to have one region in which pressure exceeds that of another. The pedagogically valuable sensation of pressure against the sternum that diverts pressure from the larynx almost certainly is created by the action of postural muscles, not the lungs pressing diagonally within the thorax [publisher].

the vocal folds to be sent by the lower ribs to the larynx, and explains why Enrico Caruso described the action of the lower ribs in the back as resembling a bellows.

Inward Bowing and Backward Bowing: Callas and Corelli

Both of these methods (or mistakes), pulling the abdomen inward or collapsing the chest, have often been disastrous for certain singers who have tried to use them. Videotapes of Maria Callas and Franco Corelli toward the end of their careers show them singing with collapsing chests, bowed necks, and exaggeratedly bulging abdomens, which allowed their points of leaning to wander downward into the extreme lower reaches of the air column. This method seems to work for a time, making the voice fuller because of the increased depth of the air column, but causes the singer to lose the ability to sing lyrically or to be able to execute coloratura singing or use *mezza voce* dynamic levels. This approach, which, if the chest were held in a high position, would resemble a dead drop type of lean, differs from the bel canto style of breath support, which requires that the chest be kept up and out and perfectly still while singing, with the pressure of the breath against the chest at all times. Collapsing the chest tends to make the head lean forward, leading to the notorious bowed neck method of singing.

Like Callas and Corelli, Christa Ludwig sometimes collapsed her chest while singing, creating a bowing inward effect of the chest. But she compensated by bowing the upper back outward and to the rear, and pressing her breath against her middle spine. The shoulders would tend to come forward as the chest would sink in. This created a kind of backward-bending breath stop, placed directly opposite the sternum around the sixth or seventh thoracic vertebra. Her method of support worked very well during a long career. Callas, toward the end of her career, changed the function of her chest from her earlier days, from holding it up and not allowing it to sink or move, to using the sinking chest method while searching for more volume and a deeper color in the voice. This would create a slight bowing of the upper back and allow the shoulders to move forward instead of holding them back. Her bowing of the back was never as obvious as Ludwig's, who seemed to deliberately lean into her back. Callas utilized the bowing of the neck to compensate for the shoulders. Ludwig never bowed her neck or arched her neck; her sinking chest was particularly obvious on long, sustained, dramatic phrases. The audience members could clearly see that she was actively bowing her upper body backwards, not at the waist, but in the middle of the back, controlling her breath in a way that was opposite from the usual, "chest forward and outward" leaning technique employed by Sutherland, Milanov, and Pavarotti.

The Gandhi/Mother Teresa Technique

This used to be a popular subject for discussion among voice students in Vienna, where the crushing of the chest downward and inward while pushing the upper back outward was the most popular new way to control the breath while singing. Although they often looked a little odd while singing, especially during extremely difficult moments in a performance, Waldemar Kmentt and Anneliese Rothenberger used this vocal method with great success at the Vienna State Opera. The secret to their success may have been that the inhalation method, drawing the breath deep into the lower back while collapsing the chest, resembled, at least, a part of the function recommended by Tetrazzini. The "downward and inward" collapsing (crushing) of the chest during the inhalation, so actively practiced in the "Viennese School," reduced the size of the drum. The loss of resonating space in the body caused the voices to have less amplitude than that provided by the open chest method, and limited the repertoire of singers who applied it to the lighter roles in opera and operetta. The crushing of the chest continued in the imagination (and sometimes literally) during the emission of the voice. The concept of singing as inhaling was practiced to the greatest possible extent. The German word for warming up the voice is *Einsingen*, which means in-sing. The whole concept of singing inward and not outward can be established psychologically as one begins the warm-up of the voice. The singers looked comical sometimes while warming up their voices in their Gandhi/Mother Teresa postures. When they used the collapsing chest method on stage, they sometimes looked ridiculous, all bent over and trying to hide what they were doing by acting! Maybe they survived vocally because they sang only light, lyric roles.

Christa Ludwig: Covering Many Possibilities

It was not known if Christa Ludwig had actually learned to sing with this method during her vocal studies, or if it was a trick she discovered that let her sing music written for soprano. She always kept the corners of her mouth extremely back, forming what seemed to be a slit with her lips through which she sang her vast repertoire. She used the mouth shape and the breathing into the back, in the same manner as Callas. Although Ludwig's natural voice was a high mezzo-soprano, she could sing a number of dramatic soprano roles in a repertoire that was high for her natural voice, and she did them beautifully! She sang some of her more difficult concert pieces, including excerpts from operas, at the *Musikverein* in Vienna, where I heard her sing the "Immolation Scene" from *Götterdämmerung*. However, I heard her most often at the Vienna State Opera. Her technique worked very well in both mezzo and soprano repertoire. She was the best Donna Elvira in Mozart's *Don Giovanni* I ever heard. But my favorite role she sang was Eboli from Verdi's *Don Carlo*, the most difficult role in the mezzo repertoire because of the high, dramatic notes in her famous aria, "*O don fatale.*" She had no discernible problems with any of these huge roles, and she could change over to a lighter mezzo role, like Cherubino in Mozart's *Le Nozze di Figaro,* and sing it perfectly. However, in dramatic phrases, she used the bowing of the upper back and the sinking chest in a very extreme way, almost bending over double toward the end of some of the longest, most difficult phrases.

Leans Sometimes Change

All of the singers mentioned above used a leaning method of some variation thereof. It was very visible in some singers and invisible in others. We have to go by the explanations revealed in their books or in interviews, or simply by observation of the physical movements manifested by the various approaches to singing, to ascertain as clearly as possible how they sang.

Because they all had a breath control method that didn't allow the breath to rise into the neck or throat, the jaw could remain unhinged and totally uninvolved in the emission of the tone. They leaned the breath against the chest, midriff, abdomen, or the upper back, using the breath prop as a technique for controlling the steady emission of the voice. Interestingly, the earliest films of Callas, Corelli, and Ludwig show them maintaining a steady, high chest position that did not collapse while singing. Perhaps the frequency of performances of dramatic roles forced these artists to experiment with different support techniques.

A Reminder of the Correct Function: Tetrazzini's support method

Luisa Tettrazzini said to "inhale the first drop of air into the lower rear quadrant of the lungs" and to "fill the lungs with air from the bottom to the top." Then, an instant before the attack of the tone to be sung, the breath should be pressed or leaned against the sternum "like leaning a ladder against a wall."

The *appoggio*, although dependent on gravity and leaning instead of force to generate the necessary energy for singing, must be sufficiently vigorous in order to gain absolute control of the emission of the tone. We are acquainted by now with some of the terminology used by great singers to describe *appoggio*. In spite of their recommendations, we must still find the necessary commands that will coordinate our voices with our breathing capabilities. Some music we sing may require a heavier lean, like leaning a heavier ladder against a wall. It is often evident that some singers, instead of leaning a heavier ladder to maintain the necessary *appoggio* in more dramatic music, begin to push the small ladder they have been using even more vigorously against the wall. We must remember that, regardless of how vigorously we apply live leans, the wall against which we lean does not move, and a bigger ladder (more breath development, both capacity and strength) will be required for heavier roles. That is the main reason for singing dramatic roles as late as possible. Give the breathing system plenty of time to develop, and more vigorous pushing against the wall won't be necessary. The weight of the heavy ladder will do all the work.

Method by De Luca: *Messa di Voce* (The measure of the voice)

De Luca's approach was slightly different. Although his concepts of breathing and *appoggio* were exactly the same as those described by Battistini, Tetrazzini, and Lehmann, he added the criterion of keeping the weight of the voice as light as possible for the attack. Robert Merrill, who coached extensively with De Luca, said that the historical singer's approach to singing was taught in steps. Each step was equally important and had to be perfected.

The first step:

Breathe silently through the nose into the lower back while pulling the abdomen inward, maintaining a gentle smile at all times (Marcella Sembrich called the correct formation of the mouth "the oval lying on its side"). Allow only the ribs in the lower back to expand.

The second step:

Keep the weight of the voice as close to the falsetto as possible, especially at the instant of instigation of the sound, without allowing the slightest hint of breathiness or nasality.

The third step:

Press the breath against the center of the chest at the beginning of the tone. Maintain the pressure of the breath against the chest as long as the phrase lasts. Then breathe again as described above.

De Luca loved to have male singers begin a tone with a soft falsetto [u] vowel. Gradually, the falsetto would be blended into a full voiced [a] vowel while increasing volume. After sustaining the *forte* for a moment, he would direct the singer to decrease the volume slowly back to the falsetto [u]. He called it *messa di voce*. This exercise was often done with a candle flame or a tissue held in front of the lips. The flame or tissue would be disturbed and move away from the mouth during the pure falsetto tone. However, if the flame moved at all when the full voice was achieved, the tone was leaking breath and was wrong. The decrescendo was done with no leaking of the breath allowed, ending with a *mezza voce* that did not leak breath instead of a falsetto tone. His concern with lightness of tone bordered on exaggeration; he would not allow any meat in the tone, no darkness, no thickness, no coloring with the throat or action in the throat, jaw, or tongue, and, especially, no nasality. The volume of the voice was built on a crescendo of the falsetto-based, non-leaking, mixed tone, while keeping the pressure of the breath against the chest. Consonants were combined with vowels and repeated with the candle flame held in front of the lips. Any movement of the flame or tissue during the articulation of any consonant was a sign of faulty *appoggio* and not permitted. No chewing or biting of the dental consonants (moving the chin up and down while enunciating and allowing the teeth to close together) was allowed. Only the tip of the tongue was allowed to move up and down to articulate the dental consonants, with the chin left loose and hanging down. The clarity of the tone was ensured by keeping the corners of the mouth back at all times.

This technical approach developed his voice into a leading Italian baritone. It was powerful enough to sing all of the dramatic roles of Verdi during his long career, but also light enough to let him sing high lyric roles. He sang Verdi's Rigoletto and Rossini's Figaro in *Il barbiere di Siviglia* with equal success.

We should all consider the advice of this great artist. He sang as a leading baritone at the Met for thirty-three years without a vocal problem. His teacher was Venceslao Persichini, the teacher of Mattia Battistini and Titta Ruffo. Persichini would hold the record for teaching historical baritones, if such facts were compared and rated! Persechini's vocal method (used by Battistini, De Luca, Ruffo, and in modern times, Robert Merrill and Kim Josephson) was revealed by the advice De Luca gave to Merrill. It was most definitely the same *appoggio* method we have encountered when studying the vocal techniques of other historical singers of the same era.

Examples of singers with great support

One Long Crescendo: Porackova, Corelli, Del Monaco, De Lucia

Some singers have enormous breath capacity that allows them to spin out a tone that seems to go on forever! Joanna Porackova once sustained a high A-natural for eighty-six seconds without any loss of volume or color. Franco Corelli held the high B-flat in the second act of Puccini's *Tosca* (*Vittoria, vittoria!*) at his Covent Garden debut performance for seventeen seconds! There is a recording of Lauritz Melchior holding the repeated *"Wälse, Wälse"* from the first act of *Die Walküre* for twenty-one and nineteen seconds respectively! Mario Del Monaco sang *"sul tuo amor infrante"* from *I Pagliacci* without breathing during the phrase, and at the slowest tempo ever recorded, surpassing even Caruso in the length of the phase. Fernando De Lucia on his recording of *"Amor ti vieta"* from Umberto Giordano's *Fedora*, started the aria with a beautiful, caressing pianissimo at the beginning of the vocal line, and sustained one long crescendo over the entire length of the aria, until he reached a gigantic fortissimo on the last phrase!

Zinka Milanov's breath capacity: Behind a Door

The greatest example of breath capacity and *appoggio* I experienced in a live performance was at the old Metropolitan Opera. Zinka Milanov, on the last note of the Nile aria in Verdi's *Aida*, began the high A pianissimo, and held it with her head tilted up and back, facing the upper balconies, until the orchestra stopped playing. But wait! She was not finished! While continuing to sustain the ravishing, perfect note, without the musical support of the orchestra, she turned slowly and walked upstage. She continued to hold the note as she exited the stage behind the curtain, and made her way to her dressing room, still holding the high A with absolute security. I was so flabbergasted that I completely forgot to time the total length of that incredible note! It was the most extraordinary feat of breath supply and *appoggio* I have ever witnessed in any singer! Needless to say, the audience went completely insane, screaming, stomping their feet, running down to the front of the auditorium and throwing flowers up onto the stage! It was an unforgettable moment.

Coloratura plus Splendor: Lehmann's and Porackova's long phrases

Lilli Lehmann was famous for her extraordinary long phrases without loss of projection or expression. That is one reason she was considered the greatest Isolde of her era. Her breath supply seemed endless. She could fulfill the criteria of Richard Wagner's music like no other soprano until the arrival of Kirsten Flagstad. Flagstad had her own seemingly endless supply of breath that allowed her to portray the heroines of Wagner with a tremendous voice of incredible width and amplitude and effortless vocal splendor. Porackova and Copley, with their enormous, beautiful voices, both sing the heaviest roles in the soprano repertoire with no problems at all. They also sing roles that require great coloratura facility. Their breathing and leaning methods are thorough and exemplary. Young singers should do all they can to hear them and coach with them if possible.

Athletic Lungs: singers, wind instruments and swimming

Development of breath capacity is definitely possible. It has its own concepts, motivations and practices. Time and techniques, including yoga, swimming, playing a wind or brass instrument, and specific breathing exercises dedicated to the development of breath capacity and diaphragmatic strength, are required if we hope to emulate Caruso's massive respiration necessary for great singing (Figure 2).[18]

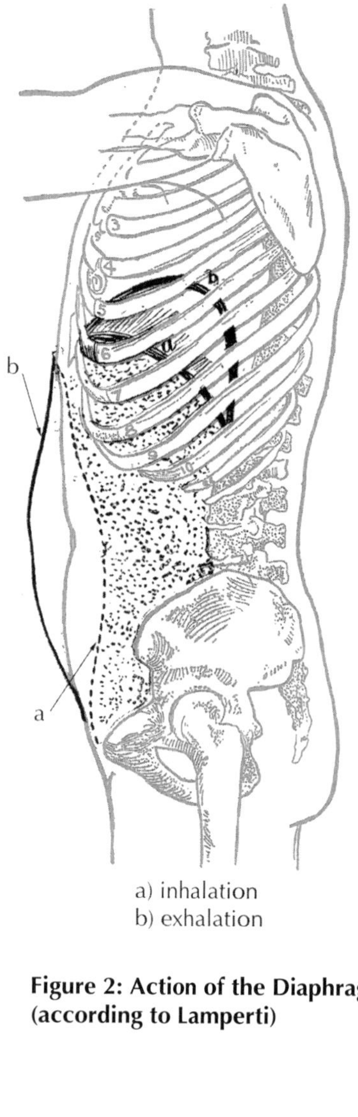

Figure 2: Action of the Diaphragm (according to Lamperti)

What do we know about the hobbies and physical activities of certain singers? Copley, like the great mezzo-soprano, Ebe Stignani and the natural phenomenon, Adelina Patti, has her breath capacity naturally, as a gift of God and nature, without having to develop it. However, there are ways to develop the strength and capacity of the breathing system. Some of the greatest singers in history were steadfastly devoted to activities that encouraged the development of a massive breath capacity. Porackova has been an avid swimmer since childhood. She is amazingly advanced in this breath-developing sport. Caruso, Melba, Hines, and Sutherland were all ocean swimmers. Gigli was a saxophonist. Ezio Pinza was a professional cyclist, and Pavarotti was a soccer and tennis player. Kim Josephson was a tuba player, while Nicolai Ghiaurov played trombone and clarinet, and Wunderlich played French horn. Merrill and Roswänge were advanced yoga practitioners. You get the idea! Extreme breath capacity rarely happens without some systematic form of exaggerated breathing activity in the life of the singer.

Caruso's massive respiration was no accident. His pianist Salvatore Fucito said in his book that:

[18] Figure 2 represents Lamperti's nineteenth-century understanding of respiration. Contemporary science shows that any inward motion of the abdominal wall during inhalation must be counter-balanced by an equivalent expansion in the back and sides, which is not shown in the image. The contents of the abdomen are incompressible, like water; if they are pushed in one direction, they must be displaced in another direction or place [publisher].

> Caruso went every day, no matter the weather, and did his forty-step walking/breathing exercise: he walked ten steps, inhaling silently through the nose as fully as possible, with the abdomen moving inward; he then walked ten steps holding the massive inhalation in the lungs while holding the abdomen in; the next ten steps were spent exhaling through the mouth with the abdomen moving outward and the breath pressed against the chest, and the last ten steps of the forty step exercise were spent with the lungs squeezed empty, leaving the abdomen in a dropped out position and the chest held high.

This exercise was repeated over and over while walking for one and one-half hours every day! He was devoted to it, in spite of the great development of the breathing capacity he had already accomplished during his childhood, by swimming and diving in the Bay of Naples.

The Most Precious Possession: Patti, Stignani, Copley

Some extraordinary singers, including Adelina Patti, Ebe Stignani, and Rebecca Copley, seem to have been born with everything needed to compete on the world stage. The rest of us aspiring mortals must spend our lives trying to perfect the art of singing through diligent, repetitive, physical, technical, and musical exercises, and plain dedication to hard work. There is no doubt that the greatest single asset a singer can possess is a developed breath capacity. It is essential for anyone aspiring to a professional singing career in big theaters with big orchestras.

Long Careers because of the right support technique

If we study the requirements of music written for singers in the great operas composed by Verdi, Puccini, Donizetti, Bellini, Ponchielli, Massenet, Bizet, and Thomas, we begin to realize one fact: they were writing music for fantastic vocalists. They couldn't have written music with such extraordinary vocal demands unless they knew that there were singers who could actually perform it. Who was going to be able to sing a title role that would be four hours long, with forty-nine high B-flats, nine B-naturals, and dozens of other dramatic high notes? These are the requirements in Verdi's opera, *Don Carlo*. For whom was he writing? The expectations of the composers were unbelievably difficult to fulfill. But, a vocal method had been discovered that would develop singers into vocal giants. They were able to sing high, low, and make endless musical effects with their voices, including coloratura, staccati, martellati (hammered notes), *mezza voce*, fortissimo, and a true pianissimo in any range of the voice that would project into any theater in the world, and they could do it for hours at a time. Many singers were able to sustain careers that often lasted fifty years: Mark Reizen, Lucien Fugere, Antonio Cotogni, Jerome Hines, Jan Peerce, Mattia Battistini, Del Monaco, Roswänge, Milanov, Merrill, De Luca, and a long list of others. They were able to execute every effect asked of them by composers, directors, and conductors, and still please the public over a lifetime. How did they sing? How did they describe their ideas of how to support and place the voice while singing?

A conductor, who performed with the baritone Mattia Battistini, asked him how he sang and what he thought about while singing. Battistini answered, "I press my chest." The verb, "press," was echoed by the greatest soprano of them all, in the opinion of Caruso and Arturo Toscanini, Luisa Tetrazzini, who said that she "kept the pressure of the breath against the sternum at all times." Another goddess in the pantheon of opera stars, Lilli Lehmann, said to "keep the pressure of the breath against the chest at all times." If I were to include all of the singers who recommended an outward pressure of the breath against the chest while singing, I would have to list almost every great singer in history.

Richard Tucker's support: The Diaphragmatic Lift

The lean against the lower chest is easily identifiable among great singers if there are films available of them actually singing. Richard Tucker and Eleanor Steber can be seen using the diaphragmatic lift. The breath would be inhaled into the lower lungs, expanding the ribs in the lower back while, at the same moment, arching the chest slightly up and thrusting it forward. The attack of the tone would begin with a pressing or leaning of the breath at a slight downward angle against the lower chest. The lean would be sustained against the lower chest by steadily closing (squeezing) the ribs in the lower back until the tone ended. This method of breath support was taught to them by their teacher, Paul Althouse. Althouse was a very successful tenor who had a wonderful, long career at the Metropolitan Opera as a leading singer.

***Tutto sul punto* (Everything on the Point): Martinelli**

Giovanni Martinelli said the breath must be *ben postato, ben appoggiato* (well placed, well leaned). When asked what he taught his students, he said, *Qui respirare e qui postare*! (Breathe here, placing his hands on his ribs in the lower back, and place it here, indicating with the tip of his finger the center of his chest). When I asked him about the new idea of focusing the voice that was gaining popularity in New York at that time (1962), he said, *"Il posto, il posto,"* pointing at the center of his chest, *"e tutto sul punto"* (and everything on the point). He was seventy-seven years old at the time, performing the role of the Emperor in *Turandot* at the Met. He, like Giuseppe de Luca, had a career at the Met that lasted thirty-three years!

The Glass Voice: Caruso's Lean

Caruso was known as "the Glass Tenor" when he began his career, because he cracked on his high notes so often (allowed the voice to suddenly slip into the pure falsetto function). The tendency to crack on high notes is an occupational hazard for any male singer, and especially for tenors with big voices. Any male singer, trained to sing close to the falsetto, will need to develop adequate strength and capacity of the breathing system in order to fulfill the criteria of a professional career without the problem of cracking.

Caruso was a master of the use of the *mezza voce* at the beginning of his career. However, his power singing left a lot to be desired. Cracking is a sure sign that consistent strength of the intensity of the lean is inadequate for the task at hand. Of course, he developed the necessary strength to sustain his incredible voice at full power when it was needed, and became the most celebrated singer in history.

Method for the right opening of the mouth

A crucial element of Lamperti's vocal technique

The great singers and teachers of the past considered the shape of the mouth during singing to be of great importance. Francesco Lamperti (the father), Giovanni Battista Lamperti (his son), and Manuel Garcia II, all insisted that the mouth be opened vertically no wider than the width of one finger in the middle range of the voice, and no wider than two fingers in the upper range of the voice with the corners of the mouth pulled extremely back. Why do singers and teachers today want the jaw pulled down extremely when the greatest teachers and singers in history insisted that the mouth not be opened vertically in a baby-bird waiting for a worm posture while singing?

A Generational Thing: Marcella Sembrich's vowel shape

Marcella Sembrich insisted that her students shape the mouth and throat "like an oval lying on its side," and keep it that way at all times by using "breathing to create and maintain the form." Her validation as an expert was indisputable. She was the star pupil of Giovanni Battista Lamperti and his father, Francesco Lamperti, and the greatest exponent of the bel canto vocal style of her era. She was known as the Second Patti, and praised as the greatest soprano of her generation. At the young age of twenty-five, she was chosen to sing at the opening of the Metropolitan Opera in New York. She advocated the same principles of singing as other great singers of her era. Her teaching was passed down to another great soprano, Leontyne Price, whose teacher, Florence Kimball, was a pupil of Sembrich. Price can be seen maintaining the oval-lying-on-its side shape while singing, and is yet another singer who proved that the old rules were the best rules.

Caruso's Vocal Technique, Practiced by Millions

Caruso, in order to sing, followed a sequential process that is described in his book in this order:

- He inhaled into his lower back with the abdomen moving inward, expanding the lower ribs (like a bellows), and raised his chest. Babies do this.
- While inhaling, he kept his tongue in contact with his lower lip, pulled the corners of his mouth back, unhinged his jaw and opened his throat. Babies do this, too.
- At the instant of the attack of a tone, he opened the mouth vertically the width of one finger, keeping the corners of his mouth back, and leaned his breath against his chest by doing a motion that was contrary to his inhaling function. Babies open wider when the get desperate and scream, but, for normal crying, they don't open their mouths very far.

He produced his vowels like a baby who is awake and crying or laughing. The [a] vowel was placed far back and low in the throat. Similarly, Manuel Garcia II said to place the vowel by doing a miniature cough. Babies make a coughing sound in their throats when they cry, which also is placed far back and low in the throat. So, one thing is obvious. Caruso used the same vocal method as practiced by millions of babies around the world!

Methods for perfect singing

Perfect Singing and Character: Helge Roswänge

The true and correctly identified natural method for making sounds (the crying or laughing baby) is the most efficient of all vocal methods. It allows a baby to cry for days (and sometimes for nights!) without straining its voice. Any singer or actor using this method will never experience problems with fatigue in the throat or irritation of the vocal folds. Roswänge, using the crying baby method, sang three times a day for fifty-five years, without a vocal problem. I should mention that he had the floppiest jaw I have ever seen. It was so loose when he sang, hanging down at the back, that it seemed like it could fly away at any moment! The only visible activity was that the corners of his mouth were kept pulled back at all times.

Crucial Point: The *Baby* Method

As we know, a baby will never pull the belly inward while crying or laughing, and a singer should never pull the stomach in while singing. A baby will never pull the jaw or chin downward into a vertical oval while laughing or crying, and a singer should never pull the jaw down into a vertical oval while singing! A baby will never pucker the corners of the mouth forward while crying, and a singer should never pucker the corners of the mouth forward while singing.

The Janus Mask: Harrell's method for a loose jaw, throat and tongue

My first semester of study with Mack Harrell at Southern Methodist University was spent on exercises to loosen the jaw, throat, and tongue, while singing scales and arpeggios. Mr. Harrell believed that the freedom of those structures was inseparable from their action/reaction relationships to the emission of the voice, and absolutely, therefore, essential to good singing. In order to eliminate any signs of tension or flexed muscles in the throat, a set of rules had to be learned. He explained that babies express emotions with a loose jaw. He used the term, *diaphragmatic expressions* (emotional colors in the voice without the benefit of text), explaining that it is possible to color a tone simply by thinking an emotion, without tensing the jaw or the muscles under the jaw or chin. In the Italian language, these colors are called *timbri* (timbres). A happy baby smiles and laughs with the corners of the mouth pulled back and the jaw unhinged, without stiffness or tension. An unhappy baby cries, sometimes desperately if the bottle is too slow to arrive, in the exact same manner. The corners of the baby's mouth are pulled back at all times when laughing or crying. It is the principal behind the design of the Janus mask. Every emotion can be clearly demonstrated by an actor or singer with the corners of the mouth pulled back. Caruso said to "open the mouth well at the sides." Tetrazzini said to "sing with the mouth in the shape of a smile." Singers can be as expressive as they need to be without puckering the lips forward, or contracting the jaw muscles, or flexing the muscles under the jaw and behind the chin.

If one studies the greatest singers on film, the gentle smile, sometimes called the open smile, seems to be an integral part of good singing. It allows the mouth to be shaped like an oval lying on its side, prescribed by the Lampertis and described and taught by their star student, Marcella Sembrich. Fernando De Lucia, considered with Mattia Battistini to be one of the greatest vocal technicians in history, was criticized during his entire career for maintaining a smile on his face regardless of the emotions being felt by the character he was portraying. Nicolai Gedda kept the corners of his mouth pulled back extremely at all times, as did Maria Callas. One notices that Caruso, in the pictures of him demonstrating the proper facial formations for each vowel, kept the corners of the mouth back, even on the [u] vowel. For those singers who worry about acting, the corners of the mouth being held back should not limit expression at all. The Janus mask allows the corners of the mouth to move slightly up for happiness and slightly down for sorrow.

Mr. Harrell's rules

Rule 1: No action in the throat

Deep, silent, and very slow breathing through the nose and into the lower back was practiced (Tetrazzini described it as "smelling a flower") until the goal of complete inaction in the throat, jaw, tongue, face and head was achieved. The only parts of the body that were allowed to move were the corners of the mouth, the larynx, and the ribs in the lower back. The larynx relaxed and moved downward as a result of the strength of the inhalation into the lower back. It was not allowed to move unless the inhalation moved it. Deep breathing will open the throat vertically as the air passes through the throat and into the lungs.

While singing, the pressure of the breath against the chest maintains an open throat and allows the larynx to float in its lowered position. There will be no need to resort to tension of the jaw or to stimulate actions or reactions in the throat muscles to keep the larynx in place while singing. Just as in the case of the ribcage, the larynx should not move unless the inhalation moves it.

Rule 2: No action in the jaw

The freedom of the jaw was assisted by repeatedly moving the jaw up and down and sideways, using only the hand or hands, without flexing the chewing muscles, or any muscles in the area of the throat, especially under the jaw and behind the chin. No muscles were allowed to assist the sideways movement of the jaw. The head was angled upward while the throat was kept in a still, inactive state. No independent action of the tongue was allowed until all the parts of the throat puzzle were under control and completely inactive. The only movements of the tongue were to allow the back of the tongue to descend reactively with the larynx at the moment of the instigation of the deep inhalation, and to allow the front of the tongue to remain in contact with the lower lip at all times, leaving the tip loose and free to articulate the dental consonants against the upper teeth.

Rule 3: The jaw must be unhinged

All movements, when exercising the extreme unhinging of the jaw, had to be performed by using the hands to provide the downward pulling force. The chin would be pulled down as far as it would go by using the thumb or index finger to press it down (not by using the chewing muscles), while trying to maintain a smile. This exercise would cause the jaw to unhinge. It was then released quickly and completely, without losing the smile, and without any controlling action of the chewing muscles of the jaw. Unhinging the relaxed, dropped jaw ever wider was accomplished over time, by often repeating the joint-stretching exercise.

While singing, the singer must not hold the mouth open or closed by means of muscular action (the chewing muscles). Ideally, gravity must be the only force affecting the dropping of the jaw while singing. Pulling the jaw down using only the hand (the fingers) exploits the natural elasticity of the tendons and muscles, requiring them to let go of any degree of tension or flexing. Some of my colleagues in Europe walked around with an apple crammed into their mouths as far back as possible. This extreme stretching exercise was supposed to eventually stretch the tendons that attach the jaw to the skull. It is not a bad exercise if the mouth is not held open with muscles after the apple is removed, and is one way to develop elasticity in the hinge of the jaw. Simply letting go of the jaw with the head facing slightly upward will automatically allow the mouth to find its natural open position as dictated by gravity. The upper part of the face, if all muscles are relaxed, demonstrates the slack-jawed, moronic expression that is ideal in singing. Olga Ryss used to say, "Drop from the eyes to under the jaw, like an idiot!" This may be the reason for the evolution of the gentle open smile while singing. It was the only muscular action permitted in the lower face while singing during the Bel Canto era. Perhaps, at one point, the singers realized that some expression would be necessary while singing. The question arose: how can a singer maintain a live expression while singing without beginning a chain reaction of tensions in the jaw and throat? The answer was simple: the only muscles that can be activated that do not react in the throat are the ones that draw the corners of the mouth back.

Great singers and history

Two Modern Divas

Lilli Lehmann included in her repertoire Norma, Konstanze, Isolde, and Brünnhilde. Not even Sutherland, Milanov or Birgit Nilsson accomplished such vocal feats. There are today only two singers who have accomplished this incredible variety of repertoire and vocal styles: Rebecca Copley and Joanna Porackova. They are fantastic sopranos, having wonderful, long careers, singing the most difficult roles ever written for soprano voice. Roles they have performed with success include Lady Macbeth, Abigaille in *Nabucco*, Salome, Elektra, Tosca, Aida, Amelia in *Un ballo in maschera*, Turandot, Brünnhilde in both *Siegfried* and *Götterdämmerung*, and the above mentioned deadly duo of Norma and Isolde. Amazingly, both can sing the Queen of the Night from Mozart's *Die Zauberflöte*, in the original key, including the high F-naturals. Very few singers have been able to sing one of these roles beautifully, much less all of them! These ladies can sing anything in the soprano repertoire with ease, fulfilling the demands of the most important conductors and audiences in the world, and they have the international reviews to prove it. They sing easily, with absolute control, and without any indication of vocal strain or vocal fatigue. They demonstrate a total absence of muscular activity in the jaw, and have done so for many years. Their fabulous technical approach to singing will let them enjoy exciting careers for many years to come.

Carlo Bergonzi: A Perfectly Still Tenor and a Perfectly Still Colleague

Bergonzi was a wonderful vocal technician who used the stillness breathing method for many years. He did not place his inhalation, but allowed it to react to the stillness of his chest and abdomen. If the chest and the abdomen were not allowed to move, the breath had to be taken in and sent out in a way that would not disturb his stillness. In this approach, the breath is taken into the lower back reactively, because it is not permitted to go anywhere else! As it developed, his respiration became strong enough for him to switch from baritone to tenor. I heard many of his performances at the old Met. He sang beautifully, and was especially admired for his smooth legato singing. He sang the most difficult roles in the Italian repertoire, and was particularly good at singing roles in the operas by Verdi. My favorite role I heard him sing was Riccardo in Verdi's *Un ballo in maschera*. During the actual act of singing, his chest and abdomen never moved. Trying to see how he breathed was almost as difficult as trying to analyze Zinka Milanov's breathing technique. Her chest was totally still while breathing and singing, making it appear as if the voice just happened without any effort at all. When I asked Bergonzi how he breathed when he sang, he answered, "*Non muovere niente*!" (don't move anything!).

I realized later, just as I had finally discovered by observing Zinka Milanov, the only movement to be seen when either of those wonderful singers sang, was in their lower backs. Their lower ribs in the back would open when they inhaled and closed when they sang. It made perfect sense, with all of the stillness in the front of their bodies, that the ribs had to move. They had no choice!

The Perfect Attack

The famous silent film of Caruso singing "Vesti la giubba" from Leoncavallo's *Pagliacci* is a perfect example of invisible singing. I have watched that film many times. The only view we have is from the front, and it is clear that there is no visible movement in his chest or belly. Unfortunately, we do not have a view from the rear, and it is impossible to see any movements that would offer a clue as to how he sang. Thank goodness we have his book, and his own words, to describe the approach to singing he used. W.A. Henderson, music critic for *The New York Sun* during the Golden Age at the old Met, thought that Caruso had the only perfect attack he ever heard. Even Patti's attack was not as good as Caruso's, in Henderson's opinion. It is hard for us to imagine what that must have been like.

More about Milanov: Downstairs and Without Noise

Meanwhile, back to the problem of analyzing Milanov's perfect breathing method. To make a long story as simple as possible, I was finally able to detect, observing her from the back of the stage and in her coachings with Victor Trucco, which I was allowed to attend as his page turner if I was absolutely silent and perfectly still, how she expanded her lower ribs in her back when she inhaled! What a fantastic discovery for a young singer! Milanov was human after all. She had to breathe, too, just like every other singer. The thing that was unique about her breathing method was that she hid it from view better than anyone I have ever seen (or heard) since. The movement of her lower ribs was never sudden or violent, but always smooth and seemingly gentle. If I had not discovered her secret, I may have believed her many admirers, who swore she never breathed at all! The only visual evidence of breathing was the opening and closing of her ribs in her lower back, and the movement had to be seen from behind. A clear view of her lower ribs was essential. Getting a proper location for viewing her from the rear was not as easy as it may sound. There were some sneaky things required in order to manage the proper view, but I won't go into that! The front of her body was deathly still when she sang. I was reminded of Olga Ryss' instructions to "stand still like a statue as still as a dead corpse!"

It was hopeless to ask Milanov about vocal technique. I tried several times (never in or around Trucco's studio) during a rehearsal or after a performance, but there was never enough time to try to translate her concepts into something I could understand and use. When I asked her how she breathed, she said "Downstairs and without noise." This remark may have been the explanation of her approach to singing, or it may have been a dig directed at Renata Tebaldi, who often was heard vocalizing upstairs in one of the empty rooms!

There was much discussion at that time among students and fans about Tebaldi's audible mini-gasps between phrases. The sounds she made between her sung tones were loud enough to be heard by the audience. Of course, no one was bothered by them, except maybe Zinka. She loved to expound on the "proper way other sopranos should sing," and had said publicly that Tebaldi, Nilsson, Callas, and Leonie Rysanek should come to her and ask about correct singing! The terminology she used when discussing singing was totally confusing. My favorite expression she used was: "Put the breath on the voice and sing without noise, and only pianissimo." Milanov had what was probably the most beautiful high pianissimo in the history of singing. However, it is often forgotten that she could also produce some of the most powerful and beautiful tones ever heard at the Metropolitan Opera! They were prodigious and often overwhelmed the sound of the full orchestra, the full chorus, and the other soloists, except maybe Mario del Monaco!

Counter Can Mean Contrary

The famous countertenor Alfred Deller used the contrary motion method of breathing exclusively, and with fantastic success. He tried to draw the tone inward using the illusion of a continuous inhalation while singing. The volume level was determined by his ability to increase or decrease the intensity of air inhaled. In order to develop the sense of the degree of intensity necessary to use different levels of volume in his singing, he would practice blowing a dangling tissue outward, achieving and sustaining different angles, from ten degrees to ninety degrees. The ten degree angle of the tissue was sustained in order to gain a mirror concept for soft singing. It was blown more intensely, and sustained past forty-five degrees to an angle of almost ninety degrees, to gain the concept that loud singing should feel like a contrary motion of a more intense exhalation.

Of course, the breath was never leaked at all when singing. The controlled blowing of the breath outward was used as an opposite and equal model of what the singer should imagine happening in the opposite function when sound is being produced. Deller said, "nothing goes outward but the sound. The breath always moves inward in the imagination while singing, and it can be perfectly controlled as to how intensely it streams back and down into the phonation process."

Italian versus German and Opera versus Lied

Variable Success: Fischer-Dieskau

In general, singers who specialize in the song repertoire do not enjoy the same level of success in Italian opera that they do in the concert field. Fischer-Dieskau's attempts to sing Italian opera were notably unsuccessful. The international critics in Salzburg who heard his attempt to sing Verdi's *Rigoletto* as part of the Festival wrote the most caustic, horrible critiques of his portrayal of the title role that I have ever read. One of them asked:

> How can Herr Fischer-Dieskau presume to dare to offer us a pitiful, weak, vocally thin, barking interpretation of *Rigoletto*? Was it really necessary to accent every note and separate every two notes? Could he not have sung a phrase legato one time in an entire performance, if only for variety? What an artistic disaster! It was the worst kind of arrogance to expect us to accept what he perpetrated on the stage as *Rigoletto*. Hopefully, he will never attempt to sing Italian opera again!

The most interesting thing about this review was the critic's surprise and anger. This same critic worshipped Fisher-Dieskau as history's greatest interpreter of German art songs!

Singers should listen to Merrill sing Rigoletto's opening line and compare it to Fisher-Dieskau's. The difference is dramatic! Merrill sings it in the Italian vocal style without accents and with every note bound to the next note. It is a beautiful example of legato singing. The line I have in mind is "*In testa che avete Signor di Ceprano*?" Then listen to Fischer-Dieskau sing the same line! There is no legato at all. Each note is separated from its neighbor. Accents are repeated where Verdi did not ask for them! Barking is probably the best word to describe this German singer's vocal approach to Italian opera! Fans familiar with his recordings of Lieder know that his usual approach to music and singing did not include barking. Wouldn't it be better to sing in the Italian style and be able to sing every kind of music beautifully? In modern times, Wunderlich, a German tenor singing German repertoire in the German language in Germany, proved that it is not only possible—it is preferable!

Germans Who Sang the Italian Way

A list of great German singers who sang with the old Italian method of leaning the breath would include Frieda Hempel, Fritz Wunderlich, Friedrich Schorr, Frieda Leider, Joseph Schmidt, Selma Kurz, Paul Schöffler, and the great Lilli Lehmann. Kirsten Flagstad, Lauritz Melchior, Lluba Welitsch, Helge Roswänge, Frederick Dalberg, and Jan Kiepura, although not Germans by nationality, should be included on this list. Their careers predominantly were made by singing the German repertoire, but their vocal techniques were completely modeled on the Italian legato style.

Trimble's advisors

Different Times, Different Reasons: Tucker, Amara, Roswänge

When Richard Tucker or Lucine Amara gave me vocal advice, I listened with respect. Both had proven for many years that their understanding of how to sing was based on solid principles. I wanted to learn those principles, and compare them to what I heard and read about vocal methods that were recommended by other great singers. It is one thing to say that a certain technical concept will work. It is quite another to have proven it over a Wagnerian or Verdian orchestra for four or five hours at a time, and for thirty or forty years!! Tucker sang at the Met for thirty years, and Amara sang at the Met for forty-one seasons and sang fifty-six roles during that time.

Roswänge, another advisor, with whom I studied during the winter of 1970-71, sang for fifty-five years, seven days per week, three times a day, and never had a vocal problem! He would rehearse in the morning, make recordings in the afternoon, and perform every night, seven nights a week! When I asked him to what he attributed such incredible longevity, he answered, "yoga, and the book on singing by Enrico Caruso."

Perspective and Outlook

Belonging to an Elite Group

Singers who wish to belong to the elite group of vocal artists, who desire to sing beautifully and have long, successful careers as performers, must reject any ideas and methods that cause action or tension in the throat, tongue, jaw, face or in the tendons and muscles of the neck. They must try to imagine that physical functions of essential parts of the throat, that are crucial to the biomechanics of great singing, can feel invisible while singing. They must learn to move the mind the way great singers of the past moved their minds. Tetrazzini said to "never get upset. It will stiffen the jaw, and singing will be impossible." Thank goodness she wrote her book before the great emotional crisis that ruined her singing. Her book was written while she was still the greatest female vocalist in the world. Ironically, it was a terrible fit of rage that turned into an uncontrollable state of chronic anger that ended her great career. She did not heed her own advice. The hysterical, sustained and unforgiving anger she felt made her jaw and breathing stiff and dominated her mind completely. She suddenly became unable to sing the way she had since childhood. Moving the mind calmly and sequentially became impossible. Tetrazzini proved she had been right all along: getting upset can ruin a singer, and tragically, in her case it did. Lamperti said, "one word can destroy a singer." That is how simple and yet fragile it can be to practice perfection.

A Consensus of Opinion

Of course, we all have our favorites. There are singers who appeal to music critics, but not so much to the general public. Some singers, such as Corelli, appeal to the general public, but not to the music critics. Some singers appeal to the public and to the critics, but the management of the theater may not like them, and no one knows why. A few singers are appreciated by their colleagues. There is no doubt, that the one singer who appealed to her fellow vocal artists and to the public more than any other during the Bing era at the Metropolitan Opera—in spite of the fact that her difficult personality made them dislike her as a person—was Zinka Milanov.

When Zinka sang a performance at the old Met, every famous singer who happened to be in New York was in attendance! Jerome Hines and George London both thought Zinka was, without question, the best singer in the world. Lucine Amara compared Milanov's standing among her colleagues with the stories of Ponselle's dominance of the vocal scene during the 1920s. Amara, trying to explain her assessment of Zinka's voice and vocal artistry, quoted Geraldine Ferrar's famous answer, when asked how to get a voice like Rosa Ponselle "by special arrangement with God!" Merrill thought that Milanov was unique. Her voice was the most beautiful and powerful voice in the world, and she was the absolute best, most reliable singer he ever heard.

In 1962, the members of *The Metropolitan Opera Club* in New York, many of them in their seventies and eighties at the time, were asked if any of the current singers at the Met could have been a star during the Golden Age of singing. They had been listening to opera since around 1900 and had heard all of the stars of that period. And, of course, they had heard all of the famous stars on the current opera scene. They certainly had a good basis of experience for forming an opinion. The surprising answer they gave to the question was unanimous: "Only one modern singer could have been a star during the Golden Age, and it is Zinka Milanov."

Advice

Advice Comes in Various Forms

There is a great deal of advice available to young singers, some of it valuable and important, some of it worthless but harmless, and some of it destructive. Unfortunately, too much of it is destructive and must be identified and avoided completely.

The best and safest advice usually has to do with common, everyday things:

- Don't drink hot or cold drinks immediately before singing (it might move the mind to the mouth and throat).
- Eat several hours before a performance (eating too close to performance time may move the mind to the mouth and/or stomach, or it can inhibit the function of the diaphragm while breathing).
- Showers and baths should be taken in the morning and not close to performance time.
- A massage, so beneficial if received the day before or after a performance, may disperse the concentration required in order to sing well.
- Spicy foods and alcohol should be avoided before and during a performance (the mind will be moved to the mouth and the tongue).

If we analyze this advice, we begin to recognize that older, more experienced singers often advise younger singers to avoid activities that can either disperse their concentration or move their minds to locations that are not beneficial for singing.

Listening to one's own voice while singing can have a disconcerting effect on the concentration necessary for the total commitment and mental organization needed during performances. Allowing one's attention to be drawn to the ears, and to the analytical and listening/receiving part of the mind instead of the giving part of the mind, especially if there is self-criticism or any form of emotional response to listening, may cause a mental distraction that can disrupt the mindset needed for great singing. It is advisable to avoid listening to one's own recordings until a year has passed, to prevent the inevitable emotional reactions that evaluation and judgment cause. It should be remembered: the greatest singers in history did not have the possibility to record themselves during their developmental years. Caruso was twenty-nine when he heard himself on a recording for the first time. Adelina Patti was sixty-three, and her response was charming. She said, as the recording began to play, and she heard herself for the very first time in her life, "Ah! Now I know why I am Patti!"

Measured in Decades

I would advise singers to watch films of the greatest singers they can find, to study the methods of those singers, and, in particular, the methods of breathing and phonation being employed. Some singers do one thing better than another, and fame is not necessarily the best recommendation. There are many fantastic vocalists who have not achieved the international stardom their talents deserve. Some of them are incredibly admired in their geographical areas of activity. Helen Donat, Mimi Côrtze, Lucia Popp, Anton De Ridder, Nellie Dutoit, Hans Van Heerden, Frederick Dalberg, Cristina Deutekom, Paul Schöffler, and countless others were superb artists. Any of them can safely be studied as examples of great singing. They should be sought on recordings and on YouTube to discern the good points of the very best. We must judge the best singers, not by the degree of their popularity with a fickle public, but by the beauty of tone, the longevity of career, the generous and free vocal style, and their ability to sing high, low, loudly, softly, fast coloratura, and sustained phrases, and do it all without making weird faces, puckering the lips, grimacing, shaking the jaw and tongue, singing through clenched teeth, or wrinkling parts of the face. In other words, the ability to fulfill the criteria of the music and remain healthy, over a period of time measured in decades, is one of the best ways to evaluate the vocal technique of a singer.

Vocal Freedom

I advise young singers to study any recordings and films of Milanov's singing they can find. She was a great example of what we should all aspire to achieve with our voices and our art. I don't mean to suggest that any young singer should imitate any other singer, no matter how famous the star may be. However, it is good to study the very best, and compare what we know about singing with what they were doing when they sang. The criteria of good singing have been listed in this book. They are there to be understood and accepted or misunderstood and rejected. In the end, it is, as it always has been, up to the individual artist to decide what is good or not good for him- or herself. The advice I have given is based on the actual concepts and applications of those concepts as used by the greatest singers in history. I can only hope that it can help some young artist along the way to vocal freedom.

Been There, Done That

Instead of blindly accepting the vocal methods that are commonly propagated today, singers should rely on the opinions of the greatest vocal artists in history who have "been there, done that." How many voice teachers have actually sung the major operas of the great composers? Only in many performances, over many years, in big theaters, and over big orchestras, can a technique be truly tested. Projection of the voice and text over the orchestra, emotional timbres in accordance with the interpretation of the text, and the stamina necessary to fulfill the criteria of an entire role, are immediate requirements in live performance. The breathing methods of the greatest singers will provide the aspiring vocalist with a technical approach for fulfilling the criteria of the most difficult roles in each singer's respective voice category.

The Proof Lies in Good Vocal Health and Longevity

A vocal method should last for a lifetime and enable beautiful singing that will fulfill the criteria of the singing profession without vocal problems. There should be no artificial factors, like nasality, tongue shaping that causes tension in the throat, lifting the soft palate in any direction but up and forward, belly-outward inhalations, or inward or upward movements of the abdomen while singing. One advantage of having taught singing for over fifty years is that I have students who are actively singing professionally after studying with me over forty years ago, thus proving the validity of the vocal method I advocate! Longevity should be a criterion for any career in any field. Unfortunately, there are teachers who have never sung anywhere, whose students have never won a competition or been hired by an opera company, who are teaching completely wrong vocal methods. Some of these methods lead to damage of the vocal folds and to total ruination of beautiful young voices. In 1974 I had three students come to me from the same teacher, each of whom had vocal nodules. What could have been so wrong in the method they had learned that would cause such damage to young voices?

As it turned out, all three had been taught to expand the belly when inhaling, to pull the belly in while singing, and to focus the voice into the narrowest part of the top of the nose. They would pinch the top of the nose right between the eyes while vocalizing! Needless to say, all three were cured of their vocal nodules within six months by applying correct breathing techniques and relaxing their throats. Their voices became healthy and perfectly responsive to an even vocal emission. Today, some thirty-five years later, all three still have clear, healthy voices!

What Do Singers Want to Accomplish?

Moving the mind in ways that guarantee a free throat, a large, resonating air-box in the chest, and an uninterrupted emission, has been clearly explained by the greatest singers in history. We have been told how to inhale to open the throat and prepare the *appoggio* by inhaling a certain way, and how to lean the breath when ready to sing. Understanding and practicing the mental commands recommended to us by Caruso, Tetrazzini, Lehmann, and Mattia Battistini will allow us to be part of a vocal tradition that has proven to be the best approach to singing ever discovered. The sequential breathing and support process described in their books and in quotes handed down to us from these greatest of all vocal artists allow a modern singer to sing beautifully and to fulfill the demands of the most difficult vocal music ever written. The *appoggio* method of singing will help a young singer make the most beautiful sounds his or her voice is capable of making, while, at the same time, avoiding vocal problems and distortions of the throat. The criteria of great singing are fulfilled as the result of the breathing method instead of requiring constant compensatory actions in the throat. No action in the throat and no change of emission become the automatic results of the method of inhalation and the *appoggio*.

I would ask singers who want to become wonderful vocalists to study and research for themselves the quotes, opinions, ideas, and writings of Caruso, Tetrazzini, Lehmann, Battistini, De Lucia, Roswänge, Sembrich, De Luca, Lillian Nordica, Maggie Teyte, Melchior, Flagstad, Milanov, Tucker, Dame Eva Turner, London, Ponselle, Ghiaurov, Frieda Hempel, Merrill, Frances Alda, and Tito Schipa. Not one of these excellent vocalists ever suggested focusing the tone, or reversing the obvious function of a megaphone and speaking into the large end, while expecting the voice to come out of the small end with a better result.

One thing we know for certain: no great singer ever recommended forming a cup in the middle of the tongue, or forming ski-slopes with the tongue by humping it up in the middle, or creating parachutes with the soft palate, or holding a banana low in the throat, or shaking the head to create vibrato in the tone, or squinting the eyes tighter and tighter as the voice ascends into the upper range. One teacher in Boston taught a nineteen-year-old tenor to use the eyes in the opposite way: "Stretch the eyes open as widely as possible while singing, like an old-fashioned automobile with huge headlights." The great teachers recommended that the mouth open no wider than the width of one finger in the middle range of the voice, and no wider than two fingers in the upper range of the voice. Now a young singer may be told to open the mouth as wide as possible when singing high notes!

No historical singer ever recommended the use of syllables like [ga – gɛ – gi – go – gu] to place the tone against the hard palate. Lehmann and Caruso said "the voice passes over the soft palate and over the hard palate." Any kind of action in the throat while singing goes against every piece of advice ever presented to aspiring young singers by great singers. Dame Eva Turner said to sing with the idea that the throat, jaw, and tongue are invisible.

Pick Up Your Legs and Run Like Hell!
Ideas and concepts that are different from the advice handed down to us by the greatest singers who ever lived should be avoided at all costs. Olga Ryss, whose teacher at the St. Petersburg Conservatory was a student of G.B. Lamperti, said: "If a teacher or coach says focus the tone, or just breathe normally, or pucker the lips for [o] and [u], or press the chin down as far as possible, or press the jaw down against the chest, or create a vertical shape with the mouth, or pull the jaw down and pinch the middles of the cheeks or the corners of the mouth together, or sing everything through an "ew" form, the singer **should pick up his legs and run like hell**!" Franco Corelli, in a master class in New York, said the American singers "all sing like they are singing through a straw and into the nose. Do they not care if anyone can hear them over the orchestra?" The only singer he liked in that class was Joanna Porackova because "she sings deep in the body with the throat open and the head faces up to the balcony."

Ideas originating with teachers who have never sung and who could never sing will not be accepted by intelligent, experienced singers. Singers and teachers have failed to have careers as professional singers because they studied singing with so-called teachers who were never successful performers themselves. It is a case of the blind leading the blind.

Grand Finale

One thing is absolutely clear and applicable to all singers: the foundation on which all great singing is built is the correct breathing method, the inhalation, posture and exhalation of the breath. This psychomotor system response and biomechanical process must be repeated correctly under expert supervision until the body responds habitually to the correct, healthy, muscular coordination of the breathing function. Remember: ritual eliminates choice. Through repetition, the body integrates the pathways that are correct and, if incorrect pathways have already been created (bad habits), eliminates those that are damaging to good singing and cause physical damage to the vocal folds.

> In fact, all bad habits of the throat are merely efforts of protection against clumsy management of the breath. Faulty singing is caused by awkward respiration...The foundation of all vocal study lies in the control of the breath.[19]

[19] Giovanni Battista Lamperti (1839-1910). *Vocal Wisdom* (New York: Taplinger), 1931/1957: 5,13

> The precept breathe low means control the breathing low in the body. In passing from low to high tones, the breath must take the opposite direction of the voice.[20]
>
> The stroke of the glottis (violent attack) which many singing teachers advise is absolutely harmful to the voice.[21]
>
> It is the training of the middle voice that brings the beautiful head voice.[22]
>
> It is indispensable, for the singer, to properly take and control the inhalation and exhalation of his breath; for breathing is, so to speak, the regulator of singing.[23]
>
> The lungs and diaphragm and the whole breathing apparatus must be understood by the singer, because the foundation of singing is breathing and breath control. A singer must be able to rely on his/her breath, just as he/she relies upon the solidity of the ground beneath his/her feet.[24]

The first two rules of the historical Bel Canto era of singing are no action in the throat and no change of emission. Every singer of the Golden Age of beautiful singing who wrote a book about the production of the singing tone repeatedly emphasizes the importance of the relaxed, totally free throat and proper breathing techniques, which permit the throat, tongue and facial muscles to remain free. Professional singers, whether specializing in opera, cantorial repertoire,[25] song, or other genres, are expected to be able to fulfill vocal demands that include beauty of tone, projection, flexibility, range, emotional expression, vocal stamina and vocal longevity. A singer should have a loose jaw, a relaxed tongue and a breathing method that releases tension instead of creating it. Tension and relaxation are words that must be carefully defined in any type of physical skill. There must be a balance of tension and relaxation somewhere in the body, of course. The singer must learn to use only the essential muscle groups at the correct time, which are necessary to produce a free and healthy tone, relative to the individual's vocal potential and the particular moment in each singer's development.

---

[20] Ibid; p.42

[21] Ibid; p. 6

[22] G.B. Lamperti. *Vocal Wisdom* (New York: Taplinger), 1957: 137

[23] Manuel Garcia II. A *Complete Treatise on the Art of Singing, Part I* (New York: DaCapo Press), 1984: 45. A Note: Manuel Garcia II is credited with the invention of the Laryngoscope in 1854.

[24] Luisa Tetrazzini. *The Art of Singing* (New York: Dover edition) 1975: 11

[25] Cantor Pamela Kordan Trimble speaks to the relationship between opera and cantorial singing as follows: "In comparing books on bel canto singing, one is convinced there was at that time a traditional way one learned to sing, an aesthetic one recognized and strived to attain, to the best of one's ability. It is no accident that the era of bel canto and the Golden Age of Singing followed each other historically. One wonders what conditions were present that allowed this to happen; that such marvelous singing should thrive sequentially in two different worlds of expression: in the world of Italian opera and the world of synagogue prayer." "Kol Hazzanit: Alternatives to the Vocal Requirements and Expression of Traditional Hazzanute for Women Cantors," *Journal of Synagogue Music,* Vol. 32 (New York: Cantors Assembly), 1972: 105

One of the reasons I am able to help and have the patience necessary to re-train singers with damaged vocal folds is that I was and still am totally fascinated with the idea that human beings can use their voices to create extraordinary musical sounds combined with emotional expression. The basic musical scales and various exercises never, for an instant, bore me. I find the process challenging because it requires intense concentration, physical development and dedication by both teacher and student. Repetition of correct function under expert supervision is essential for incorporating the physical concepts into a singer's working technique as quickly as possible. I can still sit at the piano, day after day, playing the same simple scales and feel the way a prospector or treasure hunter must feel during the search. As the singer achieves looseness of the tongue and throat, a little gold dust emerges, then a few nuggets and signs of beauty of tone begin to appear or reappear. I feel the same excitement as the prospector who first finds gold dust. Somewhere beneath the dust are the nuggets and then, with enough digging, the mother lode!

Wilbur Gould, MD was world renowned as the great throat specialist for professional singers. He was Chief of Otolaryngology at Lenox Hill Hospital, New York City. Throughout my teaching years in New York (1973-1994), Dr. Gould sent professional, working singers with vocal fold problems and damage to me for rehabilitation before he would schedule surgery. He was a colleague and wonderful, caring human being. He always encouraged the singers to take the time necessary to correct vocal breathing techniques and avoid surgery. If surgery was necessary, Dr. Gould sent the singers to me for vocal rehabilitation after the vocal folds had healed properly.

What is good for a singer?

The ability to know what is good for you is so rare among singers that it is often never discussed at all. It does not occur to many coaches and teachers to even broach the subject. Yet, when Robert Merrill presented a master class for singers during my summer opera program at Sarah Lawrence College in 1978, he answered succinctly:

> You have to have the talent, gift or intelligence to know what is good for you specifically. You have to be able to run everything through your mind... you will hear a lot of nonsense and garbage, most of which, if you followed the advice given, would eventually ruin your voice!

Mr. Merrill's insight brings to mind Mahatma Gandhi's famous quotation: "It is because we have at the present moment everybody claiming their own right of conscience without going through any discipline whatsoever that there is so much untruth being delivered to a bewildered world."[27] There will be a few people you meet who may have some good advice for you, but the thing to remember is that everyone you meet has an opinion!

---

[27] R.K. Prabhu & U.R. Rao, editors. *The Mind of Mahatma Gandhi* (India: Jitendra T.Desai,Navajivan Trust),1945/1967/1996: 42

> To be a person of truth, to be swayed neither by approval nor disapproval... Work at not needing approval from anyone and you will be free to be who you really are.[28]

You will hear: "I think the tone is too bright, I think the tone is too dark, I think it should be more accented, I think it should be smoother, etc." One hundred people in a room will give you one hundred different opinions. Which ones do you listen to and which do you ignore? Most professional singers end up listening to no one. If a singer is lucky, as Merrill was, he finds one great mentor and listens only to the advice of that individual. Merrill studied with Samuel Margolis for over forty years. (Mr. Margolis was also the teacher of Jerome Hines). In the end, the singer stands alone on the stage and will take the credit, blame or criticism for his or her performance.

> It is not everyone that can be taught to sing, even granting an exceptional gift of voice. To become a singer is impossible if you have no ear, for no mathematical combination will put that into you. Time and rhythm cannot be taught; if you do not possess them as natural gifts you cannot acquire them. They are things to be developed, not learned. Good physique is absolutely necessary to the singer; a great singer is, of necessity, strong bodily. A nervous person should not attempt to become a singer, for here again, is an insurmountable handicap. Regular digestion is absolutely essential to good voice, and a repeated course of medicine to stimulate it will only add to the intervals of physical inability to sing.[29]

I have helped countless singers over the years find and "re-find" their voices. Singers of all ages and all stages of development have been coming to me since 1959, desperately looking for help with their voices. What did I know when I was twenty-one years old? What could I know at that age? Something—very little—intuitive maybe—but I already knew something. I did seem to possess some kind of knack or talent for teaching: the ability to impart information clearly, and to empathize physically with what the singer was doing or not doing in the throat and in the breathing system that either helped or hurt the quality of sound the singer was producing. This ability permitted me to actually help singers with general and specific problems. For instance, it seemed obvious to me that a singer should not have to make faces to sing well. How could a singer act, smile, cry, look surprised, etc. if the face was always locked in a grimace, or having to show all the teeth, or having to pull the jaw down?

Criticism

Questions: criticism of today's singing method

We should ask ourselves some questions pertinent to this discussion. When did pulling the jaw downward while singing become the correct position of the mouth? Many singers today look like Edvard Munch's painting, *The Scream*. The greatest teachers and singers of the past gave specific recommendations that advised singers to use a horizontal formation

[28] Rebbe Nachman of Breslov. The Empty Chair (Vermont: Jewish Lights Publishing), 2009: 78

[29] Lillian Nordica. *Hints to Singers* (New York: Dover) 1998: 29-30

of the mouth while singing. The most often mentioned shape was the open smile with the corners of the mouth pulled back.

When did focusing the voice in the nose by singing [jing], [jang], [jong], [ming], [mang], [mong], or [gaidi], [godi], [gudi], [gɛdi], [gadi] and other similar exercises based on the search for nasal resonance, become the correct way to sing? Caruso says emphatically to "never sing into the nasal cavity. It is against all the rules of song."

When did nasal resonance and focus become the sound that defines the aesthetic of today? Great singers and teachers of the past told us to avoid such sounds and placements!

When did swelling the belly outward while inhaling become the correct way to breathe? We know that Dr. Louis Mandl, a famous physiologist in Paris (but not a singer!), recommended in 1876, that singers should breathe "like a sleeping baby." He believed that the abdomen should push outward while inhaling and collapse inward while singing. However, the greatest singers in the history of singing tell us to draw the abdomen inward while breathing and to relax it outward while singing, which is the way a crying or laughing baby uses the abdomen.

Why do teachers today teach the opposite of what the great singers and teachers recommended? Do they accept the advice of a scientist who never sang and reject the advice of the greatest singers? It would seem to be so.

FAZIT

In Conclusion

Any book written on singing today will have to deal with faulty concepts of vocal technique that have become universally acceptable to the point of being, in some respects, convention. But how can a young singer become as great as the "old" greats if he or she does not use the same criteria they used, as described in their books? Young singers today are directed as follows: no grunting; no sobbing; no slowing down; no speeding up; no holding notes too long; no cutting off notes too soon; don't wait too long; don't hurry; don't sing too dark; don't sing too bright; don't look up; don't put your head up; DON'T BREATHE (the most amazing of all bad advice!); don't, DON'T, **DON'T!**

All we can do is hope that there are young singers in the wings who are smart enough to wade through the *don'ts* and discover the *do's* that set the voice free. The true fans of beautiful, thrilling, expressive singing will be so grateful!

Instigators

Singers need a way to establish the correct function of the voice when the teacher is unavailable. The best way to do this is to have a series of vocalises that place the voice and cause predetermined reactions in the breathing and support systems. The specific exercises I recommend here will coordinate and produce the best sounds possible without anyone, including the singer, having to listen to each tone to ascertain whether or not the placement of the voice is correct.

I call these exercises instigators, because each exercise will instigate a specific reaction in the diaphragm. A predictable reaction in the diaphragm that results in fulfilling the criteria of good singing is amazingly beneficial to the voice and to the psychological state of the performer.

The most important criteria of good singing are:

- No action in the throat
- No change of emission
- Proper phonation

Below are listed some instigators that will help to fulfill the above criteria.

La messa di voce (the measure of the voice)
Tita Ruffo, Mattia Battistini, and Giuseppe De Luca all studied with the same teacher, Venceslao Persichini. What did these greatest baritones learn from this particular teacher, and how did they describe their approach to vocal technique? And for the purposes of this book, we wonder if the technique taught by Persichini would have been—or is—a good vocal technique for a tenor.

Merrill said that De Luca, who sang leading roles at the Met for thirty-three years without a single vocal problem, insisted in coaching sessions that the inhalation be placed as low as possible in the lower back, and that the voice be kept as light as possible at all times ("as close to the falsetto as possible without leaking any breath while singing").

The swelling of a note from falsetto to full voice and back to falsetto, without permitting the flame to waver, is only possible if the pressure of the breath moves with sufficient energy from the lower back to the lower chest. The procedure is to identify the necessary degree of pressure required by the singer to produce the musical phrase at hand, and thus to maintain the ideal point of leaning on the sternum at all times while singing. Merrill was fortunate to have had the opportunity to study roles with De Luca between 1945 and 1950. Battistini was quoted as saying "I press my chest." Does the technique sound familiar? There are pictures of both historical singers showing huge chests thrust out in front of the body. There are no greater examples of the sternal arch in photos of singers. The logic was simple: The bigger the air-box, the bigger and richer the sound. Caruso said to "feel the tone vibrating all down inside the body." Tucker said that the tone "is made by the big breath held in the lungs, and never by the vocal cords." Ponselle said to "feel the tone going deeper and deeper and deeper into the body" (notice that she used the word deeper three times to emphasize her point).

It is interesting to point out that the baritones mentioned above, with the exception of Ruffo, had incredibly long careers. De Luca sang lead roles at the Met for thirty-three years without any vocal problems. My teacher heard Battistini between 1921 and 1925 when the great baritone was between ages sixty-five and sixty-nine. His career continued until he died of heart trouble in 1928 at age seventy-two. His voice was pure, gorgeous, powerful, caressing, and as fresh as a young man's just starting his career.

[njam] (NnnYYAAHM)

The next instigator for the singer to practice is to sing the word [njam], which, together with some of the other Instigators we will discuss, will cause intense resonance in the mask. The danger lies in the singer's tendency to feel or listen to this. The singer must not allow his or her attention to be drawn to the facial area instead of to the diaphragm. Of course, it is exactly that resonance we want, but we must understand that the resonance is caused by a specific function of the diaphragm, and that the resonance that occurs is entirely a reactive response to the diaphragmatic function.

A definite and identifiable diaphragmatic response will occur if the [nj] plus a vowel is sustained. The combinations of the consonants, [nj], with a vowel immediately attached, will instigate an outward and downward movement of the diaphragm.

Singers can use the following combinations and achieve the diaphragmatic response necessary to sing evenly and securely:

- [njam] (NnnYYAHM)
- [njɛm] (NnnYYEHM)
- [njim] (NnnYYEEM)
- [njom] (NnnYYOHM)
- [njum] (NnnYYOOM)

There is a certain order of action that must be followed in order to achieve total relaxation of the throat:

- First, inhale deeply into the lower back
- Second, instigate the correct action in the diaphragm by using a consonant/vowel combination that results in a function of the diaphragm that becomes a support method (in this case, the [njam])
- Third, identify diaphragmatic response
- Fourth, accept the resulting sound and placement of the voice

The sound of the voice that results from the attachment of the breath to the lower chest (the reactive pressure of the breath against the front of the diaphragm) is caused by singing the word, [njam], repeatedly. This response in the diaphragm is the *raison d'être* of the exercise. The placement of the resonance and its corresponding formulation of the vowels in the pharynx are the *result* of the diaphragmatic response, and as long as we lean the breath against the diaphragm, the resonance of the voice is certain to achieve its most beneficial position (placement) in the true mask.

The exercise is actually very simple. Inhale deeply into the lower back while drawing the abdomen inward with the chest held still and somewhat lifted.

- Sing the word [njam] repeatedly, relaxing the belly outward without dropping the chest, while using various vocalises.
- Repeat [njam] on the same note and begin to sustain the [a] (or any vowel) longer and longer between the [nj] (NnnY) attacks, always observing the reaction in the diaphragm.
- As soon as the reaction in the diaphragm is identified, sing only vowels without the instigator (in this case, without the [nj]), using the same function of the diaphragm.
- As the diaphragmatic function is understood and becomes sustainable, sing text and excerpts from vocal music of different genres until the outward and downward function of the diaphragm is objectively and subjectively identified.

This support method is the same function as the *appoggio* described by Caruso, Tetrazzini, Mattia Battistini, Lauritz Melchior, Helge Roswänge, and Lilli Lehmann. It becomes the basis of all free-throated singing.

The Smiling Lip-Clamp

Simply closing the lips together while singing is how we produce the consonant [m]. Singing mmm with the lips relaxed will open the nose and cause the resonance to drop out of the true mask and into the nasal cavity (the false mask). We must remember Caruso's warning to "never sing into the nasal cavity. It is against all the rules of song."

The consonant [m] by itself, even if pronounced with the lower lip protruding in the Italian pronunciation, will not cause an automatic reaction in the diaphragm. Therefore, we must look for an exercise that will instigate a diaphragmatic response. We want the inhalation and the attack to lift the resonance of the voice into the mask (over and above the placement of the open-nosed [m]).

The first thing to understand about the smiling lip-clamp is that it really has nothing to do with an [m] as we must sing it in text. We must isolate psychologically the use of the consonant [m] from the use of the lip-clamp, which resembles an [m] but is something entirely different.

I learned the following exercise from Helge Roswänge. Instead of just closing the lips together in a normal, smiling [m], continue to press the lips together as extremely as possible with the corners of the mouth pulled back gently. Do not allow the lip-clamp to form into a pursed or puckered shape. Only when the smiling lips are pressed together as tightly as possible should a sound be made. It is important at this point to understand that inside the mouth and throat, behind the lip-clamp, only pure vowels are to be sung (formed, phonated). The lip-clamp could be called a variation on humming, but it has nothing to do with humming. Humming opens the nose and places the voice into the nasal cavity. The difference between humming and clamping has to do with the response, or lack thereof, in the diaphragm.

The smiling lip-clamp (especially if pure vowels are sung behind it) instigates a definite downward and outward response in the diaphragm. This can be observed by repeating "[m], [m], [m]" with the lips tightly pressed (clamped) together. The lower chest and upper belly wall will respond by moving outward with each new [m].

If the [m] produced by clamping the lips together is sung with a beautiful [a] behind it, the [a] and the diaphragmatic function will be sustained as the lips and mouth are relaxed and allowed to fall open. Once the diaphragmatic response is instigated, it will not let go as long as a tone is being sustained. Instigators are all about attacks and diaphragmatic responses.

The [ha-la] (Hah-LLLah)

Another Instigator is to emit a sound that begins with a short hah and then instantly change into a sustained [l], as if creating the beginning of a word. The German word for hall (*Halle*) can be used as a beginning exercise, with a sustained emphasis on the double LL. It is important to leave the mouth open the width of one finger while repeating the [l]. The [l] should be enunciated with the tip of the tongue against the back of the upper front teeth, and not by closing the teeth together repeatedly like Pac-Man. The [ha] part of the word establishes the diaphragmatic source of the support for the voice, and sustaining the [l] will instigate an outward and downward reaction in the diaphragm. Immediately sustaining the [l] with the tip of the tongue pressed against the back of the upper front teeth will instigate an outward movement of the solar plexus. The singer can practice using the [ha-la] to sustain sounds on every vowel:

- [ha-la] (HahLLaah)
- [ha-lɛ] (HahLLehh)
- [ha-li] (HahLee)
- [ha-lo] (HahLLoh)
- [ha-lu (HahLLoo)

It is always to be assumed that the singer will inhale deeply into the lower back before every instigator recommended here. Only the function of the diaphragm (based on deep inhalations into the lower back and influenced by specific instigators) should be given attention by the singer when exercising the instigators.

Resistant Voices

Some instigators are better suited to more resistant voices. Longer and thicker vocal folds are more resistant to sustained emission. The so-called *spinto* voices are resistant in the vibrating function of the vocal folds and require a more intense instigation of the diaphragmatic function to achieve the utmost freedom of the throat, the tongue, the jaw, and the larynx. This is why the Italians use the word *spinto* (pushed) to describe a type of voice that requires a more intense pressure of the breath against the diaphragm. As in every type of diaphragmatic instigator, the idea is to evoke a response that will achieve a freer, more active vibration of the vocal folds. The following wheezing instigators are not efficient for light, lyric voices, but are ideal for dramatic and *spinto* voices. It is very important to ascertain whether or not the natural weight and resistance of a voice requires an exaggerated intensity for the activation of the diaphragmatic response or if intensification is inefficient or even damaging in some way to the voice.

Wheezing

Wheezing is an intensification of the pressure of the breath that is leaned against the diaphragm. Dramatic voices will respond fantastically to this approach, while lyric voices can lose the beautiful overtones that make them so touching and delicate in their emission if the intensity of the lean becomes a form of over-supporting. Heavier, more resistant voices often are not effective in light, lyric music, because, when they reduce the intensity of the diaphragmatic pressure to express sentiment lyrically, there is not sufficient activity in the diaphragm to allow them to equalize the resistance of the vocal folds and bring out the potential overtones that are natural to them. Wheezing is possible in four manifestations, and can be instigated by deliberate action as expressed by the singer.

The Laughing Wheeze

The laughing wheeze is an exaggerated way of laughing, and is taught by having the singer sustain the laughing function of the diaphragm and ribcage while running out of breath. It is usually voiceless (silent except for the sound of the breath being compressed) and sustained. The exaggerated diaphragmatic (wheezing) intensity is used to sustain a sung tone halfway through the wheeze, before the breath is completely used up.

There was a time when the older singers of the Bel Canto era recommended that singers avoid Puccini, Leoncavallo, and Mascagni roles. The raw, primitive emotions demanded by composers and librettists in the *verismo* operas required an intensification of the pressure of the breath against the diaphragm, which sometimes led to the ruination of the most beautiful voices.

The days of Battistini, who sang until he died at age seventy-eight, or Mark Reizen, who sang until he was ninety years old, or Giovanni Martinelli, whom I met at the

Metropolitan Opera and who was still performing there until he was seventy-seven, or Milanov, who performed until she died at age seventy-four, seem to be gone forever. These great singers all used an exaggerated support method to compensate for the requirements of some of the music they were singing and they had to overcome the resistance of their huge voices.

Tucker, who sang beautifully until he died too soon at age sixty-six, taught me the intensification of breath support, as did Roswänge and Melchior. I thought, at the time, that this added compression was the secret to great singing until I spoke with some of the greatest lyric singers of my era. The most important lyric tenors I questioned personally were Björling, Kraus, Gedda, and Peerce. They all agreed that any exaggerated pressure against the diaphragm was deleterious to their voices and to their effectiveness as lyric singers! So, it became clear that lyric voices sing more effectively if they lean the breath gently against a point on the diaphragm (we will discuss Manuel Garcia's concept of the miniature cough) and dramatic voices are more effective if they lean the breath more intensely against the diaphragm.

If a lyric voice is trained to exaggerate the pressure of the breath against the diaphragm, it can severely limit the freedom of the vibration of the vocal folds and even damage the voice over time. On the other hand, if a dramatic or *spinto* voice is not trained to sufficiently energize the pressure of the breath against the diaphragm, the voice will become an inadequate, "croony" version of a lyric singer. Success will elude the singer who does not achieve the correct method and amount of compression of the breath against the diaphragm. The right amount of pressure must be tailored to the individual singer's needs.

Tito Schipa's sighing method was a perfect example of how to use the gentlest amount of compression possible. I use it with every light voice that comes to me. However, some voices require tremendous compression to equalize the resistance of the vocal folds (Del Monaco, Milanov). Those singers who possess naturally lyric voices or naturally high, more slender voices and who try to increase compression to be able to sing dramatic roles are usually not able to sustain a long career (Tebaldi, Callas).

It is important to understand that it's a question of resistance of the vocal folds and not vocal amplitude that is the deciding criterion. Some voices are huge, like Tebaldi's or Sutherland's, but are still lyric in the European sense of mellowness, fullness, and roundness in their function and efficiency. As long as Tebaldi sang lyrically, it was one of the most beautiful voices in history. But when she tried to sing dramatically, the voice narrowed, and, although huge in volume and ring, was not as effective in terms of beauty and success with the audience. Dame Joan Sutherland was smarter about her choice of repertoire and sang the huge coloratura roles. She was offered many opportunities to sing dramatic roles, but always turned them down. The result was a very long career without vocal problems.

I would like to recommend to anyone who does not know what wheezing is to watch an Abbot and Costello movie. Lou Costello was the ultimate "wheezer" and used it in every movie. He had the crying wheeze, the laughing wheeze, the frightened wheeze, and the coughing wheeze. Note that his voice was always very high and clear, and if he had sung with the placement of his wheezed voice, he would have most certainly been a *lirico-spinto* tenor.

One learns the laughing wheeze by sustaining a big belly laugh until out of breath. Trying to sing while out of breath is one of the oldest vocal methods described in some of the old Italian books on singing. It was called silent singing. In any case, the last drops of breath will require intense squeezing to keep the laugh going. Squeezing when nearly out of breath (silent singing) becomes wheezing if there is breath left in the lungs. The idea, once the laughing wheeze is understood, is to take a deep breath and commence singing as if you are out of breath. The end-of-the-breath function will cause an intense stimulation of the diaphragm and the lower ribs in the back, and will encourage the *spinto* effect of the declamation. The laughing wheeze can easily turn into a voiceless wheeze with a silent laughing expression. This is a very vigorous application of the stimulation of the diaphragm. It should be used by resistant voices and not by light, lyric voices.

The Crying/Sobbing Wheeze

Instead of laughing, cry and sob until the breath runs out and then squeeze a few sobs out by using the last drops of breath. Then take a full breath and attack a note as if you are out of breath and crying. The result, if done correctly, will be wheeze-based crying and sobbing. If music is sung with this expression, the criteria of the verismo vocal style will be fulfilled. Those interested in hearing an example can listen to the end of Enrico Caruso's recording of *"E lucevan le stelle"* from Puccini's *Tosca*. That particular recording is a perfect example of the wheezing sob method of gaining intensity of expression.

Manuel Garcia II based his teaching method on a miniature cough. The miniature cough would stimulate the pressure against the diaphragm very subtly and at a point on the chest. It became the basis of the *punto d'appoggio* (the point of leaning) method of breath support, and was taught using the staccato function of the diaphragm. It is a wonderful method and produced some of the greatest singers in history. However, along came the verismo composers and the subtle point of the lean of the breath was no longer sufficient to express the "blood and guts" emotions of the leading characters in the modern operas of the day. The *punto d'appoggio* method of support is still the best way to sing the music of the Bel Canto era, written by Bellini, Donizetti, and the most successful composers of the decades that preceded the verismo era. It allows a singer to sing coloratura, staccato, pianissimi, extreme high notes, etc. Verismo composers did not ask singers to sing coloratura, but to really suffer and laugh and cry on the stage. They wanted the true to life experience set to music and sung by singers who could express the deepest emotions that human beings feel at desperate moments.

We've discussed laughing and crying, and now we will examine how the great method based on the miniature cough evolved into another wheezing method that became useful and successful in the verismo operas.

The Wheezing Cough

The method for developing the wheezing cough is to begin coughing very slightly into the solar plexus (Manuel Garcia's miniature cough) and continue growing louder and louder until out of breath. The next step is to repeat the above, but try to sustain each cough. As soon as this is accomplished, try to sing a note on [a] that is cough-based by interrupting the sustained cough with a sung tone. Hold the note until out of breath. Inhale a deep breath into the lower back and attack the same note as if you are out of breath, and, just to affirm the action, cough in the middle of the note and see if it is still based in the solar plexus. Eventually you will not need to use the laughing, crying, or coughing to remember the lean into the diaphragm. It will become second nature, and the intensity of the pressure used against the diaphragm will vary according to the music to be performed.

The Retching Wheeze

One of the funniest stories I know from my student days at the Kathryn Long School at the old Metropolitan Opera is the tale of Bonaldo Giaiotti trying to teach young singers how to sing. He recommended imitation retching or imitation dry-heaves or, in some cases, imitation vomiting. Supposedly, imitating the act of retching would accomplish several things. First of all, the necessary pressure of the breath against the diaphragm when imitating dry heaves was intense. The entire belly becomes involved, trying to support such an extreme process. The throat spreads open exaggeratedly and the breath is stopped in the area of the sternal notch. Giaiotti was demonstrating it often in performances! He sang beautifully and everyone admired his vocal technique. The problem was that every young singer in the Met school who tried Giaiotti's retching method was choking. No one could understand why it didn't work for any of the young singers, and, most amazed of all was Giaiotti, who couldn't understand why his method wasn't working. "It is so easy to do this! Why are you choking? Listen to me. I am doing it and my voice is free and it is so simple and easy." To make a long story short, the reason it didn't work was because the young singers did not have resistant voices like Giaiotti's massive *basso-profondo* voice. His voice was so powerful and his vocal folds so resistant that he needed such an exaggerated stimulation of the diaphragm, and such a huge opening of the throat to get his voice to function. No one else could attempt his method without sounding like they were being strangled to death!

I tell this story as a warning to young singers. The instigators discussed here are very beneficial to young singers, but they should be applied only as described above. Singers with very light voices should avoid the wheezing exercises unless they see me personally. These instigators will help sort out the proper amount of diaphragmatic stimulation necessary for each individual voice.

Remember the Rules of Great Singing:

- No action in the throat
- No change of emission
- No tension in the jaw, the throat, or the tongue
- Never sing into the nasal cavity
- No closing of the teeth together (like Pac-Man) when singing the dental consonants [s, d, g, j, l, n, t]
- No pulling the jaw down (the baby bird syndrome, like expecting a worm!)
- No pressing the head down toward the chest. Always look up at the second balcony with an open smile on the face
- No pulling the tongue back

There are many more rules of great singing. If the singers will learn those listed above, the rest will probably happen automatically.

Contrary Motion

The Inhalation

Contrary motion, a particular method of breath control, was the basis for the most advantageous breathing/support method ever developed in the history of singing. Enrico Caruso was a proponent of this method. He explains how to breathe and how to attack a tone as follows in his book, The Art of Singing: "Breathe deeply into the lower ribs in the back while pulling in the abdomen and raising the chest slightly. When you sing, do a contrary motion."

The Exhalation

Contrary motion, as a concept to be used by singers, can be applied to the functions of the abdomen, the floating ribs in the lower back, and the chest. This concept of breathing can be explained as follows:

- The chest must relax downward in an amount that is exactly equal to the amount that it was raised while inhaling.
- The abdomen must relax outward, upon exhalation, mirroring exactly the amount it was drawn inward while inhaling.

The Bellows

The pressure of the breath while inhaling is directed against the lower ribs in the rear of the torso. Caruso described the function of the lower ribs in the back as being "like a bellows. They open when inhaling and squeeze together while singing."

The Diaphragmatic Lift

As the breath is inhaled and directed against the lower ribs in the rear of the torso, at the same time, the chest should be raised slightly. Richard Tucker and Eleanor Steber called this up and down method of including the front of the upper chest in the inhalation process the Diaphragmatic Lift.

The *Appoggio*

As we've now seen, in order to create a contrary motion while singing, the breath that is drawn in through the action of the lower ribs during inhalation must be leaned upon during exhalation against the lower chest in a motion contrary to the motion of inhalation. The controlled exhalation of breath and the squeezing of the lower ribs while singing is contrary (antagonistic) to their expansion while inhaling.

A Psychological Trick

Another function of contrary motion has to do with control of the deliberate, steady emission of the voice. It is very easy to demonstrate, but difficult to explain. The process of respiration is the same as described above. However, a psychological trick is used to achieve a perfectly even, smooth emission of the tone while singing. Ideally, a knowledgeable teacher should demonstrate this exercise, which requires the use of a sheet of tissue paper in front of the mouth. Begin by blowing gently and steadily through pursed lips against a vertically hanging tissue held very close to the mouth. The horizontally directed stream of air should be just enough to move the corner of a tissue paper to a forty-five degree angle away from the mouth. Sustain a steady emission of the breath so that the paper remains suspended in the air at a forty-five degree angle without buffeting, supported only by the gentle, outward emission of the breath through pursed lips.

Some singers use a soft whistle to establish and maintain the movement of the tissue to its desired forty-five degree angle. Whistling has the additional advantage of using sound to help keep the emission perfectly even. Any change in the sound is a clear indication that the intensity of the emission of the breath is not being perfectly sustained. This is also a good exercise for the development of breath control and the sustaining ability of the diaphragm. The second hand on a watch can be used as a timer to develop long exhalations. It also provides a method that allows the singer to compare day by day, month by month, the increase in the sustaining ability of the diaphragm and the lower ribs in the back.

The Imagined Contrary Motion

As soon as the singer clearly understands that the emission of the breath is something that can be perfectly controlled, proven by the ability to maintain the desired angle of the tissue paper while blowing the breath gently and steadily through pursed lips, the suggestion of an opposite function is then presented.

The singer must imagine that, while singing, the flow of the breath will now be reversed and drawn inward: one must be able to imagine that the interior angle of the breath while singing is exactly equal to the outside angle of the breath as produced while blowing or whistling. This particular concept has inspired expressions that have become part of the lore of singing through instructions including: singing is inhaling; drink the tone in; feel like the wind is blowing in your face; never allow the voice to proceed outward beyond the lips; and nothing goes outward toward the audience except sound.

Contrary Motion and the Mouth

The pursed lips, used to direct the exhalation against the paper tissue suspended in front of the mouth, are moved contrarily into a relaxed smile while singing. The corners of the mouth move from a forward, puckered position to a pulled back smiling position. This movement satisfies the criterion of a contrary motion for the posture of the corners of the mouth, and allows them to become a part of the overall contrary motion approach to voice production.

The Candle Flame

One of the oldest exercises in the history of the vocal arts is to hold a candle flame in front of the lips while singing to detect and prevent leaking breath. It is still a great exercise, both as a cure and as a preventative measure.

The Mirror
Singing to the mirror is another great exercise for singers. The idea, when using a mirror to detect leaking breath, is to not allow any fog to appear on the glass while singing with the tip of the nose touching the mirror. It is a very difficult exercise to perfect. Those who can accomplish this seemingly impossible task will cure any problems that have occurred in the vocal folds because of breathiness. Singers who leak breath are going to have vocal problems. It is not a matter of if, but a matter of when. We must remember that nothing passes through the vocal folds but air. Air (breath) is either our best friend or our worst enemy.

Defining the Open Throat
The strength of the inhalation will determine the following characteristics of the true open throat. Only a deep and powerful inhalation can create the ideal shape of the throat to which a singer should aspire. The ideal shape of the throat can be maintained while singing by continuing the inhalation process. Inhaling with sufficient strength will determine the following characteristics of the open throat:

- How extremely the throat will open vertically downward
- The degree to which the larynx is affected toward its ideal low position in the vertical tube
- The degree to which the epiglottis is opened
- The purity of the [a] shape that can be maintained in the lower pharynx
- The height and degree of forward movement of the soft palate

Magic
This is an introduction to the magic of the concept of contrary motion. It is a very safe approach to the production of the singing voice, and offers the singer a psychological path to perfect breath control. Every aspect of the creation of musical sounds that is available to the voice can benefit from the application of the concept of contrary motion.

The Laws of the Paradoxes
The Laws of the Paradoxes, believed by Zen Buddhists to be a set of cosmic laws, are based on one premise: everything is the opposite of the way it should be. The ability to distinguish between right and wrong is the criterion that proves that a state of enlightenment has been achieved by the seeker.

This set of observations, reaching back over thousands of years, teaches that everything is the opposite of the way it should be, could be, or appears to be. It would seem that we should blow out more breath if we want to sing with as much volume as possible. However, if you want to make a louder sound, according to the Laws of the Paradoxes, we must do the opposite of what seems so obvious to us and reverse our breath flow and energy direction and phonation toward the inside of our bodies.

It is my hope that singers will be able to understand the concepts of contrary logic and contrary motion and use them to their best benefit. The concept and application of contrary motion has been especially helpful and healing for singers who have some form of damage or malfunction of the nerves in the vocal folds.

Remember: Nothing but air passes through the vocal folds while singing. If the breath is utilized correctly by the vocal folds, the voice will become as healthy and resonant as it was meant to be. The ideal amount of breath that is permitted to arrive at the larynx during vocalization will be converted into beautiful, free sound, and never into a tool for causing damage or pain to the singer.

Covering the Tone

Registers and Terminology

Covering the tone, covering the break, hooking the tone, vowel modification, and many other terms have been inspired by the obvious acoustic changes that occur in every voice at certain points in the ascending or descending scale, which identify so-called registers of the voice. Registers, often identified in separate sections of the range or scope of a voice, are generally referred to as the chest register, the middle register, and the head register. They are identified by noting the similarities or differences between groups of notes that seem to have the same acoustic quality. Terminology denoting registers, breaks, and covering is so common in the world of classical singing that to try to ignore it can actually be detrimental to a singer's healthy approach to vocal production. It is better to understand registers and how to cope with them, and later to forget that they exist. Everyone who sings is aware of the acoustic changes that occur on certain notes in the range of a particular voice. But how shall we deal with those changes artistically and vocally?

The Old School

My teacher, Olga Ryss, when I asked her on which note I should cover my voice, said, "Cover?! I will give you a blanket!" She was very funny sometimes, but there was a very serious side to her clever response to my question. Covering a note was not a concept that was in common usage back in her day. She had begun her vocal studies in 1912 at the St. Petersburg Conservatory at the height of the Golden Age. Her teacher was a student of Giovanni Lamperti and the evidence of the fantastic Italian bel canto approach to the development of the voice pervaded the criteria of great singing all over Europe at that time. She actually heard Battistini perform live many times between 1910 and 1921.

I wondered if the lack of technical concern for the different registers of the voice during that time was a geographical phenomenon that affected the vocal culture of certain countries and not others. So I made it a point to ask every great singer I met if they thought in terms of registers and passing the voice and, if so, would they explain the concept of covering a tone. I wanted to know if each one of them applied such an idea to her/his own approach to singing and if they did, whether or not the concept was the same and dealt with in the same way.

Irritated Reactions

When I asked great singers like Tucker, Merrill, Martinelli, London, Melchior, Roswänge, Gedda, Björling, and Kraus to explain the idea to me, they looked at me like I was a rank amateur and became somewhat derisive in their responses. Every one of them rejected any thought of covering the tone, modifying a vowel, or doing any form of action on any particular note. The idea was to breathe and support in a way that "distorting the throat or soft palate is not necessary."

"Don't listen to the people who never sang anywhere!" said Richard Tucker. "That kind of amateur thinking is utter nonsense! It is a crime to ask any singer to distort the throat and expect the results to be beneficial. Some fantastic natural voices may be able to sing for a while with distortions on certain notes but the career will not be a long one."

"Do you think I'm going to modify a vowel or change my throat every time I ascend a scale or sing a high note? That would be insane! I sing *Wotan*! Do you know what you are asking? Don't be ridiculous!" said George London.

"The turning of the registers is none of our business!" said Roswänge. He continued:

> It is God's business! He gave us registers to make it easy to sing high notes, but we have to leave it up to Him. The notes turn when they are ready and not before and the turn can be different on each vowel, on each pitch, and at different levels of volume. A singer who sings big roles would go crazy if he had to do something in his throat every time a certain note is sung. What a nightmare! Any form of interference with the throat, the vowel, or the legato of the breath breaks a basic and essential rule of singing. The title role of Verdi's *Don Carlo* has forty-nine high B-flats and nine B-naturals, and literally hundreds of high A's and G's and G-sharps. Do you think that a tenor who sings this role will be preoccupied with committing an act of interference with each of those hundreds of notes? You are talking about flexing and forming and making actions in the throat literally hundreds of times during the evening every time you perform when even one activity in the throat is against the rules of singing. Forget it and attribute activities in the *Übergang* (the going over place) to ignorance and amateurism.

Merrill's reaction was one of shock. "What are these ideas and where do they come from?" he exclaimed. "This stuff is invented by people who never sang the big roles. Let them try their ideas out in *Rigoletto*. They will have a horrible surprise waiting for them! They will either not be able to sing the role or damage something and the career will be over very early."

One of my students asked the famous Wagnerian soprano Birgit Nilsson how to sing the upper register of the voice. She answered:[30]

> There are no registers in the voice, my dear. Just fix your deep breathing. The high notes, just like the other notes in your range, are automatic if your breath is sitting low enough in your body. Believe me, the notes know better where to go in the resonance than you know where to put them and any effort you make to improve them other than deep breathing will diminish them. Keep your head up, breathe deeply to get your throat and jaw loose, smile a lot, and your high notes will place themselves.

---

[30] Someone also asked Nilsson to name the most important consideration for a singer who wanted to sing the operas of Richard Wagner. She answered, "A good pair of shoes."

Caruso said in his book that "the original shape of the throat must not be allowed to change when singing from low to high."

According to Caruso, the shape of the throat must remain in the form of an [a] regardless of what text is to be sung, and the [a] shape is created by inhaling deep into the lower back and recreated every time the singer inhales. All of the vowels must be phonated within the [a] form in the throat, like singing text through a megaphone. The megaphone does not change its form from vowel to vowel and its shape "is maintained by the power of the respiration."

Rosa Ponselle said Caruso insisted that she "keep a horizontal rectangle in the back of her neck at all times while singing." That means the throat does not change its shape, regardless of the vowel or the range to be sung, although the acoustical quality can change dramatically when ascending into the upper range, especially in men's voices. It is not confusing if the singer, male or female, high voice or low, big voice or small, will neutralize the throat (make it utterly soft and relaxed) by inhaling deeply into the lower back. A powerful inhalation can open the throat into a horizontal rectangular shape (Lamperti's bright [a] shape), and the emission is then controlled by leaning the breath sufficiently against the lower chest. The singer must not allow the slightest change or gust of breath to disturb the completely loose [a]-shaped throat and the perfectly even emission that supports the tone. Unfortunately, some male singers sing out of Fach (in the wrong vocal category) and usually load up the vocal folds with too much breath and too much activity in the vocal folds themselves. Lyric tenors sing as dramatic tenors, heavier tenors sing as baritones, true baritones sing as bass-baritones, and lyric basses sing as deep basses. The most serious consideration when this happens is that the whole vocal fold begins to vibrate instead of just the edges. As explained to me by the most famous otolaryngologist in Vienna, Dr. Hans Ruedi, the unofficial singer's doctor in all of Europe, "the correct use of the vocal folds while singing should vibrate only their edges and not involve the entire thickness of the folds."

Weighting the voice by using the vibrations of the entire vocal folds means trouble when passing the voice from the middle range into the high range. If the voice is falsely weighted, the pure, inactive, totally reactive process of allowing the voice to pass, without any change of emission, becomes impossible to execute. It is essential to lighten the middle range as much as possible. Allow the *appoggio* and the principle of the large drum (the bigger the drum, the bigger the sound) to create the amplitude of the voice. Vibrating air in the air-box (the chest, the lungs, and the ribcage) makes the power and volume and, ultimately, the color of the voice. The vibrating reed (the edges of the vocal folds) is exactly that in its function: a vibrating pair of edges that without the air bucket under them cannot make an efficient, resonant, projecting sound.

It is important, when discussing the break (the passing note, the passaggio, the *Übergang,* the cover) to emphasize the necessity for lightening the voice, especially the middle range, and to permit the enclosed body of air in the lungs to amplify the sound.

If the vocal folds are limited to vibrations along the edges only (called *schlank singen* in German and *squillo* in Italian), the voice will pass (cover, go over) automatically if the throat is kept loose and the emission is continuous and unchanged. If the singer sings too heavily, either by vibrating too much vocal fold or by overloading the singing process in the larynx and throat by sending more breath upward than can be utilized, the passaggio will become jammed and clogged, and the easy, natural passing of the voice will not happen. Some form of active cover method may have to be employed because the singer is singing too loud or too dark. To avoid having to employ some hooking method or a vowel modification technique, just lighten the voice (do staccato exercises until the natural width of the voice is established) and sing more lyrically.

As Tucker, Merrill, Roswänge, and Melchoir said to me, "Sing as close to the falsetto as possible for the core of the sound. Use the intensity of the *appoggio* to sing with a full-voiced tone."

Björling said, "The voice is really a blown up falsetto, and that is why all good male singers can sing softly. Even Melchior and Leo Slezak with their monstrous voices could sing fantastic soft tones and entire sections of operas *mezza voce*. Listen to a recording of Melchior singing the second act of *Tristan und Isolde*. It is a fantastic example of how to use the mezza voce and how the male voice is based on the slenderest use of the core of the voice. His amazing mastery of *mezza voce* was based on the fact that he lightened his voice to be able to change from baritone to tenor."

As I've previously noted, the most powerful male voice I ever heard was that of German *Heldenbariton*, Paul Schöffler. He was world famous for the size of his incredible voice, which was unlimited in range and amplitude in low bass-baritone, Heldenbariton (heroic baritone), and bass roles. He was also world famous for singing concert repertoire that included the most subtle Schubert and Schumann art songs. His Lieder were exquisitely sung, full of ravishing pianissimi and light expression. His *mezza voce* singing was exemplary in its ease and fullness of color. The predictable result of such light singing was that he sang through his passaggio without the slightest change of emission or phonation. He was the best example I ever heard of a singer who could sing the title role of *The Flying Dutchman* or Wotan one night with an all-powerful, orchestra-smothering resonance, and the next night a recital of the lightest, most subtle art songs.

Non passare la voce!

Cesare Alfieri (Teatro alla Scala, Milano), Dick Marzolo (Toscanini's main musical assistant and rehearsal conductor), Ettore Campogaliani (the most famous coach in Italy when I was singing there in 1963-64), and Victor Trucco (head coach of the Italian and French repertoires at the Met), would scream at the male singers: "*Non passare la voce! Non passare la voce!* (Don't pass the voice! Don't pass the voice!) The Italians would use the word pass because the word for cover (*coprire*) has never been used in the history of Italian vocal music.

Where in the world did the term "cover" come from? We all know, just as the great Italian coaches knew, that there is an acoustic change in the voice as it passes from one register to another, but there should never be an action in the throat or soft palate or nasopharynx to accommodate it. The great coaches would accept the passing of the voice if it happened without action, but as a result of an even emission and a loose throat. The coaches would have a fit if the singer raised the soft palate to achieve a high note. They insisted that the voice would pass from one register to another by and of itself, if the throat was totally loose and the emission of the breath was steady and unchanging as the passaggio was reached. They were all concerned with the posture of the head, insisting that the singer pretend to look up at the higher balconies in a theater. Marzolo would say, "Don't look at me! Look at the audience! You sing for them, not for the orchestra down below!"

The throat must be free when singing, and it is almost impossible to flex muscles in the throat and tilt the head up and back at the same time. It is also more acoustically efficient if the head is facing upward toward the second balcony. The coaches mentioned here thought it was impossible to sing the Italian language with the head facing down or the jaw pulled down.

I am making a distinction between action and reaction. The deep inhalation into the lower back will cause reactions in the soft palate and the nasopharynx. The soft palate will rise up and forward as an opposite and equal reaction to the deep inhalation into the lower back. As the breath is sucked down into the lower back, the nasopharynx will open upward and create a sealed air chamber behind the eyes. When the air in the nasopharyngeal chamber is set into vibration by activating the vocal folds, the resonance will be felt there and the sensation is called singing in the mask. Vibrations lower in the face, especially in the nasal cavity, are not the result of correct breathing or phonation and must be avoided. A good exercise to identify the true mask is to hold the nose closed while singing. Only [m], [n], [ŋ] and some of the French nasalized vowels actually require the nose to be open. Practice all other sounds in classical singing by holding the nose closed.

I have frequently mentioned that Dame Eva Turner taught young singers the concept of the invisible throat. When asked about covering and registers, she said:

> I've been asked this question many times, and I still don't understand what it is that the singers want to know. I never heard of such things when I was a student or during my years as a performer. There is no action in the throat, ever, when singing. When asked what I felt in my throat when I sang, I always have to answer with the same answer: Nothing! I sang as if I didn't have a throat, and never felt a thing. I think that is why I was able to sing the most difficult roles for so many years. I simply didn't use my throat, so it was never used up! The resonance of the voice, if the throat is not involved while singing, moves from the chest to the forehead to the top of the head by itself, without the slightest guidance or interference from me. It is like the elevator in one of your skyscrap-

> ers here in New York. The elevator moves up and down smoothly without jerking or sudden swinging or shuddering. The energy for the movement of the elevator comes from the power source in the basement. The energy source for singers comes from down below, also. All that is necessary is deep breathing into the lower back. The lower back is our basement. That is the only action I ever used while singing. After the breath is inhaled, the emphasis psychologically should be on non-action in the invisible areas of the throat, the tongue, and the jaw. Every mental effort is directed toward doing nothing at all in the throat.
>
> Something must work and be constantly active while singing, but not the throat or tongue or jaw. All of the energy for singing comes from the lower back and is held against the chest at a diagonal angle that avoids the throat. I always felt that keeping the throat soft and neutral forced me to sing somewhere else. The only place to sing if you are not allowed to use the throat is in the body. I see young singers pressing the jaw down, and I wish I could show them that it is not necessary, and that the voice is negatively affected by any degree of tension in the area of the body from the middle of the chest upward through the throat, the jaw and the tongue. And pulling the jaw down or leaning the head down and forward or jutting the head or jaw forward will most certainly affect the longevity of the career.
>
> When I was young, everyone talked about not showing the slightest bit of effort while singing. It was considered amateurish to let the audience see you working at the production of the tone. How can you portray a character and the many moods and feelings of a character if you can't smile or frown or cry or laugh when you sing? Imagine a Tosca who can't smile at the tenor in the first act because when she sings, she has her jaw pulled down all of the time. And the tenor can't smile back at her because he is looking at the floor with his chin pressed against his chest. It is absurd to even contemplate, but, in reality, singers do these things and I don't know why. And when the voice must go up into the higher range, the throat must be totally invisible, with no action of any kind occurring. Only deep breathing must be involved in the production of the high notes. The body is the instrument and not the throat.

That lecture went on for a long time, and I remember it very well. The reaction among the young singers was, "How is it possible that she has such a fantastic, huge, gorgeous voice and such a long career if she didn't do anything but breathe deeply?" Later, I realized that the information Dame Eva was trying to pass on to us was the same information I received from every great singer I met or read about. No great singer who wrote a book about singing ever mentioned covering or singing into the nasal cavity. Today, everyone talks about covering and focusing the voice in the nose. And, of course, if the voice is placed in the nose, the natural passing of the voice will not occur and the singer must apply some form of assistance, usually an abrupt raising of the soft palate, to help the voice change registers. By now, you have memorized Caruso's advice to "never sing into the nasal cavity" and to "never change the shape of the throat when singing from the lower note to a high note." If the inhalation is deep into the lower back, the throat will open vertically and the correct, original [a] form necessary to sing through the break will occur. The soft palate will rise up and forward and create the access to the mask that the passing of notes requires. The key to alleviating every problem that may arise in the pursuit of vocal technique is to breathe deeply into the lower back before singing, and lean the breath against the chest while singing.

An Exercise

Do nothing in the throat. Inhale as deeply as possible into the lower back. This type of inhalation will cause the soft palate to move upward and forward. Press the breath against the chest the instant the singing begins. Maintain the shape of the throat and the legato, and don't change the emission in any way as you sing through the range of the voice, from low notes to high notes. The registration of the voice will become automatic, and the passage of the voice from one register to another will be as smooth as silk, with no separate or individual actions necessary in the throat or nasopharynx or soft palate.

In Conclusion

When dealing with the passaggio, I would like for singers to try the approach as described here. I'm sure they will find that any concerns they may have had will disappear almost as if by magic. Every true vocal artist should be free from constant concerns about actions in the throat while singing. This method became available to me when I was a young, aspiring, curious, and bold tenor. I was always asking questions and picking brains. I was and still am very grateful to the great singers who spent time with me and tried to answer my (sometimes presumptuous) questions. I offer the answers to those questions, asked over fifty years ago, to all singers who read this chapter. I wanted to know what the great singers were thinking when they were singing; I hope you will benefit from their answers as much as I did.

The Posture Method

Section One:

The Elimination of Resistance

All physical exercise should begin in a gentle manner. One should never force the muscles or tendons of the body to do anything they don't want to do. We must make every effort to neutralize resistance in the throat (and sometimes in the mind) until it disappears. If we are patient and consistently demand freedom of the voice, the psychomotor system gradually will respond to our desire by organizing the body to accomplish the task at hand. Forcing a path through muscular resistance, either by pushing excess breath against a tight, muscularly active throat, or by demanding a vocal response based on artificial criteria (nasality, focus, yawning, spreading, flexing the tongue, arching the palate, etc.) can, either as a result of action or reaction, damage the vocal folds and/or the emotional and psychological programming necessary to enhance both vocal and physical health.

A House of Cards

Nothing but breath passes through the throat while singing. Forcing the voice to respond to our desires or criteria is always the wrong solution. Regrettably, forcing breath through a muscularly active, resistant throat occasionally can be sustained for a limited time, especially in a young, healthy body. However, forcing the body to obey unhealthy commands and to try to fulfill artificial criteria will not last and can only cause problems in the long run. The collapse of a psychological house of cards, built on a confused, conflicted, muscular basis that cannot last, can become not only vocal ruination, but also an emotional disaster. For instance, finding a way to achieve a high note or notes by forcing muscles in the body to counteract and neutralize muscles in the throat will ultimately work against any long-term success. Forced air, delivered with enough pressure to overcome a muscularly resistant throat, will damage the voice at some point in the future. This is true, in spite of the relief one feels at finding a way to sing high notes and in spite of the clarity of the deceptive epiphany. In order to survive the myriad vocal, physical, mental and emotional demands made on singers, it is important to learn as soon as possible to trust the basic principles of healthy singing. The singer must ask him/herself: "Did I feel resistance in the throat when I sang that note?" If the answer to this all-important question is "yes," the technical approach is wrong. Feeling secure in a wrong method of voice production will lead to a complete vocal and psychological collapse. Security based on the compensation of a set of muscles in the body to counter the activities of a set of muscles in the throat is simply a wrong approach, and is a vocal crisis waiting to happen.

The Invisible Throat

We must become slightly paranoid about feeling resistance in the throat. It must not be allowed, ever! We've referred many times to Dame Eva Turner who encouraged young singers to sing "as if the throat were invisible." She also recommended the invisible tongue and the invisible jaw. Her concept: "it should be as if you could pass your hand through your throat and there is nothing there."

Ritual Eliminates Choice

The postures described below, in combination and in a specific order, become a warm-up method for the singing voice. They make up a physical process that can be practiced ritualistically every time we sing at home or back-stage before a rehearsal or performance. Ritual eliminates choice! Derived from the practice of yoga and the martial arts, these postures will encourage correct breathing, eliminate faulty muscular applications, and help develop the traditional Italian method of breath utilization called *Appoggio*. We will become better, healthier, more reliable singers when tension and resistance in the throat and the muscular actions that cause them are neutralized and eventually eliminated completely.

Postures While Exercising the Voice

It seems obvious that in order for the throat to remain free while singing or speaking, something must happen (or not happen) elsewhere in the body. It is this process and the combined activities of the muscles of the body and the breathing system that we will explore, and begin to understand and practice correctly.

The principles of yoga include many of the same criteria that apply to the development of the singing voice. For example, both yoga and singing require deep breathing, physical stillness and balance, control and development of the breathing system, and effective postures that develop total freedom of the chest, legs, pelvis, neck, and head. All of these activities will combine and produce a positive effect on our vocal instrument, which is, in reality, our whole body. In our busy modern world, anything that calms the mind, is a low-impact form of physical exercise, is developmental of the breathing system, and is conducive to the organization of the body-mind connection, can only be good for singers.

Helpful and not Harmful

As in all exercise systems, the physical and mental condition of the person involved is all-important. Exercise should be helpful in every way and not harmful in any way. That is not to say, however, that a little discomfort from stretching is to be avoided. Almost every physical exercise system we practice can cause some physical discomfort if we are not accustomed to exercise. That is the price we pay to get into and maintain good physical condition. Before anyone commits to a rigorous, extensive exercise program, a complete physical examination by a physician familiar with the individual aspirant's physical condition should be performed. If a doctor approves of physical exercise for you, I would recommend that everyone commit themselves to the ancient exercise systems.

Charisma

Taekwondo helps develop extreme breathing capacity and endurance, and contributes to the physical freedom needed to become a good actor on the modern stage.

Stage directors love singers who are physically free and able to move well on the stage. The days of standing still while singing are gone. That is why one of the postures listed below requires movement of the arms and legs while standing on one foot and singing. The postures are designed to help singers move dramatically without losing control of the even emission of the breath while singing.

In addition to the many benefits claimed by the posture system so far, in every case they seem to contribute to that rare form of radiating energy called charisma. Elvis Presley, one of the most electrifying performers who ever lived, earned an advanced black belt in hard-style Japanese karate. Is it a coincidence that his fame lives on to this day? His estate still earns about forty million dollars per year! We can only attribute his energy and incredible success that has lasted so many years after his death to the magical force of charisma.

Hara

Ask any martial artist where the source of his or her amazing energy lies and he or she will tell you that it comes from the center of the abdomen, about one and one-quarter inches below his or her navel. Locating the center or core of a person is the result of a process known in martial arts as centering, which is the result of constant physical and mental awareness of breathing into the lower back and leaning the breath against a point in the center of the abdomen. The mental awareness of the abdominal point is achieved and combined with postures taught in the physical exercise systems, and in some cases, the fighting systems developed over many centuries.

The preoccupation of the practitioner with the point of the source of the field of energy (called a chakra in yoga) is based on the teachings of Buddha. It is called the tanden in the Japanese language, the tantien in Chinese and the tanjun in Korean, and is the point of meditation for all Buddhists and the focal point of all breathing, posturing, and movement in the Eastern martial arts. This should be the starting point for singers, also.

I recommend *Hara: The Vital Center of Man,* written by Freiherr Graf Karlfried von Dürckheim, which explains the positive aspects of the vital center of man to every aspiring performer, as a source for understanding centering and the release of chi. We want to understand the concept of hara because we need to be charismatic in auditions and performances. Charisma is a specific manifestation of chi, and it becomes part of the art of the individual singer.

Chi for any Purpose

It is important to realize that chi can be used at any time for any purpose. Obviously, singers don't need to break concrete. However, the same energy can stimulate the diaphragm and ribcage, the legs, and the mind. Young practitioners of martial arts do better in school, seldom catch a cold, and memorize very easily. Fatigue becomes an unknown state for those singers who get their centers lowered down. Huge roles become possible because there is no need for effort and strain. The energy is provided, almost like magic, by emptying the mind and maintaining a state of clear-headed concentration, with no psychological conflicts filling the mind. And, most importantly, centering and its resulting chi can be channeled into performance energy.

East Meets West

In the world of martial arts as practiced in East Asia, the different styles of fighting are divided between two basic sources of energy and power. One school of fighting philosophy is called hard-style, which means fighting with hard, flexing muscles and techniques designed to exploit the energy sent to the muscles that control striking and kicking. The other school, soft-style, is based on the use and exploitation of the force of gravity as the basic source of energy to provide movements that are designed to neutralize and absorb the energy coming from one's opponent.

Yoga and tai chi are ancient, as are the hard-style Arts (Japanese karate, taekwondo) practiced in Eastern Asia. Any of these systems taught in a reputable school by a qualified instructor are safe for the average, healthy practitioner. If a singer wants to commit to a more active hard-style exercise program, I would recommend trying taekwondo. While not as strenuous or hard-style as Japanese systems, it is a seriously active Korean system of exercises and movements especially designed to develop the many kicking maneuvers used in fighting without weapons. The ancient Koreans had no horses. In order to defend themselves against men on horseback, they developed the high kicking style. The high kicking routines are very beneficial to singers because of the balance and agility required by the system. They emphasize the development of the strength and stamina of the legs.

Historical singers, according to their descriptions of the vocal techniques they have employed, have approached the art of singing by using what could be called either a hard-style or a soft-style approach. Some singers depend on their obesity to pull the breath down deep into the body as if the breath actually has weight. It rests low in the body, firmly seated on the pelvic floor, without the slightest push downward or any form of holding the muscles in a fixed state. Gravity controls the diaphragm and the drop of the abdomen, and they are able to sing effortlessly. This is a good description of a soft-style approach to singing. It is crucial that the chest remain high and still in this method. Allowing the chest to collapse will create a downward pressure of the breath. The downward pressure will cause an opposite and equal reaction in the throat and create tension and muscular activity. Action or reaction in the abdomen will require muscular control as a means to equalize the response in the throat.

Because the flow of energy is strictly based on gravity, this style of singing is very difficult to imitate, and unless the student is obese, he or she will have great difficulty with breath control. Some very famous singers have developed problems because they began to add actions to the equation, such as lifting the soft palate mechanically instead of allowing it to operate reactively. One famous exception to the obesity rule for soft-style singing was Norman Treigle, a tall, lanky bass-baritone who seemed to produce his magnificent tones without the slightest sign of effort. When I asked him how he sang, he said: "I drop everything down to the bottom of my body and relax it there. I always try to breathe and sing like I am nine-months pregnant." Treigle was a great singer, with the ability to sing clear, crisp, very fast coloratura. He could sing loudly, quietly, very low, and had wonderful high notes that seemed to come from his toes. According to his explanation, they did.

Transformations

We know that transformations from dull personalities to charismatic personalities happen to people. Many of us have seen it happen with our own eyes and heard it with our own ears. In the world of opera, the most famous case of a singer becoming suddenly charismatic was Luciano Pavarotti, who was a working Italian tenor before he went on tour in Australia with Joan Sutherland. Giancarlo del Monaco, stage director and the son of the great tenor Mario del Monaco, told me in Stuttgart in 1964 that: "the new tenor, Pavarotti, has a nice, small voice without an especially beautiful quality. The man himself is a nice person, but fat, and cannot act at all. He is not particularly musical, being unable to read music. He has to learn everything by ear. I find him totally uninteresting as a performer."

Pavarotti was not causing excitement in Europe at all. Then he went to Australia on a long concert tour with Joan Sutherland. When he came back from that tour and started performing around Europe, everything had changed. All of a sudden, the whole world began to talk about him. What happened? All we know is that Pavarotti, while on tour, began to imitate Sutherland's performance postures while singing, especially the exaggerated forward lean with the head thrown back. By the time the tour was over, he had changed his performance stance completely, from a straight up posture based on standing on two feet while singing, to an extreme forward-leaning posture based on standing on a front foot while singing with no weight on the back foot. He looked like he had been studying yoga. His chest was open and thrust outward and upward, his head was tilted up and backward, and he often bent over, especially for the highest notes. He gained a new contact with his audiences who, in turn, began to worship him. He actually drew an audience of over a half-million in Central Park, New York! Not even Caruso had drawn such an immense, live audience.

Examples of Low-Centeredness

Study the bent over postures of Mother Teresa and Mahatma Gandhi, the constant footwork and twirling of Michael Jackson, Mick Jagger's pumping of the knees up and down while in a bent over posture, Tina Turner's constant movement of the legs with the knees bent, the footwork of James Brown, and the under-slung hips of Frank Sinatra. We can observe the strange, subtle crossing of the knees evident in the walks of John Wayne, Bruce Willis and Marlon Brando (watch Brando's walk in the movie, *One Eyed Jacks*). Charismatic people always have a peculiar low carriage while in motion (observe the famous walk of Groucho Marx). Watch the movie called *The Quiet Man* with John Wayne, Maureen O'Hara, and Victor McLaglen for a study of three charismatic stars. Observe their postures and walks and the way they move while sitting or standing.

During the latter part of her career, Maria Callas bent over, sank her chest, and dropped her abdomen outward while singing, which exaggerated the lean into the abdomen. Could this postural characteristic have made her one of the most charismatic opera singers of the modern era? Could all of this be just coincidence? Or is it a state of being that can be learned through posturing and certain prescribed movements? A postural instigation of chi can be achieved by anyone willing to pursue it through ancient physical systems of exercise that release chi. It is the same energy that stimulates the heart to beat. It is the energy of the life force itself. Certain physical postures and movements allow the individual who seeks them to increase charisma, energy, stamina, strength, and good health. And, the most fantastic thing of all is that it is yours to acquire if you desire it.

Accidental Chi

There is a mystery surrounding the seemingly spontaneous occurrence of chi in certain people. A few sad examples are provided by Elvis Presley, Michael Jackson, and Maria Callas. These performers had extraordinary levels of chi and its manifestation as charisma without the controlling influence of a systematic program of regulation like the study and practice of yoga to calm and mete out the chi only as it was needed and to slow things down when the chi began to be too much for the moment or the task at hand. Chi can cause a performer to "burn up inside" with an overabundance of energy unless some way to control it is found. Unfortunately, the most common coping mechanism, abusing drugs and alcohol, is ineffective in the long run. A chemical that deadens the mind is at best a temporary solution, and we have witnessed what can happen at worst. The proper control mechanism should be to empty the mind when necessary through yoga or meditation. A martial art, with its endless, organized body movements, will achieve empty-mindedness by totally occupying the mind with procedural commands and the execution of those commands.

It is important to understand that chi makes everything more intense, including sorrow and suffering. Extremely charismatic people will feel things more than normal people. That is why they usually require special consideration in everything they do. Any physical activity that lowers the center is good for the regulation of chi. Examples of center-lowering activities would be any of the martial arts, and other sports including:

- Boxing
- Wrestling
- Fencing

Active sports that require balance, including:

- Surfing
- Skiing
- Extreme hiking
- Horse-back riding
- Ski-boarding,
- Mountain climbing

Body control systems that require extreme stillness and control, such as:
- Yoga
- Archery
- Rope-walking
- Meditation

The list could continue, but the reader must understand that there are many ways to relieve the pressures of overwhelming chi that are not dangerous to general health.

Common Exercises
Running is good for general conditioning and muscle tone and will contribute to the lowering of the center but, although it tones muscles necessary to the function of breathing, it does not seem to increase the actual capacity of the chest and ribcage. Running can cause gasping and exaggerated breathing through the mouth. This natural response to the need for more oxygen can be terribly drying to the throat and the vocal folds.

Yoga and swimming will dramatically increase breath capacity and also strengthen the muscles of the breathing function. Any form of Asian martial arts and the passive system of yoga posturing will increase stamina.

Playing a wind or brass instrument will increase the pressure function of the breathing muscles. Some instruments require too much pressure, like oboe or French horn. Others, like the Flute or Harmonica, don't ideally require enough pressure to develop the sending muscles of the breathing system. They are better than nothing, though, and will do a lot of good if practiced regularly for several years.

Section Two:
The Postures

1) Lolling About
This posture is practiced with the body leaned back in a big chair, nearly horizontal but not fully. The head should be higher than the feet, although the entire body makes a straight line at an angle of twenty to thirty-five degrees above the horizon, depending on the individual and the chair or couch used. The activities we practice in this posture are concerned with the relaxation of the abdomen and the throat before any actual singing is done, and the emptying of the mind of any other concerns. At this beginning point, the overriding goal is to achieve total looseness of the throat. The relaxation and softening of the abdomen will allow equal softening and relaxing of the throat. Once the abdomen is relaxed, the subsequent postures will accomplish the process of organizing the parts of the puzzle that make up what we call vocal technique.

Sit in a large easy chair and lean back all the way. Slide the pelvis forward toward the edge of the seat while relaxing the head and neck and leaning well back. The head and neck should be supported by the back of the chair, thereby avoiding any form of tension in any part of the neck. Relax everything but the desire for total freedom of the throat. Place both hands on the lower abdomen, right above the pubic bone. Inhale through the nose silently as if smelling a flower for as long as possible, with the lips closed in a gentle smile. Draw the abdomen inward slowly with the hands pressing inward against the lower abdominal wall. The breath should be drawn deeply into the lower rear quadrant of the lungs.

The Bellows

Expanding the chest and filling the lungs completely will be developed during the postures that follow. At this stage, we are concerned with the freedom and expansion of the back and the lower lungs while maintaining a totally loose throat and neck. The lower ribs in the back do all of the work of drawing air into the lungs. This is Caruso's concept: "the lower ribs in the back work like a bellows. They open when inhaling and squeeze together when singing."

Hold the breath for a moment while the lower halves of the lungs are expanded to full capacity. This is the beginning of the development of Lilli Lehmann's pause after breathing. There should be no tension in the neck or the throat. Do not allow a glottal stop to hold the breath in the lungs. The sensation while retaining the breath should be as if the inhalation were continuing.

Reverse the process by slowly relaxing the belly (abdominal wall) outward at the moment of attack of a singing tone. The lower ribs in the back will immediately begin to close. The sung tone should be a bright [a] vowel (*stai*) on a low, comfortable pitch without any particular criteria in terms of volume or quality. Comfort and ease are the main criteria at this point.

- Avoid a glottal stroke or any form of tension or resistance in the throat.
- Avoid any flexing of the muscles in the abdomen.
- The lower ribs in the back do all of the work.
- Drop the abdomen and allow it to relax and fall outward when singing or exhaling.
- Do not use an outwardly directed pushing function to influence the abdomen! Use only gravity and relaxation as the controlling energy to let the abdomen fall outward. Pushing outward will cause an opposite and equal reaction in the throat.
- Use the hands to help maintain the muscles of the abdomen in their softest state while pulling inward during the inhalation.
- While sustaining the sung note as the belly (abdomen) moves continually outward, use the hands to deliberately disturb the tone by moving (shaking) the abdominal wall in and out (not up and down) fairly rapidly until a rhythmic disturbance of the sung tone is achieved.

It is sometimes better to make a fist with one hand and use the other hand to press it inward. Some singers use a foot roller by pressing it inward end first and alternating the in and out motion. It's important to note that while inhaling, the movement of the fist or the hands (or the foot roller) against the abdomen must be in an inward direction (toward the spine) and outward direction (away from the spine) while singing or exhaling. The angle of the movement of the hands is at ninety degrees relative to the spine.

As soon as the rapid in and out movement causes an audible response in the voice, change the pulsing with the hands to a slower or faster tempo, eventually creating a range from slow to very fast and back again to very slow. Important: the movements of the hands should be perpendicular, not be vertical in relation to the spine. This exercise is similar to the "Heng-Haah" breathing exercise taught by the ancient tai chi masters. The tai chi exercise is to sustain "Heeeennnnngggg" while pulling the abdomen inward for seven to ten seconds, and say "Haaaaaaaaahhhhhh" while moving the abdomen outward for seven to ten seconds.

Singing until Empty

All of this outward movement should be done while holding a long note in a comfortable part of the voice. Different vowels can be practiced once the procedure is clearly established. The pitch can be lower or higher, and even to the very highest notes of the range, as long as the voice responds to the pulsing movement of the hands in and out against the abdominal wall and the lower belly remains flexible. It is important that the sound be continuously sustained until the breath is completely expended, and not crack or break while the abdomen is being moved. At the end of the available breath, the empty state of the lungs should be sustained for a few seconds before inhaling again.

Supplying the Voice with Breath

The abdominal wall should be completely loose while moving inward during inhalation and moving outward during exhalation. This can be achieved by continually moving (shaking) the belly in and out with the hands during inhalation and exhalation. The object of this exercise is to loosen all tension in the abdomen and throat, and in the viscera. Lolling is particularly beneficial to the practitioner's psychological state, because it encourages a total letting go of the concerns of the day while beginning an activation of the breathing process. The low breathing and relaxing will contribute to low-centering and begin the release of chi.

Singing While Pregnant

Everyone agrees that the larger the fetus becomes, the looser the belly becomes, and the only way to breathe is into the back. Therefore, the larger the fetus grows, the better the future mother sings! A pregnant woman has the nearly impossible task of pulling the belly in while singing, which can lead to severe conflict between her voice and her diaphragm. It is better to do what comes naturally and breathe into the back with the belly hanging out and the muscles in the belly completely neutralized and relaxed. After all, the reason some singers pull the abdomen inward while inhaling is to get the deepest breath possible into the lower back. Singers who are not pregnant should practice pulling the abdomen in while inhaling in order to eliminate the possibility of tension in the abdomen, and to assure the development and benefits, physically and psychologically, of lower back breathing. However, any singer who, for some reason, already breathes into the back doesn't need to pull the abdomen inward while inhaling. Of course, there is nothing wrong about breathing the way Caruso, Lilli Lehmann, Geraldine Farrar, and Olive Fremstad recommended! The activity of pulling the abdomen inward while inhaling and letting the abdomen fall outward while singing assists the singer psychologically to center himself or herself due to the repetitive thought process of seeking and activating the tantien. Joan Sutherland's description of her breathing method as "breathing up the rectum" would have caused a mental penetration of the base chakra at the tip of the tailbone. This activity, using each and every breathing opportunity to think of moving of the mind downward would definitely stimulate the center of the core (the tantien), and would instigate a steady flow of chi into the performing singer.

Constipation and Neutralization

The ultimate goal is to forget the abdomen entirely while singing. As soon as breathing into the lower back becomes a habit, it will no longer be necessary to pull the abdomen in consciously while inhaling. However, until it does become a habit, it is essential to eliminate the abdomen as a place to breathe. Freedom of the abdomen is crucial to good singing. One need only flex the abdominal muscles while sustaining a tone to understand how the reaction can interfere with the throat. Singers who activate abdominal muscles while breathing or singing must compensate by creating an opposite and equal force somewhere else in the body to neutralize muscular contractions or reactions in the throat. Unfortunately, the throat reacts to every flex and tension that occurs in the abdomen. A push downward or outward, as opposed to a relaxation of the belly wall downward or outward causes a reaction upward which must be neutralized in order for the vocal folds to be free to vibrate at their maximum level of efficiency. It is much better to avoid tension in the first place, avoiding any necessity for compensation and/or neutralization. The constipation method of support demands a pressing downward of the breath. It is one of the worst applications of abdominal tension. Pushing downward while singing in an exaggerated manner requires intense equalization in the throat; therefore, it should be completely avoided.

2) Floor Postures

While lying flat on the floor, facing upward with the legs straight and stretched out, breathe the abdominal wall in and out at a ninety degree angle relative to the floor. The inhalation and exhalation procedures and the shake of the lower abdomen are the same actions as in the lolling posture. This floor posture is a completely horizontal variation of the lolling posture. The same movements of the abdomen with the hands are used to achieve the total looseness of the abdominal wall and the throat.

Keep the Legs Straight
After achieving total looseness of the abdomen, lift the legs ten inches off the floor, keeping the knees straight. This exercise will create a muscular process in the lower abdomen that releases the throat completely. The secret is to keep the knees straight. Do not do crunches. Bent knees while lifting the weight of the upper body will cause the upper abdomen to flex and harden. This places the breath too high in the body and can create tension in the lower abdomen as a sympathetic reaction. We want the placement of the breath to sit in the lower back, right behind the pubic bone. All hard-style methods (using the contractions of muscles to achieve proper functions) such as the leg-lift exercise, must be more exact than soft-style methods (using relaxation and gravity to achieve proper functions). Therefore, leg-lifts must be absolutely correct with no bent knees.

Crossing the Body
Swing the left leg slowly across the body creating a ninety degree angle with the right leg (many singers cannot accomplish this in the beginning, so just do the best you can). Do not allow the shoulders to lose contact with the floor. Let the crossing leg (at this point, the left leg) reach over until the left foot can make contact with the floor. Maintain the position for a few seconds. The non-crossing leg (the right leg) remains lying straight out without bending the knee. Reverse the process, crossing the opposite leg over the body. Try to maintain the ninety-degree angle between the legs as perfectly as possible.

Lifting and Spreading the Legs
Go back to the straight legs position with the back of the body and the backs of the legs and heels completely touching the floor. Slowly lift the legs ten inches off the floor and hold. Then spread the legs apart as far as possible while keeping them ten inches off the floor and hold. Slowly bring the legs together, returning to the elevated legs-together position, hold for a few seconds and then let the legs gradually sink to the floor. It is possible to do the bicycle and the plow based on these floor postures. Singers who are curious about yoga will want to attend a serious class and learn many new postures, all of which will be beneficial to the voice, health, and career.

The Head on the Floor
From the position of lying face up on the floor, raise the upper body to an upright, sitting position. With the upper body erect, creating a ninety degree angle relative to the floor, spread the legs apart as far as possible, keeping the knees straight and in contact with the floor. Bend over and touch the forehead to the floor (or as far as possible) while blowing breath out until completely empty. Some singers can't bend over much at all. Don't worry about it. Just do the best you can without forcing anything. After holding the emptiness of the lungs for a few seconds, inhale as deeply and for as long as possible while maintaining the head on the floor. Gradually sit up, singing a scale or a sustained tone, regulating the emission of the tone so that you are empty when you reach the vertical position of the upper body. It is a good exercise to sustain notes in the upright posture if the supply of breath is sufficient.

Bouncing the Buttocks

While sitting erect, if enough residual breath is available, bounce on the buttocks while sustaining a tone in the middle voice. The mind of the singer should seek the lowest point of the bottom of the bounce and concentrate the beginning of the sung tone from that deep spot. To facilitate bouncing, and with the legs still spread apart, place one hand in front of the body on the floor and the other hand behind the body on the floor. The lower belly should be relaxed outward while singing any tones. Bouncing is a good loosening exercise in almost every posture we will discuss here. It uses gravity to lower the center. Singing at the bottom of the bounce helps to gain the lowest connection of the voice and the deepest level of the body and the breath.

Singing scales or sustained notes while sitting up slowly will assist the muscles and the ribs in the lower back with the important primary control of the emission of the voice. The tempo of the sitting up will have to be adjusted to the individual singer's breath capacity. Do the scales faster if necessary to leave enough breath in the lungs for sustained singing and bouncing in the upright position.

3) The Primitive/Campfire Squat

Heels on the Floor

From a normal standing position, squat down all the way, with the heels on the floor. Some adults cannot squat down with the heels touching the floor the first time they try. However, it can be learned! In some cases, it is as difficult as learning to ride a bicycle or learning to ski because it is all about balancing and centering. Every child we see playing in the sand on the beach squats this way. It will require a lot of practice in some instances, but it is possible to learn to squat correctly. All primitive people squat this way around their campfires. Most adults squat down on the balls of their feet. This is not as developmental for breathing or for centering as the primitive squat, and should not be the compromise position. The squat with the heels down on the floor is superior, especially for developing the breathing in the lower back. It requires a total drop of the body down between the legs, which aids in centering and the generation of chi.

Do not despair if you fall over backward in the beginning. It is a common problem and will go away with practice. The squat with the heels down is essential to maximizing proper energy flow and must be learned. It is actually easy for most children and for some adults. The rest of us must try repeatedly until it becomes one of our main postures. Some singers compromise by holding on to a wall molding or to a heavy couch or chair. This compromise should be temporary at best, and, preferably not used at all.

How to Proceed (Squatting)

From a normal standing position with the arms hanging down and completely relaxed and the feet spread apart at shoulder width and (ideally) pointed straight ahead, bend the knees deeply and completely until the body is resting against the calves of the legs and the heels are flat on the floor. It may be necessary to shift the weight forward with the arms well in front of the body as the body descends. Ideally, the squatter will be able to rock back and forth with the feet flat on the floor without any loss of balance. Some people lose their balance and fall backwards. While comical and sometimes a little embarrassing, this is harmless and is a natural part of the learning and adjusting process, just as falling off a bicycle is a part of learning how to ride. Don't give up! Keep trying until you are successful and find your center!

Improving Breath Capacity
Once accomplished, this posture induces the breath to seek out the space it needs in the lower back. It's a continuation of the breathing method begun in the lolling posture. The dome-like rear half of the diaphragm will descend as the breath is drawn into the lower back. It's not enough to depress only the front of the diaphragm. Drawing the inhalation extremely down into the lower back will cause the rear half of the diaphragm to descend to its lowest possible level. This approach may increase usable breath capacity by causing the lower rear quadrant of the lungs to fill with air. These postures and the ones described in the following examples cause the singer or speaker to breathe in a complete way, utilizing the total diaphragmatic function, and thus providing a deeper tone and more freedom of the throat, which leads to more control of the voice.

4) The King of Dancers

Stretch! Don't Strain!
While standing on the right foot/leg with the knee straight (later, you can practice bending the knee), raise the left leg behind you, grabbing the top of the left foot with the left hand and pull the left leg up and out behind you until the thigh of the raised leg is parallel to the floor and the sole of the foot is facing upward. The knee should be opened and the lower leg and the thigh form an "L" in the air with the left thigh as the horizontal component of the "L" and the lower portion of the left leg as the vertical component. Don't strain! Go as far as you can in the beginning and don't despair! This is a difficult position for some people. Do it as well as you can and practice every day. Coax the muscles and tendons gently and slowly to let go and relax and stretch. Caution is the key word while stretching the body, even among the very flexible practitioners of yoga.

A Scissors-like Alignment
The right arm should extend out in front of you slightly above shoulder level with the elbow slightly bent and the point of the elbow pointing toward the floor. All components of the posture should be as soft and relaxed as possible. The hand should be held in the palm forward position, fingers pointing upward, with the wrist bent. The nose, arm, and right foot, which is on the floor at this point, should be pointed in the same direction and the head should be slightly lifted and held in a straight position in alignment with the standing leg. The head should not be leaned to one side or the other. The leg being held in the air behind the body should be in alignment with the arm in front, creating a steady front-to-back line like a pair of scissors. The standing leg (the right leg, in this case) can be straight, slightly bent, or deeply bent. All three

ways should be practiced. After this has been accomplished, switch to the other leg and repeat everything on the opposite side.

The Abdominal Hinge

Yoga postures tend to constantly exercise the flexibility of the abdominal hinge (the bending point of the body across the middle of the abdomen, approximately located at the waist) by causing the lower belly and the lower back to bend either extremely forward or extremely backward. This is all part of centering, balancing, and aligning the body. It has the added advantage of causing the chest to open and extend forward, automatically creating the form of the sternal arch and helping to open and develop the air-box or air-bucket, which later becomes an important factor in the richness and fullness of the voice.

5) The Cobra (With/Without Bounce)

Cobras and Dogs

There are several ways to do the Cobra, depending on the style of yoga one studies. The Cobra posture I recommend is the one that seems to help the vocal process the most. The leaning of the breath necessary for good breath control and vocal production occurs as a reaction to the breath as it leaves the back and moves to the front of the body during singing or exhalation. Many singers and actors have found the Cobra to be the most beneficial of all the yoga postures. However, the extreme curving of the lower back is very difficult and even painful for some people, as is the form called Upward Facing Dog (to be described later). Both Cobra and the Upward Facing Dog are hard on the wrists and lower back and can be uncomfortable. As always, when practicing yoga postures, if you begin to feel a degree of discomfort that becomes too uncomfortable to sustain, do the best you can for a few minutes and tackle it again tomorrow. There is no way to force the body to obey our desire to hurry! We must be patient and consistent, and wait until the stretching begins to feel comfortable before we can develop our air-boxes and begin to exploit the full potential of our voices.

How to Proceed (Cobra)

Lie face-down and flat with the belly and forehead touching the floor and slide the hands back to waist level, placing the palms flat on the floor with the forearms vertical relative to the floor (the wrists will bend at a ninety degree angle, fingers pointed forward toward the head) and in contact with the sides of the body. The legs are completely extended with the fronts of the legs and the tops of the feet in contact with the floor. The heels are spread apart with the big toes touching and crossed. Push down on the palms and raise the upper body until the elbows are straight and the head is slightly tilted back. The shoulders should remain as level as possible. The chest will be completely open and the air-box will be at its most extreme state of expansion. This will create an extreme curve of the back and exert breath pressure (lean) on the lower abdomen and the chest. Ideally, the pubic bone should remain in contact with the floor at all times during the Cobra. This criterion will require the lower back to curve extremely.

Adjustments to Discomfort

If the extreme curve of the back is too uncomfortable, adjust the posture to make it bearable by allowing the elbows to bend. People with back problems or health problems of any kind should ask their physician before they do any exercise program, as some of these postures may be too extreme for some singers. The Cobra may cause some discomfort to even the healthiest lower back. However, many singers would be happy to testify that there is no posture that is better for the development of *appoggio*. The extreme lean caused by the Cobra posture is especially beneficial for singing the upper range of the voice. Despite a feeling of resistance in the ribs of the lower back, this is where breathing will necessarily be accomplished. The exhalation will occur with breath pressure directed against the chest. Be ready to lie down slowly at any point during this posture. The secret is to never move quickly or violently, especially when changing from one posture to another.

6) Child Resting

It is important to note at this point that when moving from the Cobra into the Child Resting position, one should never walk forward or backward with the knees from one posture to the next. Child Resting is one of the best postures for the development of lower back breathing. It should be practiced every day by conscientious vocal artists at every level of achievement. It is very popular with practitioners of yoga because the uncomfortable curve of the lower spine required by the Cobra is reversed and any discomfort is almost instantly relieved! The move from Cobra to Child should happen as described below.

How to Proceed (Child Resting)

Starting from the Cobra position, lower your body to the floor until you are lying completely flat. Keep the head, arms and chest in contact with the floor. Allow them to slide backward along the floor while bending and drawing the body backward but do not allow the knees to move. The buttocks will rise into the air and move towards the feet while the upper body slides along the floor toward the knees. The head and chest should not leave the floor. Gently lower the buttocks until they are resting in the space between the spread-apart heels. The forehead should be leaned against the floor and the arms should be pulled backward along the sides of the body until totally extended to the rear with the palms of the hands facing upward.

People who have children or who have been around very young children will recognize this posture. It is one of the most observed sleeping postures in the crib. Adults who practice this posture will find it very relaxing and comfortable. There are several points to be made concerning this posture. First, it is very conducive to the development of lower back breathing. Second, it is the most relaxed and relaxing of all yoga postures. Third, the movement and posture of the lower back are extremely reversed from that of the Cobra, the Upward Facing Dog, or the King of Dancers.

Avoid Twisting the Spine

Advanced yoga practitioners learn how to twist the spine without danger of injury. However, twisting the spine can be very dangerous for some people and should be attempted only in slow motion and under the supervision of an experienced instructor. This list will suggest only one posture that turns the spine. It is the last posture we do and is called the Corkscrew.

7) The Zen Meditation Posture

The next step in this particular sequence is the Zen Meditation posture. It can be practiced as the second half of one exercise by joining it to Child Resting. This combination will allow for an inhaling posture (the Child Resting posture) and an exhaling posture (the Zen Meditation posture). As soon as the lungs are filled with breath in the bent-over posture, sit up with the back straight and seat the buttocks down between the heels. This becomes the Zen Meditation posture, called Sitting. The upper body should be almost vertical, with a slight lean forward. The hands should rest on the lap with the palms facing upward and resting on each other and the head should be tilted back slightly and facing upward. Everything should be loose and free of tension, especially the neck and throat. During the sitting up action, the breath should be slowly exhaled while the abdomen is slowly relaxed into the dropped downward and outward position without dropping the chest. This action has been described as dumping the wheelbarrow.

Vocalizing During the Posture Sequence

A vocalizing sequence can be coordinated with the same procedure. Start the scale or tone while bent over in the Child Resting posture, after the exhaling-inhaling sequence described above. After holding the breath in the filled lungs for a moment in the bent-over posture, begin the scale and gradually sit up straight. Ideally, the scale will finish with a sustained tone just as the sitting posture is reached. The scales or the sustained tones can be extended until the lungs are completely empty of breath. Before breathing in again, bend over completely while exhaling any residual air in the lungs. Inhale only when the bent over position is complete and the lungs are completely empty.

8) Upward Facing Dog

Dog Facing Upward is based on and started in the Cobra posture. It is really an advanced form of the Cobra but is more extreme and can be delayed until the body has developed the elasticity necessary to execute extreme postures. Starting from the Cobra, raise the fronts of the thighs, knees, and shins one inch off the floor while maintaining the curvature of the lower back. Some singers will have to adjust the feet by turning the toes up and forward in order to provide a support basis for the legs and the weight of the lower body. The Upward Facing Dog is considered more difficult than the Cobra because the lower body is no longer resting on the floor. The hands and the feet are holding up the weight of the body. Nothing should be touching the floor except for the toes and hands.

The legs should be kept straight and as close to the floor as possible without actually touching the floor. It is acceptable to spread the legs apart slightly, if necessary. The head is held tilted back and facing slightly upward and forward. Keep the body as close to the floor as possible, again without actually touching except for the hands and feet. The upper body remains, as in the Cobra, reared up in a vertical posture with the chest completely open. Each inhalation should be placed in the tip of the tailbone as if breathing in through the lowest point of the body in the rear.

9) Downward Facing Dog

Downward Facing Dog is a good example of the basis of yoga posturing and centering in that it provides an opposite posture to the Upward Facing Dog. With the hands remaining where they were during the Upward Facing Dog, the back will now be bent in the extreme opposite direction (upward) by raising the lower back and buttocks up toward the ceiling while simultaneously dropping the head down between the arms and letting the neck go completely loose (the dangling head). The soles of the feet, which were in a vertical position relative to the floor, should now drop down backward toward the horizontal with the heels in contact with the floor. It is very important for the heels to touch, even if the posture, which, ideally, creates two forty-five degree angles with the upper body angled upward and the pelvis and the legs angled downward, must be modified. With enough practice, the Achilles tendons will become elastic and enable the student to perform the Downward Facing Dog posture completely extended. The head should hang down between the arms with the neck totally relaxed.

Singing in the Postures

This posture in particular is one of the best for loosening the neck and throat. Downward Facing Dog encourages the breathing to occur in the lower back while allowing the throat and neck to be completely relaxed. It's important to note that the Cobra and the Upward Facing Dog posture create a closing of the lower back and place emphasis on the lower abdomen (the low front lean). In the Downward Facing Dog, the emphasis is reversed and the lower back is opened in order to better receive the breath. The abdomen is loose and hanging outward and downward.

10) The Tree

From Floor to Standing

Up to this point, we have concentrated on floor postures with much bending forward and backward. Now we are standing up (one of the standing group of postures) and straightening the body. The inhalation should continue to be very slow, deep and directed toward the tailbone and buttocks. The abdomen should be drawn inward during the inhalation and released outward during the exhalation. This is a very good posture for the practice of octave exercises beginning from a very low note. Absolute stillness of the torso is the most important consideration when singing intervals. Singing should not cause any loss of balance or any loss of the correctness of the posture. Good technical singers can sing entire operas without losing balance or control of the posture.

Stand up on the right foot with the leg straight and do not allow the knee to bend at this time. Grasp the top of the left foot and turn it upside down so the sole of the foot is facing upward. Pull the heel of the left foot back into the crotch (bottom of the foot facing upward) until the heel is well back and the outside edge (known in martial arts as the knife edge) of the foot is resting against the inside of the upper right thigh. Press the knife-edge of the left foot against the inside of the upper right thigh, high up against the groin tendon. The bent left knee will protrude away from the body toward the left side. Raise the arms with the elbows bent and pulled back somewhat, and touch the fingertips together above the front of the head. Be sure that the space formed around the head by the arms is as equal as possible. Allow the arms to relax with the feeling that they are falling against each other without losing their posture above the head. Keep the bent elbows well back and even with the plane of the chest and the shoulders. The shoulders should be dropped as loosely as possible and the entire body should feel soft and relaxed without compromising the perfection of the posture. Reaching upward with the arms should not cause the shoulders or the tendons in the front of the neck to tense. As soon as one side is under control, switch to the opposite side, standing on the left leg and placing the right foot high up against the inside of the left thigh. Continue the process as a mirror image of the posture already accomplished while standing on the right leg.

The Vertical Drop

One of the rules of the *Posture Method* is that once a posture is established, the singing should not cause any lack of balance or any change in the perfection of the posture. This posture is the only one discussed here that is dedicated to the development of the pure, vertical lean. This is the posture that best develops the brick in the bucket concept of a straight down, completely relaxed, invisible upper body approach to singing. There is a total vertical drop of the breath into the pelvic floor with nothing to hold it down but gravity. Bouncing develops the vertical concept of the dropping of the breath into the pelvic floor even more clearly if the bottom of the bounce can be identified. However, bouncing is not a posture. It is an action technique, using the concept of the bottom of the bounce to help with finding the connection to the pelvic floor. It can be used to good advantage in almost any yoga posture.

Gravity and its Power

Gravity is all we need to hold us down on the earth. Therefore, it makes sense that gravity can draw the breath, viscera, and diaphragm toward the pelvic floor if we can relax and allow it to happen. This is the secret of those obese singers who seem to sing so beautifully without the problems and tendencies that seem to plague most slender singers. We know that obese singers who lose a lot of weight in mid-career invariably develop vocal problems. Some are very famous cases such as Maria Callas and Eleanor Steber, who were magnificent vocalists until each lost one hundred pounds. Although each maintained her high level of artistry, the voice was never again as free as it had been before the extreme weight loss. They had lived with the vocal advantage of having been obese since childhood. They were able to rely on fat to keep everything pulling downward into the pelvic floor, which functioned as a breath control method. When the weight was no longer there, Callas developed a wobble in her high notes and Steber's voice became hard and strident.

High Notes and the Pelvic Floor

In the Tree, the feeling of heaviness and weight are all-important. The breath itself seems to become weighty and heavy (but not in the negative sense of causing the voice to become dark and thick), as if each tone weighs several pounds and is sitting right in the center of the floor of the pelvis. The feeling of the body being heavy helps especially with the high pianissimo tones (very quiet notes). This is one of the most important postures for developing the upper register of any voice. According to Lauritz Melchior, Helge Roswänge and George London, the dead-drop method of breath control was the approach described by Kirsten Flagstad as being the secret to her phenomenal voice and the apparent ease with which she sang.

11) Lion/Cow

The Lion is done on hands and knees, slowly rolling the head backward until the face is looking directly at the ceiling, while protruding the tongue as far out and down toward the bottom of the chin as possible. Some people can touch their chins with the tip of the tongue, but can they do it on their hands and knees while facing the ceiling? This is a stretching exercise that will arch the small of the back with the belly hanging down and outward. The extreme version of this posture should not be sustained very long at one time. It's better to bring the head forward and relax for a moment and then repeat the stretch than to try to sustain it for too long.

The point is to stretch and not to strain!

In spite of the activity of the tongue and the small of the back (the arching back is an important part of this exercise), the lower belly remains totally relaxed, hanging down and out. In fact, the name of the variation on this posture, The Cow, evolved due to the similarity of udders hanging from a dairy cow's lower belly! However, in the Cow, the tongue must relax back into the mouth with the front of the tongue maintaining contact with the lower lip from corner to corner. At the same time, the head must roll forward to a comfortable position slightly above level.

Singing should be done in the Cow posture and not in the Lion posture. While alternating the postures, use the knees and one hand for support. With the other hand, reach down to the lower abdomen and repeatedly press the lower belly inward while inhaling. Then, let it fall down toward the floor (outward) while sustaining a tone in the middle range. A friend can assist with the belly lift/drop if it's too difficult to do alone. In my experience, the singers can learn to do these exercises without assistance through practice and commitment. The inhalation should be, as always, directed toward the lower back. At the beginning of the emission of the voice, the belly should drop out and toward the floor.

12) The Leg-Up: bend over and blow

The Leg-Up is another standing posture, but begins to combine the erect posture with the movements of the bending of the back. After all of that bending we did on the floor and the standing posture we accomplished in the Tree, we will now try to combine standing and bending and singing. Bend down forward and, placing the hands behind the legs, grab the back of the ankles or calves. The success of this exercise depends a lot on the flexibility of the individual. It is important to challenge oneself as much as possible without causing any pain. All of the postures should be done in slow motion.

How to Proceed (Leg-Up Exercise)

After emptying the lungs extremely, inhale as deeply as possible. Stand on one leg while pulling the other leg up by the knee. Press that knee against the chest by pulling with the hands and arms. The exhalation or the vocalise should occur during the rising up slowly. Sustain a note at the peak of the leg-lift, while standing in a vertical position with the knee of the pulled-up leg pressed tightly against the chest until the lungs are emptied of breath. The emptiness should be sustained for a few seconds.

Bend over while still empty and don't breathe in again until the position at the bottom of the bend is reached. Breathe in again as fully as possible and begin the sequence again. Singing during this exercise should begin while rising up with the knee in the hands on its way to the chest. Raise the body slowly while singing a scale or arpeggio and hold the upper note, squeezing the leg to the chest as tightly as possible, until the breath is completely gone and then some. Bend over and do the steps again, changing legs each time.

Movement and Variations

We are now standing up to sing and getting closer to the posture of the chest and the function of the ribcage that we will assume most of the time while singing before the public. Public performance requires a standing, upright posture most of the time while singing lead roles. However, it is important that singers who sing comic (buffo) roles maintain the angle of *appoggio* consistently.

A variation of this posture is to drop the leg after squeezing the knee against the chest and swing it while singing. This type of exercise is very important for singers who desire to become theater performers instead of concert singers because the idea is to be able to move freely while singing. The singer can add extra movements by swinging the arms while singing. It is important that the chest remain still during a lot of movement in order to keep perfect control of the emission of the breath. There must be no loss of balance or loss of coordination, and the body should remain perfectly balanced on one leg regardless of the intensity of movement of the limbs.

13) Bending Backward (The Limbo)

We use the Caribbean dance called the Limbo as our example. Lean as far back as you can with the head back and the arms hanging loosely down (without holding on to anything) and try to sing. If you don't choke to death, you've got it made! This is the posture that reveals to you if you've been singing with a brick in the throat instead of a brick in the bucket. It is amazing how many singers cannot look up and sing at the same time. Meanwhile, the greatest singers with the longest careers—Caruso, Sutherland, Pavarotti, Caballé, Kraus, Tucker, Milanov, Merrill, Roswänge, Melchior, Flagstad, Nilsson, McCormack, and everyone who sang beautifully into their later years—*all* sang with their heads up! They sang to the upper balconies and the public loved it! Some of them, like Sutherland, Caballé, Kraus, Pavarotti and Milanov, who had the longest careers of all, were the singers who threw their heads back the most extremely!

Pleasing Stage Directors

I remember back in my student days watching Cesare Siepi throw his head back for the high G's at the end of the serenade in *Faust*. It was amazing to hear such a big, heavy, bass voice sing so beautifully and so easily in the highest part of his range. Another low bass, Jerome Hines, sang those same notes very easily and securely, and always with his head thrown back.

In the beginning, if you put your head back extremely with the breath held too high in the body, you will feel like you are going to choke when you try to sing. A few singers, who, for some reason, breathe very low in their backs, can do it right away, but they are rare. The rest of us must practice, perhaps increasing the angle of the head in increments of a few degrees at a time, singing different vowels on low notes only. Leaning back while singing has a practical side, too, because a stage director may demand that you look up, or around and up, or directly behind you and up.

It should not be necessary to sing with our heads so far up and back, but we certainly should be able to sing with our heads in any position we choose. The number one goal should be to sing with a free throat. The ability to sing to the upper balconies is a major step toward that goal because it is impossible to do if there is tension or action in the throat. There will be some funny moments when you sound like you are choking to death. As Tetrazinni said: "Keep trying in spite of cracking and making strange noises. The tone is seeking its proper path."

How to Proceed (The Limbo)

Stand up straight with the feet apart as wide as the shoulders. Bend the head all the way back while inhaling deeply into the lower back. With the head already leaned back and the inhalation placed in the lower back, bend the knees and move them forward and lean the body back as far as possible without falling. The shoulders should be relaxed and the arms should hang loosely behind the body. The angle of the body varies from singer to singer in the beginning. The goal should be to touch the heels with the fingers by reaching down behind the legs. Some singers finger-walk down the legs until they reach the heels.

Stand up after approximately ten seconds or at any time when discomfort occurs that begins to dominate the situation. The body comes slowly up to a straight posture first with the head still leaned back. As a last movement, the head rolls forward to its normal, level posture. Always move very slowly, leaving the head as the last thing that comes back to a straight up position. As soon as the body is up straight, the head can roll forward. The idea is to never use muscles in the throat or neck to assist with the lifting of the head to a level position.

Many singers cannot sing at all in this posture. If fear of falling is the reason, practice backed up against a bed or easy chair. If you do fall, the landing is very soft and you will lose your fear. The only muscular work is done by the legs (especially the fronts of the thighs) and the ribs in the lower back. With practice, the lean of the breath will move down into the pelvic floor, which will allow the throat muscles to be completely free. Some singers, who have learned to never flex a muscle in the throat while singing, can sing arias in this posture!

14) The Layout

Joan Sutherland would lean her body forward with the chest thrust out (the sternal arch in action) and keep her head leaned far back while looking upward toward the second and third balconies. I heard her many times at the Metropolitan Opera sing all of her roles, but the most exciting performance I heard her do was in Bern, Switzerland. She sang a selection of fabulous coloratura scenes from opera and also from the concert repertoire. Arne's "The Soldier Tired" and Bishop's "Lo, Hear the Gentle Lark" were on the program. I was accustomed to the fact that the greatest singers at the Met all sang looking up at the higher balconies when they sang. The concert hall in Bern had only one balcony, and she threw her head back even though there were no additional balconies! She also raised one foot off the floor behind her, with her body leaned forward. I had often noticed at the Met that the long dresses and skirts she wore that hung down to the floor would suddenly begin to rise in the rear, along the hemline, creating a large bulge of some kind pushing upward and extending outward behind her. Dame Joan was not only lifting her foot off the floor, but also raising and straightening her leg out behind her. The posture of her head, the leaned forward body position, and the leg extended to the rear were all part of her way of singing.

Imitation or Understanding?

There were singers in the past who employed a number of physical movements and postures that resembled those employed by Sutherland and Pavarotti. For example, Jan Kiepura, the most famous Slavic tenor to make a huge career in Western Europe and the United States, leaned forward with his chest thrust out while singing. His head was tilted back and held up high in a position to maximize his vocal and facial contact with his audience. His back leg was extended well back (though it did remain in contact with the floor) and one hand was kept pressed against the center of his chest. Kirsten Flagstad can be seen on YouTube singing "Brünnhilde's Battle Cry" from *Die Walküre*. Notice the forward lean of her body and the lifted head, with the chest thrown forward and outward.

We could continue naming singers who have employed the essence of the Layout posture while singing. Perhaps we should learn this posture well enough to actually use it while vocalizing and rehearsing repertoire. Once a singer has learned to sing in the Layout posture, the reasons why many great singers have used its essence will become clear.

Reasons and Results

The Layout Posture is fairly simple to understand. Its purpose is to cause a reaction in the lower back that will affect breathing and centering based on the hinge at the bending level of the abdomen/lower back. The muscles at the base of the spine contract on both sides. This influences the lower ribs to support the arching back and creates a lean of the breath into the chest and belly. Each inhaled breath meets resistance in the lower back without compromising the locations of the respiratory functions. Singing sustained tones in this posture will develop stamina in the muscles that close the ribs in the lower back.

Think of this posture as a hard-style breathing exercise. Just as leg lifts will cause the lower belly to contract and force inhalation down into the back of the lower body, the contractions of the muscles of the lower back will cause the lean of the breath, the *appoggio,* to be placed against the chest. Maintaining either posture will exert influence on the location and process of both the inhalation and exhalation and the point of leaning of the breath. The orientation of hard-style breathing changes the psychological attraction from the front of the belly in the leg lift to the lower back during the Layout.

How to Proceed (The Layout Posture)

Stand with the feet together and raise the arms straight up above the head, with the head all the way back facing the ceiling. While maintaining the position of the head and arms, bend forward at the waist until the upper body reaches a ninety degree angle relative to the legs. The head is now pulled up and back, facing straight ahead, with the view parallel to the floor. With the upper body and the arms now parallel to the floor, raise and extend the right leg behind the body at a slight upward angle while maintaining the knee as straight as possible. Sustain the posture while singing vocalizes and phrases of repertoire.

The Chalice

The position of the body in the Layout Posture, as seen in profile, has been compared to a goblet or a drinking cup (the Chalice). The leg that is angled upward with the knee unbent creates one side of the chalice. The arms lifted at an upward angle with the elbows straight and the head up create the opposite side of the chalice. The pelvis becomes the bottom of the drinking cup and the standing leg becomes the stem or base of the drinking cup. The point where the leg joins the hip becomes the fulcrum of the balanced posture and the base support of the centering hinge. The resulting placement of the breath against the chest and the closing action of the lower ribs develops *appoggio.*

15) The Sumo

Perhaps you've seen a Sumo wrestling match. Do you remember the way in which the wrestlers warm up? Two gigantic men squatting and rocking from side to side is a strange sight, especially if you try to connect it to singing. The low point of centering in this particular posture with its peculiar movements provides an answer. Doing the Sumo on a regular basis helps to seat the viscera in the lowest part of the pelvic floor. This particular spot and the exaggerated way the Sumo wrestlers seek it can be very useful to anyone whose choice of activities demand unusual stamina and power. The Sumo posture is one of the best postures for developing the necessary stamina needed while singing the most difficult roles in opera and for singing long concert programs. It is also one of the best ways to develop volume in the voice that is not deleterious to the totality of the vocal organ.

How to Proceed (the Sumo)

The Sumo is a posture dedicated to the generation of maximum and specifically applied chi. Sumo wrestlers do not develop kicks and punches. Their entire concern has to do with the amount of power needed to push an opponent out of a prescribed ring. The Sumo posture will generate more chi than a combination of other postures, and is most applicable to singers who have to perform long, dramatic roles over huge orchestras. It is only one of the many postures we can use to generate chi, but it is one of the most efficient ones, and should be included in every warm-up routine. It is a fantastic exercise for developing stamina in a singer. It is done in the following steps.

From a standing position, spread the legs apart as widely as is comfortable. Place the hands under the lower thighs from the front, close to and above the knee joint. Bend the knees and slide the feet far out to the sides in equal increments with the feet pointing straight ahead. Slowly allow the body to sink downward while looking straight ahead. Stop the movement of the body downward when the butt is almost as low as the bent knees. Some singers can lower the body all the way to the floor. This is not a competition, and each singer should do only what is possible and comfortable. Ideally, the feet should be pointed straight ahead, flat on the floor. The upper body should be leaning slightly forward of vertical with the arms reaching down in front of the body in order to place the hands under the thighs above the knee joints. The head is slightly above level and facing straight ahead and the spine is straight with the pelvis turned slightly under. Lean to the left and rock yourself over onto the left leg while lifting the right leg into the air, assisting the leg lift with the right hand under the right thigh above the knee joint. The left arm reaches for the sky at a forty-five degree angle. Do not allow the thighs to close or draw closer together while rocking over to one side and lifting. Ideally, the angle created by spreading the thighs apart will not diminish at all but will increase as the leg is lifted. For now, we do not allow the thighs to close. The right leg will rise into the air as high as possible without bending the knees of either leg. The standing leg will straighten completely if the practitioner is flexible enough, as will the lifted leg. The right foot should maintain directional control with the toes pointed forward as the leg is raised. The knife-edge (outside edge) of the foot should be turned downward as far as possible. Hold the posture for a few seconds. As the leg lift begins, the groin tendons, as they are stretched horizontally, begin to pull the core of the body downward (vertically), lowering the physical focus to the tantien and increasing chi flow.

Lateral Energy

It is not a disaster if the thighs close, but it is to be avoided while practicing this exercise if possible. The closed position of the thighs will not produce the same results in terms of stamina and amplitude of the voice. It should be said, however, that letting the thighs close can produce tremendous power, but the manifestation of chi in martial arts will be better exploited in kicking, especially kicking to the side. The equivalent energy available to the singer from the practice of kicking to the sides is lateral energy, which stimulates the flank muscles and contributes to an easy approach to high notes and coloratura. The secret of success is to practice stretching the groin tendons until the ease and balance necessary to correctly perform the Sumo posture have each been accomplished.

Wide and Apart

Vocalizing while performing this posture is done in the same way as during other exercises. Once the beginning position of being spread wide and apart is established, breathe into the lower back, which is assisted by drawing the abdomen inward. As you begin singing the scale (remember to let the abdomen relax outward and downward when you begin to sing), rock to one side, and time the scale or arpeggio so that you arrive at the upper note just as you achieve your balance on the selected leg. If you are low enough in your range, you can sing ascending intervals of fourths, fifths, and octaves at this point while trying to suddenly elevate the lifted leg even higher. Hold the position until you are nearly out of breath. When the lungs are completely empty, lower the leg back under smooth control to its beginning point on the floor. Change keys up and down the scale by half steps and repeat the exercise and the vocalises on the opposite side.

16) The Balancing Posture

The Balancing Posture begins like the King of Dancers posture. Stand up straight, feet together and arms relaxed at the sides of the body. Reach back with the right hand and lift the right foot up behind the body. Grab the top of the right foot with the right hand and press the heel against the right buttock, keeping the knees on an even plane from front to back and together. At the same time, lift the left arm straight up above the left shoulder with the wrist bent backward at a ninety-degree angle. The elbow should not bend. The relaxed left hand and fingers will fall backward into a position perpendicular to the arm and parallel to the ceiling. The left hand should feel as if it is resting against an imaginary, flat ceiling. The last step of the exercise, and the most difficult part for singers whose breath is too high in the chest and not low enough in the lower back, is to throw the head back as far as it will go with the face parallel to the ceiling. The face should be held at a ninety-degree angle in relation to the vertical arm, and be parallel to the ceiling and the floor. Facing the ceiling is very difficult for some singers. It demands perfect balance, coordination, and anchoring the stillness of the body by breathing deeply into the lower back while drawing in the lowest part of the abdomen. Shallow breathing or breath pressing upward against the throat will prevent the success of this posture. On the other hand, success with this posture will guarantee a free throat.

17) The Corkscrew

The Corkscrew is the only exercise recommended in this book that rotates the spine. The upper body must be kept perfectly vertical in order to avoid turning the spine and bending it at the same time. Bending the spine forward and backward is not dangerous if done slowly and carefully. Rotating the spine is not dangerous if done carefully with no bend in the spine at the same time. The danger arises when people try to bend over and rotate (turn to the side) *at the same time,* especially if they attempt to lift something heavy. However, sometimes a simple leaning over with a twist is enough to injure this vital part of the body. That is why we wait until all of the other postures have been completed and the body is stretched and warmed up. And then we proceed very slowly.

How to Proceed (the Corkscrew)

Start like the Sumo, with the feet pointed straight ahead and spread very wide apart and the knees deeply bent. The hands should rest on the hips with the shoulders relaxed and the elbows bent. Inhale deeply into the lower back while drawing the abdomen inward. As you begin to sing a scale, maintain the spine in an erect, straight position. Very slowly, as if in slow-motion, turn the body to the left ninety-degrees and stop. Continue turning the head an additional ninety degrees until you are facing in the opposite direction from where you began. The feet should not move from their original spot on the floor. They may turn sideways, but do not allow them to step away from where they started. At this point, breathe again into the lower back and sing while allowing the belly to fall outward. If you start the scale low enough, you can sing a wide interval from low to higher, such as an octave, as your shoulder is pulled around toward the rear as far as comfort will allow. Sustain the note and gradually return the head and body to the original starting position while still singing. Repeat the exercise in the opposite direction.

The spine is being slowly twisted in this exercise. It is very important to move gradually while keeping the spine straight. At the slightest twinge of discomfort, reverse direction or desist. Avoid sudden moves. Try again in the opposite direction. Do not hesitate to end the exercise at any time if your instinct tells you that the resistance you feel may hurt you. The main concern is to do no harm.

Reliability and Relearning Every Day

Believe me, there will be days when your voice will not want to function. My colleagues would sing pretty well most days, but I began to notice that the singers who managed to perform at the most consistent high artistic level were the ones who had a warm-up technique that was always exactly the same every time I heard them warming up backstage. If a performing artist is going to maintain a high niveau, it is necessary to have a warm-up ritual that is utterly reliable and gets the voice to work on the worst days.

Too Much of a Good Thing

Believe it or not, I've known singers who vocalized for hours before a performance. Anneliese Rothenberger was notorious at the Vienna State Opera for singing hours backstage before a performance. Even the great Pavarotti wrote in his book that, on the day of a performance, he would vocalize six times, starting in the early morning and repeating the vocalises every hour and a half. Around six p.m. he would take a limo to the theater, rush to his dressing room as soon as he arrived, and vocalize again to see if he had lost his voice on the way to the theater! A reliable, ritualistic approach to warming-up the voice is the key to professional reliability and success if the basic technique is based on breathing and posturing. Every singer needs a reasonable, reliable warm-up method. Ritual eliminates choice!

A Ritual in Action

I could list many great singers I heard backstage in various opera theaters in the United States and in Europe who had thorough warm-up methods. One of my favorites was Elena Obratsova, the great Russian dramatic mezzo-soprano. Her method included a lot of coloratura vocalises in spite of the huge size of her voice. She had the biggest mezzo voice I ever heard in any theater except for Belen Amparan, who was considered more of a contralto. Young singers who were allowed back stage at the Met, usually members of the Kathryn Long School, would stand in the hallway outside Obratzova's dressing room and listen to her sing an organized series of vocalizes. She sang exercises using her entire vocal range, always with piano accompaniment, from low C to high D, before every performance. The session would last for approximately forty minutes and seemed to be the same every time we heard her.

In Summary

A Dedicated Student

One summer in Aspen I was teaching a class on relaxation of muscles not essential to singing. A young soprano sang for me and asked my opinion about her technical approach. I had immediately noticed that the muscles under her jaw and chin were contracted as if to defend herself from attack. Her chin was tucked down and the audience could see only the top of her head. I used the opportunity to demonstrate to the class how to relax those particular muscles by massaging them with the index finger across the chin and the thumb pushing up against the tensed muscles under the jaw and chin while singing. Many of the students tried it and found it to be an easy solution to general tension in the entire area of the throat. As soon as the muscles were relaxed under the jaw, our young soprano was able to lift her head and look at her audience while singing.

Four days later, one of the members of the voice faculty called me and asked, "Michael! What are you teaching the students in your class on relaxation? One of my students is black and blue under her jaw from rubbing it so hard!" As we later found out, the young lady had gone to a practice cabin and rubbed the muscles under her jaw with her thumb violently for hours each day over a period of several days. No wonder she was black and blue! This is exactly the kind of ambitious, determined student teachers love. However, the most energetic, dedicated students are the ones who need the most supervision in order to learn how to control their avid willingness to work so hard.

Sachte, Sachte

Teachers should not worry about lazy students exaggerating the exercises you give them. They never work hard enough to accomplish anything. It is the energetic, dedicated students who may have the tendency to exaggerate things. Too much of a good thing is not always wonderful!

In cases of overly ambitious students, the Germans say, *"sachte, sachte"* and the Italians say, *"piano, piano."* Translated, these phrases mean the same thing: take it easy! This is especially true for any form of physical exercise. Singers should not force the body to do anything that is too strenuous or painful, and it is very important to learn to never hurry. Either do the exercises slowly and correctly or don't do them at all! If the singer decides to do them, and does them as recommended, then it is certain that good things will start to happen, and, in some cases, the improvements are dramatic and quickly noticeable to the new practitioner.

A Proven Approach

I wish every aspiring vocal artist the very best. Every singer who dreams of becoming a great singing artist can glean from these pages many concepts and recommendations that will help them along the way. Theoretically, if a singer does these exercises daily and over a period of several years, he/she will have no choice but to sing well. A few great singers I have known personally have practiced yoga during their entire careers.

The Ultimate Example of the Posture Approach

Helge Roswänge never had a voice lesson. His entire approach to singing was based on extremely advanced yoga and the technical concepts as presented in Enrico Caruso's book. I studied with him in Munich in 1970 and his solution to every problem I had vocally was to encourage me to stand on one foot in the King of Dancers posture and breathe as deeply as possible into my lower back. And, as far as I can tell, after over fifty years of being totally involved in the world of vocal music, as student, fan, performer, and teacher, Roswänge was right. He certainly proved it with his fifty-five years of incredible singing, seven days a week, three times a day (rehearsals, recordings, and performances) without the slightest vocal problem. He never cancelled once during all those years, and that includes rehearsals.

It is perfectly safe to assume that there are no bad or unproven ideas being suggested here. Every singer who practices the postures and breathing as described above will improve in ease, freedom of the throat, range, volume, stamina, and reliability. Using a combination of moves and the respiration that accompanies each posture will provide the singer with a complete warm-up method. The warm-up method will place the voice in the mask every time it is used, and inspire the diaphragm with chi. Remember:

Ritual eliminates choice!

Appendix I: Notable Names and Dates:

Althouse, Paul	1889-1954
Amara, Lucine	1924-
Ameling, Elly	1933
Amparan, Belen	1927-2002
Aragall, Jaume (Giacomo)	1939-
Archipova, Irina	1925-2010
Arne, Thomas	1710-1778
Arroyo, Martina	1937-
Bartoli, Cecilia	1966-
Bastianini, Ettore	1922-1967
Battistini, Mattia	1856-1928
Beal, Eula	1919-2008
Bechi, Gina	1913-1993
Beecham, Sir Thomas	1879-1961
Behr, Jan	1911-1996
Bellini, Vicenzo	1801-1835
Bergonzi, Carlo	1924-
Besanzoni, Gabriella	1988-1962
Bing, Sir Rudolph	1902-1997
Bishop, Sir Henry	1786-1855
Björling, Jussi	1911-1960
Bonci, Allessandro	1870-1940
Borge, Victor	1923-2005
Breisach, Susan	1896-1987
Buddha (Siddhartha Gautama)	566-486 BC (traditional) 490-410 BC (revised)
Bumbry, Grace	1937-
Butt, Clara	1872-1936
Caballé, Montserrat	1933-
Callas, Maria	1923-1977
Campogalliani, Ettore	1903-1992
Campora, Giuseppe	1923-2004
Caruso, Enrico	1873-1921
Caruso, Dorothy Benjamin	1893-1955
Chaliapin, Feodor	1873-1938
Cleva, Fausto	1902-1971
Confucius	551-479 BC
Corelli, Franco	1921-2003
Cotogni, Antonio	1831-1918
Crespin, Regine	1927-2007
Dalberg, Frederick	1907-1988
Dalla Rizza, Gilda	1892-1975
De Haviland, Olivia	1916-

Deller, Alfred	1912-1979
del Monaco, Giancarlo	1943-
del Monaco, Mario	1915-1982
De Los Angeles, Victoria	1923-2005
De Luca, Giuseppe	1876-1950
De Lucia, Fernando	1860-1925
De Reszke, Jean	1850-1925
De Sabata, Victor	1892-1967
Descarte, Rene	1596-1650
Donizetti, Gaetano	1797-1848
Dukakis, Olympia	1931-
Eddy, Mary Baker	1821-1910
Eddy, Nelson	1901-1967
Einstein, Albert	1879-1955
Farrell, Eileen	1920-2002
Ferrar, Geraldine	1882-1967
Ferrier, Kathleen	1912-1953
Finney, Albert	1936-
Fischer-Dieskau, Dietrich	1925-2012
Flagstad, Kirsten	1895-1962
Fleming, Rene	1959-
Forrester, Maureen	1930-2010
Fremstad, Olive	1871-1951
Frick, Gottlob	1906-1994
Fucito, Salvatore	1875-1929
Fugere, Lucien	188-1935
Galeffi, Carlo	1882-1961
Galli-Curci, Amelita	1882-1963
Gambon, Michael	1940-
Gandhi, Mahatma	1869-1948
Garcia II, Manuel	1805-1906
Garden, Mary	1874-1967
Gatti-Cazzaza, Giulio	1869-1940
Gedda, Nicolai	1925-
Ghiaurov, Nicolai	1929-2004
Giachetti, Ada	1874-1946
Giaiotti, Bonaldo	1932-
Gigli, Beniamino	1890-1957
Giordani, Giuseppe	1751-1798
Giordano, Umberto	1867-1948
Glossup, Peter	1928-2008
Gluck, Alma	1884-1938
Gould, Dr. Wilbur	1919-1994
Gueden, Hilde	1917-1998
Guelfi, Giacomo	1924-2012

Harrell, Mack	1909-1960
Hempel, Frieda	1885-1955
Henderson, W.A.	1855-1937
Herrigel, Eugen	1884-1955
Hines, Jerome	1921-2003
Ivogun, Maria	1891-1987
Janssen, Herbert	1892-1965
Jerusalem, Siegfried	1940-
Kennedy, Jaqueline	1929-1994
Kiepura, Jan	1902-1966
Kimball, Florence Page	1888-1977
King, James	1925-2005
Kipnis, Alexander	1891-1978
Kmentt, Waldemar	1929-
Konetzni, Anny	1902-1968
Konetzni, Hilde	1905-1980
Kozub, Ernst	1924-1971
Kraus, Alfredo	1927-1999
Kurz, Selma	1874-1933
Lamperti, Francesco	1811-1892
Lamperti, Giovanni Battista	1839-1910
Lao-Tzu	unknown (600-300 BC)
Lauri-Volpi, Giacomo	1892-1972
Lehar, Franz	1870-1948
Lehmann, Lilli	1848-1929
Leider, Frieda	1888-1975
Lewis, Richard	1914-1990
London, George	1920-1985
Lorenz, Max	1901-1975
Ludwig, Christa	1928-
MacNeill, Cornell	1922-2011
Mandl, Dr. Louis	1812-1888
Marafioti, P. Mario	1878-1951
Marchesi, Blanche	1863-1940
Marchesi, Mathilde	1821-1913
Mardones, Jose	1869-1932
Margolis, Samuel	1883-1982
Martinelli, Giovanni	1885-1969
Mascagni, Pietro	1863-1945
McCormack, John	1884-1945
Melba, Nellie	1861-1931
Melchior, Lauritz	1890-1972
Melis, Carmen	1885-1967
Meneghini, Giovanni B.	1896-1981
Merrill, Robert	1917-2004

Milanov, Zinka	1906-1989
Munch, Edvard	1863-1944
Muzio, Claudia	1889-1936
Nachmann of Breslov	1792-1810
Newton, Sir Isaac	1643-1727
Nilsson, Birgit	1918-2005
Nordica, Lillian	1857-1914
Obraztova, Elena	1939-
Olivero, Magda	1910-
Olivier, Lawrence	1907-1989
Olvis, William	1928-1998
Onassis, Aristotle	1906-1975
O'Toole, Peter	1932-
Paine, Thomas	1737-1809
Patti, Adelina	1843-1919
Pavarotti, Luciano	1935-2007
Peck, Gregory	1916-2003
Peerce, Jan	1904-1984
Persichini, Venceslao	1827-1897
Pertile, Aureliano	1885-1952
Peters, Roberta	1930-
Piccaver, Alfred	1884-1958
Pidgeon, Walter	1897-1984
Pinza, Ezio	1892-1957
Podles, Eva	1952-
Ponchielli, Amilcare	1834-1886
Ponselle, Rosa	1887-1981
Prey, Herman	1929-1998
Price, Leontyne	1927-
Puccini, Giacomo	1858-1924
Reizen, Mark	1895-1992
Rescigno, Nicola	1916-2008
Ricordi, Giulio	1840-1912
Rilke, Rainer Maria	1875-1926
Robinson, Francis	1910-1980
Rootham, Daniel Wilberforce	1837-1922
Rossini, Gioacchino	1792-1868
Roswänge, Helge	1897-1972
Rothenberger, Anneliese	1924-2010
Ruffo, Titta	1871-1953
Rysanek, Leonie	1929-1998
Ryss, Olga	1896-1983
Schipa, Tito	1888-1965
Schmidt, Joseph	1904-1942
Schöffler, Paul	1897-1977

Schoen-Rene, Anna E.	1864-1942
Schorr, Friedrich	1888-1953
Schumann-Heink, Ernestine	1861-1936
Schwarzkopf, Elizabeth	1915-2006
Scotto, Renata	1934-
Sembrich, Marcella	1858-1935
Serafin, Tulio	1878-1968
Shadur, Lawrence	1935-1991
Shakespeare, William	1564-1616
Shaw, George Bernard	1856-1950
Siepi, Cesare	1923-2010
Sills, Beverly	1929-2007
Simionato, Giuletta	1910-2010
Simoneau, Leopold	1916-2006
Slezak, Leo	1873-1946
Sousa, John Philip	1854-1932
Steber, Eleonor	1914-1990
Stignani, Ebe	1903-1978
Stratas, Teresa	1938-
Strauss, Richard	1864-1949
Sutherland, Dame Joan	1926-2010
Tagliavini, Ferrucio	1913-1995
Tauber, Richard	1891-1948
Tebaldi, Renata	1922-2004
Te Kanawa, Kiri	1944-
Teresa, Mother	1910-1997
Ternina, Milka	1863-1941
Tetrazzini, Luisa	1871-1940
Teyte, Maggie	1888-1976
Thill, Georges	1897-1984
Thoreau, Henry David	1817-1862
Tibbett, Lawrence	1896-1960
Toscanini, Arturo	1867-1957
Tourel, Jenny	1900-1973
Tucker, Richard	1913-1975
Turner, Dame Eva	1892-1990
Verdi, Giuseppe	1813-1901
Verrett, Shirley	1931-2010
Viardot, Pauline	1821-1910
Vickers, Jon	1926-
Vinay, Ramon	1911-1996
von Dürckheim, Graf Karlfried	1896-1988
Wagner, Richard	1813-1883
Warren, Leonard	1911-1960
Welitsch, Ljuba	1913-1996

West, Mae	1893-1980
Wunderlich, Fritz	1930-1966
Zeffirelli, Franco	1923-
Zola, Emile	1840-1902

Appendix II: The Trimble Vocal Institute

Development of the Professional Voice
Michael and Pamela Trimble, Directors
10758 Madison Avenue NE
Bainbridge Island, WA 98110
206.780.8391
TVI@biwifi.com
trimblevocalinstitute.com
A Member of the Bainbridge Island, WA Chamber of Commerce

The aim of the Trimble Vocal Institute is to develop the body, mind and spirit of each individual performer entering the Trimble vocal studio. Mr. Trimble, General Director, tailors each student's program of study to the specific needs and desires of that student and follows her/his progress closely. The Course of Study offered by **The Trimble Vocal Institute** is intense and challenging, demanding each student's commitment to the development of vocal technique; foreign language fluency; a vast repertoire of operatic roles; acting and a knowledge of stagecraft and theatrical make-up.

Supplemental Material

The TVI Study Program for Aspiring Singers

Vocal Technique

Breathing (inhalation)

As described in the books of Enrico Caruso, Luisa Tetrazzini, Helge Roswänge, and Lilli Lehmann, and described in articles and quotes by Alfredo Kraus, Rosa Ponselle, Richard Tucker, and many others. In their books, they clearly describe a method of inhalation that is exactly the same as the natural method of inhalation used by a baby when laughing or crying.

During a silent, smiling inhalation through the nose, Luisa Tetrazzini said, "to breathe in deeply into the lower back, like smelling a flower." She also said, "The first drops of air must be inhaled into the lower rear quadrant of the lungs. The lungs should be filled from the bottom to the top."

Lilli Lehmann said to "jerk the abdomen inward at the instant the inhalation begins and breathe into the lower back. Continue pulling the abdomen inward until the maximum inhalation is accomplished."

Amelita Galli-Curci said to "glue the abdomen to the spine when inhaling."
Enrico Caruso said, "to inhale by pulling the abdomen in and raising the chest at the same time."

Helge Roswänge, a lifetime practitioner of yoga, said that the difference between yoga breathing and breathing for singing is the difference between "a sleeping baby and a laughing or crying baby." In sleeping baby breathing, the belly and lower abdomen are relaxed outward when inhaling, and pulled inward when exhaling. In laughing or crying baby breathing, the process is reversed. The abdomen is must be deliberately pulled inward before each attack or phrase when inhaling, and allowed to drop outward while singing, like a laughing or crying baby.

Expansion of the Ribs

The process of inhaling as described above by some of the greatest singers in history will cause the ribs in the lower back to expand to their greatest extent. At the same time, the back half of the diaphragm will be contracted downward, greatly increasing the capacity of the lungs and chest. Enrico Caruso called the function of the lower ribs in the back as "opening like a bellows when inhaling."

One of the oldest sayings in the history of singing is: "The bigger the drum, the bigger the sound."

Some singers want to expand the upper ribs and pull the abdomen in while singing. This concept is contrary to the advice given by the greatest singers in history, and creates a small drum instead of a large drum. Lauritz Melchior said: "Nothing should move unless the breath moves it. There should be no opening of the throat or movement of the ribs without a powerful inhalation."

Expanding the ribs without inhaling creates a rigid, shallow drum, like a snare drum. Let the inhalation move the ribs in the lower back, as deeply as possible (Caruso used the term, "massive respiration") in order to get the largest drum possible and the best tone possible.

Support (controlled exhalation)

Using the *appoggio* (leaning the breath, stopping the breath, propping the breath against the chest, like leaning a ladder against a wall, or pressing the breath against the lower chest while singing) in order to gain control of the accumulated breath in the lungs that is not yet needed to produce the voice. Luisa Tetrazzini said to "maintain the pressure of the breath against the sternum at all times."

Luciano Pavarotti said to "push, push, push [lean, lean lean] the breath against the lower chest while singing."

Lilli Lehmann said to "keep the pressure of the breath against the chest while singing."

Richard Tucker said, "Breathe behind you and sing in front of you! The abdomen must go in and the chest must be lifted when inhaling and the back must fill up with air. Do the opposite when singing. Use the breath in the back to maintain the position of the chest. Don't collapse the chest while singing!" (He and Eleanor Steber called the movement of the chest while inhaling the diaphragmatic lift).

It is important to understand that breath is pressed against the chest while singing by closing (Enrico Caruso said "squeezing") the ribs together in the lower back. The "squeezing of the bellows" will compress accumulated breath from the lower lungs at a diagonal angle upward against the front of the diaphragm (the lower chest). The chest and the epigastrium will respond by moving outward and becoming firm. However, there must be no independent flexing of the muscles (as if defending one's body against a punch) in the solar plexus or in the lower belly. Activity of the belly and the epigastrium must be reactive to the impetus of the breath actively sent from the lower back. They must never be flexed outward independently or pulled inward while singing. Activity of the belly and lower chest is not like doing leg-lifts or crunches, but resembles the relaxation of belly muscles after a leg-lift is completed.

Phonation of the Vowels

The shape of the mouth and throat should be created when inhaling. It should resemble "an oval lying on its side" (Marcella Sembrich, leading exponent of the Lamperti School), or an open smile, with the corners of the mouth pulled back, created by the "power of the inhalation" (Enrico Caruso, Luisa Tetrazzini, and Helge Roswänge).

The correct shape of the mouth can be seen on film as demonstrated in performance by Richard Tucker, Leontyne Price, Beniamino Gigli, Christa Ludwig, Peter Glossup, Lauritz Melchior, Maria Callas, Jan Kiepura, Nicolai Gedda, Leonard Warren, Helge Roswänge, Elena Obratzova, Giacomo Lauri-Volpi, and many other great singers of the past. The open throat as described by Giovanni Lamperti is the same horizontal shape as the bright [a] in the Italian word *stai*.

Rosa Ponselle agreed with the concept of the open smile, and said Enrico Caruso told her to "keep a rectangle in the back of the neck at all times."

George London pulled the corners of his mouth back as far as possible with the lips closed while inhaling and called it "opening the mask."

Nicolai Gedda was even more extreme in maintaining his corners back while breathing and singing, and called it "opening the throat."

Marilyn Horne, Beverly Sills, and Kiri Te Kanawa can be seen using a variation of the open smile. They keep the corners of their mouths back by keeping the cheeks lifted while singing.

An "Ah" Shape

It is very important to understand the difference between singing a bright [a], formed and sustained by using muscles in the throat, and singing through an [a] shaped throat, created and maintained by the strength of the inhalation and maintained by the *appoggio*. Any muscular action in the throat is wrong, and maintaining a stiff, white or blatty [a] vowel by resorting to muscular action in the throat is to be strictly avoided.

The correct [a] is a color, a form, a shape of the throat, through which all vowels are to be sung.

During master classes in 1962, Dame Eva Turner described the condition of the throat while singing as totally relaxed, and called it "the invisible, smiling throat." The only way to accomplish complete relaxation of the many components that make up the entire vocal organ is through deep inhalation into the lower back. Breathing in this manner creates and helps to maintain this invisibility. Dame Eva compared the correct form of the throat to a megaphone. Just as a megaphone has a predetermined shape through which all vowels are pronounced, the throat should be maintained in one form, the "smiling [a] form," and all vowels should be sung through it. The megaphone function of a singer's throat is created by deep, silent breathing through the nose and into the lower back, while, at the same time, pulling the corners of the mouth back in the shape of an open smile.

Dame Eva Turner, Dramatic Soprano, and Clara Butt, the greatest Contralto in history, had the two most powerful voices the British Empire has ever produced. They both studied with the same teacher, Basso Daniel Wilberforce Rootham. Both singers used the megaphone created by deep inhaling into the lower back through a smiling, invisible throat. Both singers had very long careers without vocal problems.

Emission of the breath

There must be no change of the emission of the breath while singing. The singer must learn to be perfectly still in the chest and maintain the sternal arch at all times. It is obvious that some part of the body must collapse as breath is used for singing. The singer must guard the chest (the sternal arch) to make certain that it does not collapse, and that the belly does not move inward while singing. Only the ribs in the lower back may move (collapse). As they close (squeeze together as breath is used for singing), only they are allowed to send the proper emission of the breath to the vocal folds as needed to produce the voice. Any other part of the body that is not essential to the breath control system can move if necessary while acting. However, the smooth, constant emission of the breath required to produce the legato basis of singing and the security of the upper range of the voice, depends on absolute stillness of the interior of the chest, perfect control of the diaphragm and the sternal arch, and perfect smoothness of the closing (squeezing) of the ribs in the lower back.

Breath Development

- **Yoga** (Helge Roswänge and Robert Merrill were very advanced practitioners of yoga)
- **Martial Arts** will teach the performer how and when to be assertive, and when and how to yield and relax. The singer who practices martial arts will increase stamina, performance energy, and immunity against colds and illness in general.

- **Long distance swimming** develops breath capacity and breath stamina like no other exercise. The Breast Stroke and the Crawl are the best swimming strokes to develop breath capacity. Enrico Caruso, Nellie Melba, and Joan Sutherland were ocean swimmers.
- **Learn to play a wind or brass instrument**. Beniamino Gigli was a saxophonist, Fritz Wunderlich was a French horn player, Kim Josephson was a tuba player, and Nicolai Ghiarov was a trombonist and clarinetist.
- **Bicycling**. Ezio Pinza was a competitive cyclist.
- **Rowing** (also a rowing machine), and the breast stroke in swimming, help to open the chest, develop the sternal arch, and expand the capacity of the lungs. It is important to increase the size of the air-box during the singing career, but only in a natural, healthy way. "The bigger the drum, the bigger the sound." Less effort will be required when singing over large orchestras if breath capacity is fully developed.
- **Hiking or going for long walks** while practicing Enrico Caruso's favorite, 40-step breathing exercise:
  - Walk ten steps while inhaling. The lungs should be completely full at the count of ten.
  - Hold the breath in the filled lungs and walk another ten steps.
  - Walk ten steps while exhaling until the lungs are empty, exactly at the count of ten.
  - Maintain the emptiness of the lungs while walking another ten steps.
  - Repeat this exercise while walking or hiking for long periods if possible. Enrico Caruso did this exercise, according to his secretary, for 1 1/2 hours every day! If the series of ten steps times four segments is too strenuous, reduce the number of steps per segment until a possible number is found. Ten steps are ideal, and can be accomplished with time. Counting teaches the body/mind connection not only to operate from full lungs to empty lungs and back, but also teaches the singer to regulate the inhalation and the emission of the breath.

Fluency in Languages

- Italian
- German
- French
- High English (The Queen's English, or Classical Theater English)

Diction and articulation in all four languages. High, classical, European theater pronunciation must be learned in every language studied. High Italian is best learned in Tuscany (Florence or Siena), High German in Hanover, High English at the *Old Vic School* or from an actor who has been trained as a Shakespearian actor, and High French in Paris from an actor who has been trained at the *Comédie Française*.

For concert singers add:

- Russian
- Spanish

- Latin
- American English employing as many pure vowels as possible. Some sounds, like the American [er] should be avoided if possible. Most successful singers who sing American Art songs use the schwa sound in place of the [er].

Musicianship

- Piano. Competence at the keyboard is a big help to singers in many ways. It will assist and improve the singer's abilities in other areas of music. For instance, the list of aspects of music as recommended below:
- Music theory which includes
  - sight singing
  - ear training
  - chord structure
  - harmonic progression
  - harmonizing
  - The Italian system of Solfeggio, used commonly in Europe.

Study and learn operatic repertoire suitable to the voice type in the most popular languages:

- Italian
- German
- French
- English

Learn Art Song repertoire suitable to the voice type

- German
- French
- Russian
- English
- Spanish

Read Books written by great singers:

- Enrico Caruso
- Luisa Tetrazzini
- Lilli Lehmann
- Maggie Teyte
- Lillian Nordica
- Mary Garden
- Giacomo Lauri-Volpi

written by great teachers of singing:

- Giovanni Lamperti
- Manuel Garcia II

written by novelist, Anne Rice:

- *Cry to Heaven*

written by philosophers:

- Graf Karlfried von Dürckheim (*Hara: The Vital Center of Man*)
- Eugen Herrigel (*Zen in the Art of Archery*)

Study interviews with great singers and quotes attributed to them:

- Rosa Ponselle
- Mattia Battistini
- Zinka Milanov
- Alfredo Kraus
- Dame Joan Sutherland
- Dame Eva Turner

Study audio recordings and videos of great singers in performance:
(YouTube is a great resource)

Sopranos

- Luisa Tetrazzini
- Nellie Melba
- Adelina Patti
- Kirsten Flagstad
- Rosa Ponselle
- Amelita Galli-Curci
- Frieda Hempel
- Helen Donath
- Rebecca Copley
- Joanna Porackova
- Claudia Muzio
- Renata Tebaldi
- Zinka Milanov
- Maria Callas
- Nellie Dutoit
- Mimi Coerzte
- Birgit Nilsson
- Elisabeth Schwarzkopf
- Helen Donath
- Lucine Amara
- Joan Sutherland

Mezzo-sopranos

- Ebe Stignani
- Irina Akhipova

- Elena Obratzova
- Christa Ludwig
- Giulietta Simionato
- Janet Baker
- Jenny Tourel
- Agnes Baltsa
- Eva Podles
- Marilyn Horne

Contraltos

- Clara Butt
- Louise Homer
- Ernestine Schumann-Heink
- Belen Amparan
- Maureen Forrester
- Marion Anderson
- Kathleen Ferrier
- Eula Beal

Tenors

- Luciano Pavarotti
- Tito Schipa
- Jussi Björling
- Fritz Wunderlich
- George Thill
- Beniamino Gigli
- Enrico Caruso
- Helge Roswänge
- Leo Slezak
- Lauritz Melchior
- Aureliano Pertile
- Richard Tucker
- Fernando De Lucia
- Mario Del Monaco
- Nicolai Gedda
- Franco Corelli
- Jan Peerce
- Joseph Schmidt
- Alfredo Kraus
- Ferrucio Tagliavini
- Michael Trimble (You can hear the author of this book on YouTube or on his website: trimblevocalinstitute.com)

Baritones

- Mattia Battistini
- Tita Ruffo
- Giuseppe De Luca
- Kim Josephson
- Paul Schöffler
- Robert Merrill
- Leonard Warren
- Lawrence Tibbett
- Nelson Eddy
- George London
- Tito Gobbi
- Friedrich Schorr

Basses

- José Mardones
- Nicolai Ghiarov
- Cesare Siepi
- Jerome Hines
- Giorgio Tozzi (early recordings only)
- Gottlob Frick
- Feodor Chaliapin

Acting should be studied, ideally, with a stage actor who has extensive experience in live theater. It is essential for singers to keep the air-box still while singing. It is possible to move the arms and legs, to bend over, to lie down, to throw the head back or from side to side, to do somersaults, and just about any physical move the performer might wish to make while singing while protecting the integrity of the air-box. However, it is the singer's responsibility to never allow the acting to become more important than the internal stillness of the chest, the firmness and stability of the sternal arch, the openness and expansion of the drum, the air-bucket, the air-filled space created by the chest and the lungs.

Stagecraft: Singing in the Opera can sometimes be problematic because of the slow-motion acting caused by the dictates of the music. Stagecraft becomes more important than actually portraying character if the music is extremely slow and each word of text is sustained in a way one would never use in real life. Stagecraft can help a singer get through the very slow, often repeated conventions of opera. The slow, sustained sections of the music and the text may drive real actors crazy, and especially stage directors who come directly from straight theater. As soon as they try to read the lines themselves at the crawling speed of some sections, they become a little more sympathetic to the singers who are doing the best they can to try to make sense of it all!

Make-up: Knowledge of the effects of make-up can be very important to a performer. All people do not look the same or respond the same way to a standard make-up situation. Most professional make-up artists know what they are doing, but it cannot hurt for each singer to know which colors work best for her/him.

Foods singers should avoid completely on the day of a performance:

- chocolate
- bananas
- citrus fruits and juices
- nuts
- wine, especially white wine. It contains chemicals that act as a preservative.
- spicy foods, especially hot seasonings
- milk and foods containing milk products
- very cold or very hot foods

Foods to avoid before singing in a humid environment:

- chocolate
- bananas
- nuts
- tomatoes
- citrus fruits and drinks
- ice cream
- spicy dishes
- beer

The foods mentioned above tend to produce mucus. Some of them may be helpful in a very dry climate because they prevent the throat from feeling dry. The individual singer must test them for himself/herself on performance-free days and find out what keeps the throat moist and what can produce an overabundance of catarrh.

If in a dry environment, avoid the following drinks that tend to dry the throat:

- wine (both white and red)
- tea, especially black (and some herbal teas can exacerbate dryness)
- alcohol (spirits) except beers and ale. Beer can actually help alleviate dryness in the throat if taken in small amounts
- citrus fruits or juices

The individual singer must experiment with food and drink and find out for himself/herself what helps and what does not.

Two hours before singing, avoid the following:

- alcoholic beverages, especially beer or ale in a humid climate
- champagne or wine in a dry climate
- iced or refrigerated drinks

- hot drinks, including apple juice. Any drink taken before a performance or during a performance should be no hotter than lukewarm.
- fizzy, bubbly drinks (never!) Colas should have the fizz shaken out of them before a singer drinks them.
- any kind of nuts or seeds
- black tea in a dry climate
- drinks with caffeine, especially very hot or iced

Ideal Behavior and Lifestyle for Singers

- No Smoking! We all know that smoking is bad in many ways, but singers in particular can irritate the edges of the vocal folds by sucking smoke through the throat and blowing it out through the throat. Some singers smoke and it does not seem to bother them. We will never know if their voices may have been fresher, more beautiful, or more full of ring if they had not smoked. Caruso and Chaliapin were chain smokers, and managed to sing fantastically for many years. They are best considered the exceptions to the rule. Most singers suffer from increased catarrh (phlegm) if they smoke, and are constantly clearing the mucus off of the vocal folds. After a while, the voice can begin to lose beauty and clarity because of the constant irritation of the vocal folds. It is better in every way not to smoke, and that includes any substance that can be smoked!
- Practice yoga every day and its extreme breathing exercises.
- Practice yoga breathing with every breath taken during the day.
- Practice a martial art to learn how to assert yourself and how to back off when necessary without losing charisma.
- Learn to play a brass or other wind instrument and commit to regular practice times. The need to sustain the pressure of the breath against the reed or mouthpiece will train the muscles in the lower ribs in the back of the body to support a constant, even emission of the breath.
- Become a great swimmer, unless allergic to chlorine. Take lessons if necessary. Freestyle and Breast Stroke increase breath capacity. Push your breath capacity: i.e. go for 2, 4, 6 stroke breath-holding in Freestyle for increased control of inhalation and emission.
- Stay away from noisy environments, except laughing or crying babies who are perfect examples of how to get the most out of inhaling, leaning and phonation.
- Observe the tummies and lower backs of laughing or crying babies (the instinctive breathing and support systems), and the instinctive shape of the laughing/crying mouth at every opportunity.
- Do not talk or spend time in noisy or smoky environments.
- Avoid exposure to pets. Some pets can cause allergic reactions.
- Avoid massage the day of a performance. The relaxation of the muscles that is wonderful the day before a performance is bad on the same day of a performance. Do yoga postures instead.

- Avoid cold rehearsal rooms.
- Always dress warmly, especially the head, the throat, and the feet.
- Do not speak in cold rooms or outside in cold weather.
- Learn to inhale only through the nose. The cold air will have time to warm up before it passes through the throat.
- Do not yell for any reason, ever.
- Do not argue for any reason (it is better to get up and leave the room).
- Avoid high emotional states, both your own and anyone else's.
- Avoid loss of sleep.
- Avoid talking.
- Learn to love silence.
- Communicate with gestures as much as possible. Save the vocal folds and the diaphragmatic, mental energy for singing.
- Avoid extreme dryness or humidity, and employ measures to neutralize them by using humidifiers or dehumidifiers.
- Avoid dusty environments. If a hotel room seems dusty or extremely dry, let the hot shower run with the bathroom door left open. The steam will add moisturize to the room and help to neutralize the dust.
- Avoid exposure to allergens, especially pets indoors that are not your own. Sometimes it is better not to go for a walk outside if the season is producing allergens among plants and trees.
- Avoid perfumes and perfumed lotions and shampoos and detergents. If a colleague is using tons of perfume, complain or change rooms.
- Avoid singing low roles, dramatic roles, or roles that are accompanied by heavy orchestrations. A role that combines all three characteristics should be eliminated from the singer's repertoire unless the singer is very mature and experienced.
- Avoid unhealthy relationships. Emotions can ruin the necessary state of mental calm needed by professional singers, especially tenors. Many careers have been ruined by an emotional, selfish spouse or sweetheart.
- Listen as much as possible to a broad spectrum of classical music, both vocal and instrumental.
- Listen to live performances of classical music and opera as often as possible.
- Don't trust anyone who can't prove what they are saying. Beware of the "blind-faith" approach to teachers and coaches. Demand to hear the teacher's recordings or YouTube examples.
- Only take advice from a teacher who has had an established professional career as a singer of opera and classical vocal music. Even if he/she has difficulty passing on information, it is a great deal safer than information passed on by someone who never actually had a singing career.

Appendix III: Genealogy of Michael Trimble's Voice Teachers

<table>
<tr><th>Lamperti School</th><th colspan="2">Garcia School</th></tr>
<tr><td rowspan="2">Francesco Lamperti
↓
Giovanni Battista Lamperti
↓
Alma Frosström
↓
Olga Ryss*
↘</td><td colspan="2">Manuel Garcia
↓
Manuel Garcia II</td></tr>
<tr><td>↙
Ernesto Ferrí
↓
Frederick Dalberg*
↓</td><td>↘
Pauline Viardot-Garcia
↓
Anna Schoen-René
↓
Mack Harrell*
↙</td></tr>
<tr><td colspan="3">Michael Trimble</td></tr>
</table>

***denotes** teachers with whom Trimble personally studied

References

Alda, Frances. *Men, Women and Tenors*. Los Angeles, CA: Hunt Press (modern edition),2007.

Caruso, Enrico. *The Art of Singing*. New York: Dover edition. 1975. (First Publication by The Metropolitan Co. 1909)

Chiulon, Jacques. *Mattia Battistini: King of Baritones and Baritone of Kings*. Translated by E. Thomas Glasow. Maryland: Scarecrow Press, 2009.

Drake, James A. *Rosa Ponselle/A Centenary Biography*. Portland, Oregon: Amadeus Press, 1997.

Dürckheim, Graf Karlfried. *Hara: The Vital Center of Man*. Rochester, Vermont: Inner Traditions, 2004.

Garcia II, Manuel. *Hints on Singing*. Translated from the French by Beata Garcia. London: E. Ascherberg & Co., 1894.

Garcia II, Manuel. A *Complete Treatise on the Art of Singing, Part I & II*. New York: DaCapo Press, 1984.

Hempel, Frieda. *My Golden Age of Singing*. Amadeus Press (republished in 2003)

Herrigel, Eugen. *Zen in the Art of Archery*. New York: Vintage Spiritual Classics, 1989.

Lamperti, Giovanni Battista. *Vocal Wisdom*. New York: Taplinger, 1931/1957.

Lamperti, Giovanni Battista, *The Technics of Bel Canto*. New York: G. Schirmer, 1905. (The book is dedicated to his pupil, Marcella Sembrich)

Lehmann, Lilli. *How to Sing*. New York: MacMillan, 1949. (First Publication Berlin 1902)

Marafioti, P. Mario. *Caruso's Method of Voice Production*. New York: Dover Press, 1949.

Nordica, Lillian. *Hints to Singers*. New York: Dover Press, 1998.

Prabhu, R.K. & Rao, U.R., editors. *The Mind of Mahatma Gandhi*. India: Jitendra T. Desai, Navajivan Trust, 1945/1967/1996.

Tetrazzini, Luisa. *The Art of Singing*. New York: Dover edition. 1975. (First Publication by The Metropolitan Co. 1909)

Michael Trimble

"Judging from the enthusiasm of opera lovers last night at the second production of the ***Opera Piccola!*** *series at the Naples Philharmonic Center, Naples might prove to be an ideal place for an American version of England's Glyndebourne... The performances throughout the evening were on a very high level... Under the direction of opera coach Michael Trimble, the format of the program, with charming commentary about the "verismo" operas on the program, was ideal for those who prefer their opera in concert form... it was a fine night for singing!" Naples Daily News*

Michael Trimble was a winner of both the Metropolitan Opera Auditions and the American Opera Auditions in 1963 and made his debut in Milan at the Teatro Nuovo as Cavaradossi in Puccini's *Tosca*. He studied voice with Mack Harrell and Olga Ryss. He has sung over 60 leading tenor roles of the Italian, French and German repertoire throughout Europe, Canada and the United States. Mr. Trimble performed with such celebrated conductors as Karl Böhm, Christoph von Dohnanyi, Charles Mackerras, Nello Santi, Ferdinand Leitner, Wolfgang Sawallisch and Karl Richter. He served as Chairman of Vocal and Choral studies at the Cleveland Institute of Music, Associate Professor of Voice at the University of Texas at Austin, Guest Professor at University of Miami, and as a member of the voice faculty of the Aspen Music Festival for over fifteen years (he created and directed the Aspen Vocal Institute). In 1990, upon the recommendation of George London, Opera America recognized Mr. Trimble as the leading authority in the voice training and development of young singers. In 1992, he formally established the Trimble Vocal Institute, consolidating under one roof his innovative development and performance programs, and his professional voice studio. *Opera Piccola!*, the performance division of the Trimble Vocal Institute met with extraordinary success during the 1996-98 Naples (Florida) Philharmonic Center Seasons with concerts of Opera and Musical Theatre Highlights. Mr. Trimble is recognized internationally as a voice teacher and repertory coach and, despite his attempt at retirement, still maintains an active voice studio and vocal consultation service. His students are singing in opera houses throughout the world. The Trimble Vocal Institute is thriving on Bainbridge Island, Washington in the beautiful Pacific Northwest where Mr. Trimble and his wife, Cantor Pamela Trimble, relocated in May 2001.

Richard di Renzi

Internationally-known tenor Richard di Renzi appeared with L'Opera de Montreal as Radames in *Aida* and Macduff in *Macbeth*, Michigan Opera Theater as Don José in *Carmen* and Cavaradossi in *Tosca*, Opera Pacific as Pinkerton in *Madama Butterfly*, Vancouver Opera as Don José, Pittsburgh Opera and National Grand Opera as Turridu in *Cavalleria Rusticana*, Atlanta Opera as Cavaradossi and Utah Opera as Radames. He also made a notable debut in Carnegie Hall as Pollione in *Norma* with the Opera Orchestra of New York and in concert at the Hollywood Bowl with the Hollywood Bowl Orchestra. Mr. di Renzi made his European debut in a series of concerts in Bilbao, Spain and has also been heard in Italy, France, Hungary, England, Scotland and Wales and extensively in Canada.

Elsewhere, he appeared on stage with Westchester Opera as Manrico in *Il Trovatore* and as Cavaradossi in *Tosca*, the Aspen Music Festival, and as featured soloist in opera galas for Hudson Opera Theater and La Follia di New York at Alice Tully Hall.

In addition to his opera credits, Mr. di Renzi has appeared in over twenty musical theater productions in a wide variety of roles from Curly in *Oklahoma*, Matt in *The Fantastiks*, Freddie Hill in *My Fair Lady*, and Abner in *Lil' Abner*.

Richard is a winner of the 1992 International Enrico Caruso Voice Competition and a two-time winner of the Mario Lanza Scholarship Award.

Mr. di Renzi may be heard as Pinkerton on Vox Classics' recording of *Madama Butterfly* featuring Maria Spacagna in the title role.

After his retirement from singing, Mr. di Renzi taught voice and speech production for three years in the Master of Fine Arts Program of the world-renowned Actor's Studio at New School University in Manhattan. He currently maintains private voice studios in both New York and New Jersey. In addition, he has been both an adjudicator and master class presenter at teen arts festivals in New Jersey.

Mr. di Renzi had the opportunity to study for three years with renowned the tenor Franco Corelli and considers Corelli, along with Emile Renan and, above all, Michael Trimble as the teachers who most influenced his singing.

Christopher Arneson

Christopher Arneson is a professional voice trainer and Vocologist who works with singers and actors to build powerful, effective voices. In 2003, he joined the voice faculty at Westminster Choir College of Rider University where he is Director of Voice Pedagogy, and teaches Voice, Voice Pedagogy, Literature for Teaching, and Speech for the Actor. Dr. Arneson is the co-director of the CoOPERAtive Program, a young artist program for singers, held at Westminster Choir College.

His students have gone on to further study in the Master of Music, Artist Diploma, and Doctoral programs at Cincinnati Conservatory of Music, Boston University, Ithaca College, Eastman School of Music, Indiana University and Yale School of Music. They have also appeared in young artist programs at Chautauqua Opera, Central City Opera, Santa Fe Opera, and Washington National Opera. His professional-level students have appeared at the Metropolitan Opera, Los Angeles Opera, San Francisco Opera, and Lyric Opera of Chicago.

He is a frequent guest speaker regarding the training and care of the professional voice. He is a faculty member for the New York Singing Teachers Association's (NYSTA) professional development program, where he teaches classes in vocal repertoire and applied pedagogy. Dr. Arneson is chair of the NATS Pedagogy Curriculum Committee and has recently published articles in the NATS Journal of Singing; *"Teaching Teachers* and *Performance Anxiety: A 21st Century Perspective."*

Dr. Arneson was the co-director of the Voice and Speech department in the MFA program at the renowned Actors Studio of the New School University in New York. In addition, he taught voice and vocal pedagogy at the Mason Gross School of the Arts at Rutgers University in New Brunswick, New Jersey. Dr. Arneson completed Vocology internships at the Grabscheid Voice Center at Mt. Sinai Hospital and the Vox Humana Laboratory at St. Luke's-Roosevelt Hospital, both in New York, where he continues to collaborate with otolaryngologists and speech-language pathologists in the remediation of voice disorders. Dr. Arneson holds both Bachelor of Music and Master of Music in Opera degrees from Binghamton University, completed post-graduate studies at Cornell University where he studied with renowned Verdi scholar Roger Parker, and earned a Doctor of Musical Arts degree from Mason Gross School of the Arts at Rutgers University where he studied seventeenth-century Venetian opera with Dr. Irene Alm. Dr. Arneson is an editor for NATS Journal of Singing, and he served on the editorial board for the new revised edition of the Royal Conservatory of Music's Vocal Repertoire Collection, published by Frederick Harris, Ltd. He is a member of the American Academy of Teachers of Singing, and he has been designated as Master Teacher for the NATS Teaching Intern Program and served as the Program Chair for the 2014 NATS National Conference.